PHILANTHROPIC STUDIES
David C. Hammack and Dwight F. Burlingame,
GENERAL EDITORS

Philanthropy in Communities of Color

BRADFORD SMITH

SYLVIA SHUE

JENNIFER LISA VEST

JOSEPH VILLARREAL

INDIANA UNIVERSITY PRESS

Bloomington & Indianapolis

This book is a publication of

Indiana University Press
601 North Morton Street
Bloomington, Indiana 47404-3797 USA

www.indiana.edu/~iupress

Telephone orders 800-842-6796
Fax orders 812-855-7931
Orders by e-mail iuporder@indiana.edu

© 1999 by The University of San Francisco

Library of Congress Cataloging-in-Publication Data

Philanthropy in communities of color / Bradford
    Smith . . . [et al.].
        p.   cm. — (Philanthropic studies)
    Includes bibliographical references and index.
    ISBN 0-253-33493-4 (cl : alk. paper)
    1. Minorities—Charitable contributions—California—San Francisco
Bay Area. 2. Ethnic groups—California—San Francisco Bay Area.
3. Voluntarism—California—San Francisco Bay Area. 4. Helping
behavior—California—San Francisco Bay Area.   I. Smith, Bradford.
II. Series.
HV99.S53E75   1999
361.7'089'00979461—dc21   98-27909

1 2 3 4 5 04 03 02 01 00 99

Contents ∽

Philanthropy in Communities of Color

⌒ Introduction

"Philanthropy" often refers to the altruism of the wealthy, John D. Rockefeller and Andrew Carnegie a century ago, Bill Gates and George Soros now. Yet, as John Gardner once remarked, philanthropy in America is largely a "Mississippi River of small gifts." Of the $150 billion donated in 1996, the largest portion came not from billionaires and mega-foundations but from individuals giving the proverbial widow's mite to their churches, scout troops, and local soup kitchens.

After countless studies of elite philanthropy, scholars have recently begun to give some attention to the altruistic behavior of laborers, farmers, immigrants, women, people of color, and the poor. The social history of American immigration has revealed an astonishing array of mutual assistance groups, ethnic/religious organizations, and other mechanisms by which immigrants helped each other as well as needy people in their homelands and, as time went on, society at large. Feminist studies have thrown much light on the philanthropy of middle-class and poor women as well as that of wealthy women. Very little attention, however, has been given to charitable behavior within communities of color. Minority people are often portrayed as takers rather than givers, significantly less generous than white Americans; but there has been little research to evaluate this characterization.

This book focuses on ethnic philanthropy, the phenomenon of sharing and helping within communities of color. The book reports an ethnographic study which examined in close detail the altruistic behavior, attitudes, and values of 260 individuals from eight communities of color in the San Francisco Bay Area. The Mexican, Guatemalan, Salvadoran, Filipino, Chinese, Japanese, Korean, and African American participants were interviewed by members of their own ethnic groups in two phases of the study, in 1991 and 1993.

This Introduction gives the background and conceptual framework of the study, a brief description of the methodology and research team, and a summary of the principal findings. Chapters 1 through 8 describe customs of giving money, goods, and services in each of the eight communities studied. The Conclusion discusses the study's principal findings. The methodology is described more fully in Appendix A.

⌒ BACKGROUND

During the last two decades, there has been a dramatic increase in the quantity and quality of literature on the charitable activity of Americans. Since the path-breaking work of the Filer Commission (Commission, 1975), research on philanthropy has grown steadily. For example, the Rockefeller Brothers Fund commissioned a major study of personal charity in the mid-1980s, with the research conducted by Yankelovich, Skelly, and White and the analysis done by Independent Sector. That study, *The Charitable Behavior of Americans* (Hodgkinson and Weitzman, 1986), explored giving behavior, motivations for giving, and attitudes toward charitable giving and volunteering. Independent Sector and the Gallup Organization have conducted subsequent survey research studies of giving and volunteering in the United States approximately every two years (Hodgkinson and Weitzman, 1988, 1990, 1992, 1994, 1996). These studies have included the variables "black," "Hispanic," and "non-white" and have reported significantly lower levels of giving and volunteering by these groups. Carson (1987a, 1987b, 1987c, 1987d, 1989, 1990) reported extensive giving and caretaking networks in the African American community, noting that blacks have traditionally relied on kin-based, self-help mechanisms and supported local community programs through black churches and in a variety of other ways. Kasberg and Hall-Russell (1996) surveyed black giving and volunteering in several midwestern states and conducted an extensive literature review of material related to African American philanthropy. Tonai (1987), Lee (1990), and Ko and Howe (1990) found significant levels of charitable behavior in Asian American communities. Bowen (1990) examined attitudes toward fundraising and volunteerism within the Filipino community. Cortés (1991) investigated philanthropic behavior in the Hispanic community and noted the need for more research in this area.

Research on ethnic philanthropy, however, has hardly kept pace with the growth of minority groups. While U.S. total population increased by less than 10 percent from 1980 to 1990, the Korean and Chinese population more than doubled, the Filipino population increased 82 percent, the Hispanic population went up more than 50 percent, the Native American population increased 38 percent, and the African American population increased 13 percent (see Appendix B, Table B-1). The California total population increased at nearly three times the national rate between 1980 and 1990 (see Appendix B, Table B-2). More than three-fifths of the state's six-million-person increase was in communities of color. The Asian population increased 117 percent, the Hispanic population 66 percent, the black population 21 percent, and the Native American population 7 percent. In the San Francisco Bay Area, the growth rate in the Asian (98 percent), Hispanic (43 percent), and black (15 percent) communities far exceeded the white population growth of 6 percent (see Appendix B, Table B-3). Virtually all recent population reports and demographic projections make clear that the nation as a whole, and certain states and metropolitan areas in particular, are experiencing and will continue to experience rapid growth in communities of color. For example, in 1989–90 non-white students made up the majority of California K–12 school enrollment for the first time in the state's history. Demographers project that the state's total population will be over 50 percent minority by the year 2000.

⬡ CONCEPTUAL FRAMEWORK

Culture

Not only has research on ethnic philanthropy failed to keep pace with the rapidly increasing size and importance of America's minority groups, but the cultural dimensions of philanthropic behavior within these ethnic communities remain virtually unexplored. All cultures construct reality differently; within each unique cultural community, beliefs and behavior have meanings that are often not shared or understood by the outside world. Some cultural meanings are manifest and easily recognized; others are latent and subtle, requiring systematic observation in order to produce accurate analysis. Thus, the cultural dimensions of gift-giving, financial assistance, sharing, and the distribution of income and wealth all have a variety of meanings from culture to culture. For example, the use of food can symbolize wealth, prestige, humility, conflict resolution, healing, honor, peace-making, or sanctity. In the Guatemalan community, it is very important for a mother-in-law to bring several meals to a newly married couple; not to do so indicates a lack of acceptance. Other types of gift-giving have meanings, forms, and functions that vary dramatically from culture to culture (Mauss, 1954 [1925]).

In most cultures characterized by traditional patrilineal systems of kinship, authority, and inheritance, the extended family is the main source of support, assistance, caretaking, and self-help for individuals. In the Chinese tradition, for example, principles of filial piety dictate that elderly family members receive respect, care, and support from the younger generations (Chang, 1983). Particularly in rural Chinese communities, this eliminated the need for community-based care for the elderly. Chinese people entering American urban settings are likely to perceive non-kin-based support services as unnecessary and even shameful. Similar tenets of family- and community-based self-help permeate the Hispanic and African American cultural traditions as well. Understanding patterns of cultural and family tradition is essential to understanding giving and volunteering within a particular cultural group.

The uses of wealth, prestige, and power are also important to the cross-cultural analysis of charitable behavior. In some cultures, for example, gift-giving and charity involve formalized systems of wealth redistribution which annually reaffirm the power base of local leaders. In other cultures, gift-giving may signal a wish for reconciliation or improved relationships between families or clans (Gibbs, 1973; Gulliver, 1977). Subtle gift-giving rituals can signal appropriate degrees of honor and shame, reaffirm cultural precepts, and allow positive channels for "face-saving" behavior. In such cultural contexts, giving a gift or being asked to give (particularly to a stranger) can easily create suspicion on the part of the potential donor or create a situation in which the gift-giver perceives that he or she has been placed in a subservient position (Van Loo, 1990).

Acculturation and assimilation into American society, however, tend to weaken traditional practices. Each generation's experience with family caretaking and the use of external community services creates a different set of attitudes about the value and appropriateness of community programs and charitable support for such efforts. Acculturation is not a uniform process; it varies with location and length of residence in the dominant culture, entry of new immigrants, and historical patterns of discrimination. It also varies depending on the congruence of dominant-culture and minority-culture values.

Philanthropy

No one suggests that goods and services given to nuclear family members should be counted as philanthropy. Nor does anyone count as philanthropy goods and services directly exchanged for money or some other economic value. What interests students of philanthropy is *the giving of goods and services outside the nuclear family without any apparent expectation of economic return.* In accounting terms, a gift or grant results in the net assets of the grantor being reduced by an amount equal to an increase in net assets of the grantee (Boulding, 1981). This definition leaves open the question of the role of non-economic values such as status, recognition, control, acceptance, face, spiritual insurance, and feelings of self-worth. A giver may receive social rather than economic goods in return for a gift. The notion of "social exchange" will be probed further in the Conclusion. This study will focus on giving as defined above, in relation to eight ethnic communities, and will explore ethnic giving in the context of its roots in the nuclear and extended family as well as in the larger context of social and economic exchange.

The fundamental question in any study of philanthropy is, Why do individuals give money, goods, and services to others? Altruistic or apparently altruistic behavior among humans and animals has long intrigued philosophers, psychologists, economists, anthropologists, biologists, and historians, not to mention fundraisers. This book does not present or assume any general theory of charitable behavior but rather investigates indigenous conceptualizations and patterns of giving within the eight ethnic communities studied. This primarily descriptive material may, however, contribute to a general theory of philanthropic behavior. For example, some patterns of giving emerge in all the groups studied, while other patterns are highly unique to one or a few groups. The differences are unsurprising given the sharply different historical experiences of the eight groups. The similarities, however, may help us understand philanthropic behavior generally.

This study focused on enumerating and describing the specific practices and customs of giving money, goods, and services within each of the eight communities. One of the common patterns identified in this study is that the giving of money, goods, and services originates in the nuclear family and moves outward through a series of roughly concentric circles of beneficiaries. These beneficiary groups are defined as follows:

- Nuclear family: Mother and/or father and unmarried children. (Members of the nuclear family are not considered as beneficiaries of *philanthropy* in this study).
- Extended family: People related by marriage, common ancestry, or fictive kinship not necessarily living together.
- Nuclear community: People known by the individual who is giving money, goods, or services.
- Extended community: Organizations with whom an individual feels a cultural identification.
- United States: Organizations within the United States.
- The world: Organizations throughout the world.
- Other: Ancestors, nature, and deities.

This study examines the ever-changing boundaries that exist between nuclear family support, economic exchange, social exchange, mutual assistance, and gifts. Such boundaries are inevitably arbitrary, as are the boundaries between the beneficiary groups. The definitions of the beneficiary groups emerged from the research team's discussions about how to conceptualize and interpret the interview material. This conceptual structure helped the research team to see patterns in the customs and practices of giving within each of the cultural communities. Observations made within one cultural setting began to inform observations made in other settings. Also, knowledge of specific terms used to describe various customs greatly facilitated the interview process. Mentioning a single term would often release a flood of memories or associations.

Ethnicity

The principal focus of this study is ethnicity: specifically, the relationship of ethnicity to charitable behavior. Do people of color give and volunteer, and if so in what ways, to whom, for what reasons, to what degree? Do minority Americans give more or less than, or about the same as, white Americans? As suggested above, the evidence on this last question is somewhat contradictory. National survey research done by Independent Sector and others consistently shows that the larger minority groups (Hispanic and African American) give and volunteer only about half as much as white Americans, relative to their resources. However, studies focusing on minority groups report extensive giving and volunteering. The present study suggests that these findings may be less inconsistent than they first seem. The survey research studies tend to focus on more formal giving and volunteering practices, such as sending a check to the American Cancer Society or volunteering for church work or Red Cross relief efforts. For example, most of the language in the Independent Sector survey questionnaire (Hodgkinson and Weitzman, 1996, pp. E-191 to E-212) speaks of giving to or volunteering for charitable *organizations*. The same is true for two San Francisco Bay Area surveys of giving;

only information about amounts given to organizations was collected (Market Opinion Research, 1989, 1991). The ethnographic studies pay more attention to informal giving and volunteering, such as bringing food to a needy neighbor. The research reported in this book found that, in all eight minority groups, respondents were much more likely to speak of giving to or helping needy individuals, families, and informal groups rather than organizations. Much of the giving described in the following eight chapters occurs outside of organizations. However, it still serves the same function as giving to organizations: instead of providing aid to many people, most of whom are unknown to the donors, the groups studied here focused their giving on fewer people, but people they knew and could count on to return the favor if needed.

Further, the terminology of questions asked in ethnic philanthropy research may significantly impact the conclusions. The survey research studies use words such as "charity," "contributions," "volunteering," and the like. The present study found that such terms did not work at all for the participants, who were much more likely to describe their experiences as "sharing" and "helping." The word "charity" carried negative connotations for some groups.

The present study suggests that the *amount* (relative to personal resources) of minority giving may be roughly consistent with that of white America but that the *forms and beneficiaries* of minority giving may be quite different. It will be clear from the description of methodology in this chapter and Appendix A that no claim is made here to "refute" the survey research studies; but the present study makes clear that definition of philanthropy, questions asked about philanthropy, words used to ask those questions, and methods used to gather data all significantly shape the data obtained and conclusions drawn.

It is worth noting that the customs and practices of giving described here strongly resemble the "sharing and helping" traditions of earlier Americans, who often shared goods and services prior to the development of more formal government and philanthropic aid organizations (Boorstin, 1969, chapter 3; Hawke, 1988; Schlesinger, 1944–45). Historically, American life was filled with interdependent networks. Quilting bees, barn raisings, and harvest-time cooperation are just a few of the more familiar examples of groups coming together to help individuals. These cooperative arrangements continued into the industrial age. As time went on, various forms of mutual assistance were replaced by more formal and organized government and philanthropic aid. However, familial and communal networks still play an important role in the giving habits of many Americans—perhaps especially in communities of color, due to recent immigration, discrimination, and cultural factors.

A note on terminology: Following the general usage of the 260 participants, this book uses "African American" and "black" interchangeably and, for the other seven ethnic groups, generally uses single-word descriptions such as "Chinese community" and "Filipinos" rather than "Chinese American community," "Filipino Americans," and so forth.

⮒ RESEARCH APPROACH AND METHODOLOGY

This cross-cultural ethnography focused on giving and volunteering in eight communities of color. The eight ethnic groups were selected primarily because of their prevalence and importance in the San Francisco Bay Area. Focused interviews, typically an hour and a half in length, with 260 individuals were conducted by members of the same ethnic groups. While an attempt was made to select respondents representatively across age, generation, and gender, the interviewee group was not intended to be and was not a true random sample. The interviews were conducted at the participants' homes or places of work from January to September of 1991 and from April to September of 1993. The first phase included five groups: Chinese, Japanese, Filipino, Mexican, and Guatemalan Americans. The second phase added Salvadoran, Korean, and African Americans. During the second phase, earlier findings were reevaluated by returning to the original five communities for validation and criticism of the study from key informants. The second phase also included more attention to physical versus cultural survival, reactions to racism, and comparative analysis of giving customs in the various groups. The addition of three new ethnic groups led to the reevaluation of some of the analysis and assumptions made in the first phase of the study.

These interviews provided the principal data from which the conclusions of the study were drawn. Additional insights came from participation in informal group sessions in each ethnic community. Some participants were interviewed more than once, particularly community leaders and individuals conversant with social science concepts and methods. A more detailed description of the methodology is presented in Appendix A.

⮒ AUTHORS AND RESEARCH STAFF

This book is the product of a team effort at the University of San Francisco's Institute for Nonprofit Organization Management. The principal investigator and director of the study was Bradford Smith, director of research at the Institute from 1990 to 1995. Principal co-investigators were Sylvia Shue, Jennifer Lisa Vest, and Joseph Villareal. Research assistants were Richard Castaniero, Erlinda Juarez, Cindy Kemakorn, Mi Kim, Dawn Martin, Melissa Moreno, and Cecili Sin. Volunteers Patria Fermin and Andrea Matsushima made significant contributions to the study. Ken Koziol, director of publications at the Institute, assisted in the initial editing. Michael O'Neill, executive director of the Institute, was responsible for the final editing preparatory to publication of this book.

∞ FINDINGS

The following are the principal findings of this study, which will be discussed further in the Conclusion. The reader is again reminded that the 260 individuals interviewed for the study were not selected in a way that permits statistical generalization.

- Ethnic philanthropy is inextricably linked with family and kinship.
- Religion plays a very important role in ethnic philanthropy.
- Little ethnic philanthropy is directed toward mainstream charitable organizations other than churches. Most ethnic philanthropy is personal and informal.
- There is a similarity of giving-related customs (and even terms) across the groups studied.
- Significant amounts of money and goods are sent to family, kin, and communities outside the United States.
- Members of ethnic communities often report caretaking activities which in the mainstream society are more likely to be performed by government and nonprofit organizations.
- Higher income respondents consistently spoke of their obligation to help others in their community achieve success in the same way they themselves were helped by members of their family and community.
- Knowledge of people's ethnicity does *not* help to predict the proportion of their total yearly household expenditures or total number of hours a year they give outside their nuclear family. Knowledge of people's ethnicity *does* help to predict the forms and beneficiaries of giving and volunteering outside the nuclear family.

The research reported in this book was made possible by grants from the Ford Foundation, the Rockefeller Brothers Fund, and an anonymous donor.

- The African American church is the focal point of much charitable giving in the black community.
- Direct giving to individuals is more valued in the African American community than giving to nonprofit organizations.
- Donating time, skills, and knowledge is often seen as more desirable than donating money.
- Definitions of family that include relatives, friends, neighbors, and strangers are important to understand African American giving patterns.
- African Americans who do well are expected to give back their skills, money, and knowledge to the community.

The majority of African Americans living in this country are the descendants of those Africans who were kidnapped and enslaved during the seventeenth, eighteenth, and nineteenth centuries by British, French, Portuguese, and Spanish slave traders. Their original status in this country was little more than a piece of property. They were routinely beaten, tortured, raped, malnourished, neglected medically, forced to lived in inhumane dwellings, and worked sometimes to death. Blacks provided much of the labor that made possible the southern agricultural and subsequent northern industrial development of the country. They were granted their freedom in 1863 but did not obtain the full legal rights of citizenship until the 1960s.

Under slavery and afterwards, blacks established strong networks of mutual aid and support. A spirit of cooperation and charity in the face of adversity was one of the elements of their culture that helped them to survive the harsh and brutal conditions of slavery. Large extended fictive kin networks were established to replace the families torn apart by slavery and other forms of racial oppression. African Americans formed separate all-black neighborhoods, churches, schools, and other institutions. Many informal patterns of sharing and helping were established.

African Americans have historically been involved in a number of philanthropic ventures. Much of their formal giving and mutual assistance was channeled through the church, civil rights and social improvement organizations, or fraternal organizations. African Americans utilized all these types of organizations to found schools, homes for the elderly, hospitals, day-care facilities, and other social welfare programs (Nelsen, Yokley, and Nelsen, 1971; Banks and Grambs, 1972; Mukenge, 1983; Lincoln and Mamiya, 1990).

The creation and evolution of the black church has been the most significant factor in the political, social, cultural, spiritual, educational, and philanthropic development of African Americans in this country. The term "black church" refers to religions that were founded and congregated by African Americans. The first such churches were founded in South Carolina in 1773 and in Virginia in 1776, but the first significant developments in this movement occurred after Richard Allen founded the Bethel church, in a split from the white Methodist church in 1794. Absalom Jones founded the African Protestant Episcopal church at about the same time. The movement begun by Allen spread to other cities, and African American Methodists throughout the country began seceding and forming what came to be known as the African Methodist Episcopal (AME) Church. During this time the African Methodist Episcopal Zion church was founded in New York by African members of the Methodist and Episcopal churches there. Blacks in Maryland, Virginia, Georgia, Kentucky, Boston, New York, and Philadelphia organized independent Baptist churches during this same period.

This movement away from the European and European-American churches allowed African Americans to create the first black-owned and operated institutions. The church has since played an important role in the history of African Americans and their philanthropic ventures because of the centrality of religion in the lives of black people and because the church was for a long time the only organization in which blacks, both free and slave, were allowed to participate.

Each of the major African American church denominations—the African Methodist Episcopal Church, the African Methodist Episcopal Zion Church, the Colored Methodist Episcopal Church, and the Negro Baptists—established and maintained secondary schools and colleges during the nineteenth century. The churches also went into the community to care for the elderly and sick, and started homes for the elderly and child-care centers.

The church has been the center and the financier for many endeavors which have benefited African Americans. Before and after the Civil War, African American churches assisted in the education of blacks, both enslaved and free, through Bible study and through the schools and colleges they had founded and financed. The church has also always played a central role in political movements and civil rights organizing. Many African American leaders such as Nat Turner, Adam Clayton Powell, Leon Sullivan, Sojourner Truth, Ralph Abernathy, Martin Luther King, Jr., Malcolm X, and Jesse Jackson received their training in the church. Many important political and civil rights organizations such as the Southern Christian Leadership Conference (SCLC), the Black Muslims, the Montgomery Improvement Association, the National Committee of Black Churchmen, the interreligious Foundation for Community Organization, and the Deacons for Defense in Louisiana were affiliated with the church. Other organizations such as the Student Nonviolent Coordinating Committee, the Urban League, and the National Association for the Advancement of Colored People (NAACP) have historically maintained important alliances with church leaders and church organizations (Lincoln, 1974).

Out of black churches grew mutual aid societies, schools, and, ultimately, civil rights programs. The first recorded African American mutual aid society was the Free African Society, organized in Philadelphia in 1787 by the founders of the African Methodist Episcopal and the African Protestant Episcopal churches. The African Union Society was founded in Rhode Island in 1780 to curb illiteracy and provide job training. Other major benevolent societies include the New York Society (1810), the Clarkson Society (1812), the Wilberforce Benevolent Society (1820), the Union Society of Brooklyn (1820), and the Woolman Society (1820). By the early 1800s there were several hundred such organizations (Harris, 1979). These organizations typically concerned themselves with job training, assistance with schooling, death and sickness benefits, money for medical expenses, grants for widows and orphans, and care for the elderly. Many African American financial institutions which came into existence during this period, such as the National Benefit Life Insurance and the Central Life Insurance companies, owe their origins to mutual aid organizations.

Other mutual aid organizations with which African Americans have traditionally been involved are the fraternal benefit organizations and secret societies. In addition to forming their own chapters of existing fraternal organizations such as the Masons (1784), the Odd Fellows (1842), Knights of Pythias (1864), Eastern Star, Foresters, Shriners, Household of Ruth, Elks (1897), and the Daughters of Isis, blacks also began new orders such as the African Blood Brotherhood, the Knights of the Invisible Colored Kingdom (1923), the Colored Consolidated Brotherhood, the African Legion (1905), Friends of Negro Freedom, the Colored Brotherhood and Sisterhood of Honor (1886), the International Order of Twelve (1846), and the Grand United Order of Galilean Fishermen (1856). Many of these fraternal organizations were involved in charitable activities such as establishing homes for the aged and for orphans.

Traditionally, social welfare, philanthropy, and political struggle have all been linked for African Americans. Many black organizations pursue economic, philanthropic, and political projects or objectives simultaneously. The Urban League, the NAACP, and the National Council of Negro Women are some of the better known national organizations of this kind. Such organizations, in addition to promoting rights of African Americans, have also fought for the rights of other ethnic groups and provided charitable services for these groups.

African Americans have also traditionally used their involvement in college fraternities and sororities as a vehicle for establishing community service programs. Many of these organizations provide scholarships for students. In addition, their members are often expected to participate in community service programs established by the fraternities or sororities.

Although the black church today is less intimately connected to historically black colleges, there still exist college and scholarship funds at many churches. Church programs today also include homes for the elderly, services to the sick in local hospitals, food pantries, community centers, athletics programs, drug treatment efforts, and tutorial programs.

The following excerpts from interviews with 20 African Americans show that black philanthropy is largely informal and takes place primarily within the black community, although some giving and volunteering take place within formal organizations and some is directed at non-black organizations.

∞ KINSHIP AND COMMUNITY

African American families are often characterized by large kinship networks related both by blood and association (Willie, 1970; Aschenbrenner, 1975; Martin and Martin, 1978; McAdoo, 1988). The existence of fictive kin among African Americans is widespread, and definitions of kinship play an important role in giving and sharing patterns and choice of beneficiaries. Appeals made to blacks by other blacks to give money or time are often made with reference to the importance of helping out one's "brothers and sisters." The assumption is that one is responsible for one's "kin," whether they are related by blood or not.

There are different degrees of fictive kin. The broadest circles may include all African Americans, all people of color, and one's neighbors, classmates, fellow workers, or fellow church members, whom one may casually refer to as "brother," "sister," and "mother." More formal designations of fictive kin include friends who take on permanent labels and roles such as those members of one's family who are not related by blood but who have been included in the family through informal adoption or long-time acquaintance.

Black people tend to define the family broadly. For example, when asked to define the family, few respondents in the present study restricted their definition to include only blood relatives. One middle-aged male said: "I define family as people you truly love who love you back. I got a lot of relatives who are not really my blood, but I've known them just as long as I've known my blood relatives so it's almost the same." A young, college-educated, female respondent said: "There are times when I define family as people I don't know, especially when we are a few African Americans in a largely white atmosphere."

A form of fictive kinship prevalent in the African American community is described by the term "homies." A homie is usually a member of one's age group, neighborhood, or school grade, of the same gender. Homies are often from the same hometown and share the same background and experiences. After growing up together, these childhood friends form a special bond and turn into an extended family. Homies, also called "homegirls," "homeboys," or "partners," were defined by one 30-year-old female respondent as "a friend, someone who's there, somebody I grew up with . . . who was there to give support, understanding. It takes a long time to create homies." A 33-year-old male respondent defined homies in the following way: "My homies would be my 'boys,' my friends who I grew up with and am still friends with, or the guys I went to college with—and we still hang out." One respondent spoke of the importance of homies and the role they play in family relations and the practice of giving:

> There are things you do for your homies you wouldn't do for just anybody. Your homies are almost like your other network of family. What's in your home, you know, your blood. Sort of the other part of your extended family. You have some sort of kinship building with them, too, and you work almost as a familial unit. So you would do for them as you would do for any valued family member and not what you would do for just a regular old acquaintance or someone you could call a friend.

The extended family was defined differently by different respondents. For some the extended family consists of distant relatives and godparents; for others it includes family friends, "homies," neighbors, or all black people. One young female respondent had the following to say about the extended family:

> I have a lot of extended family members. I think people define it differently. It means different things to different people. Like the guy I used to date, his parents are considered my extended parents 'cause I still go over there a lot and they feed me and give me good advice. They genuinely care about me. They are close with my parents and they treat me as one of their own when I'm there.

One older male respondent, comparing his generation to that of his children, included neighbors and church folk in his definition of extended family:

> There were always people beyond my parents who cared for me on a daily basis. If I was down the street and did something I shouldn't—by the time I got home my mother knew about it. People cared enough, and that's very different from the sense of community we have now. . . . I saw my grandparents almost every day and maybe stayed with them most of the time . . . everybody in the church I went to was either a relative or felt they were a relative.

Another popular designation of fictive kin is the "cousin." When children growing up feel especially close they often begin to refer to one another as "cousins." "Cuz" or "cousin" is a popular colloquialism used by African Americans as a greeting. It is used to denote a sense of kinship among strangers. In addition, often the "homies" of one's parents will become one's "aunties," "uncles," or "godparents." One female respondent had the following explanation:

> There's the cousin, the person that you grew up with who's not really related to you but you spend a lot of time with them so they become your cousin. And your uncles and aunts who aren't really your uncles and aunts. Your mother's friends or your dad's. It was a given. Almost anybody who was in our parents' life who was an adult . . . if they're around a lot, then you added on "auntie" or "uncle."

Another form of fictive kin is the godparent, the definition of which is often loose. Homies, for example, are often seen as godparents. One respondent said: "I know a lot of people in the black community who say they are godparents. . . . Most people I know have godkids. I think it is a usual thing. You know, usually the person who had the child, their best friend or a relative or someone who was a homie of theirs became the godparent to help take care of responsibility."

Some people are given godparents at birth, others acquire them later in life. Some godparents are expected to play a role in the child's life, while others are expected to play a role in supporting the child emotionally, financially, and morally. One respondent described godparents in the following way:

> The godparent is usually the mother's good friend. They would be the ones that would take care of me outside my family. If my blood relatives couldn't take care of me, if anything happened to my parents. So godparents, I think, are people that when they went on trips or vacations, I'd get a gift from my godmother or godfather, or at graduation and birthdays. They're the ones who give you extra money.

Another respondent, a godmother herself, described her role as follows:

> I have a godson. He's seven years old. I buy his shoes. So when I see him and I take him out we go buy shoes. And he knows that what we're gonna do. Shoes are expensive. I don't get to spend a lot of time with him but that the one thing I do for him and his mom is to buy all his shoes. It helps. 'Cause his feet really grow. It would be every three months almost.

✆ THE HOOK UP

The extended family plays an important part in sharing and helping among African Americans. In the hierarchy of giving within the black community, one might be expected to help one's family first, one's extended family (if the distinction exists), and then homies, neighbors, and church members (all of whom may be included under the heading of extended family), followed by strangers, including especially African American people, people of color, and disadvantaged or needy people. The practice of "hookin' up" is often associated with these types of relationships.

Hookin' up involves the giving of food, shelter, information, job opportunities, discounts, business patronage, and/or money within a kinship or other group. It can also mean helping people out, putting them in touch with resources, opportunities, or other people. There are people whom one is expected to hook up and others to whom one has no obligation. Some feel obligated to hook up only with blood kin. Others feel obligated to hook up their extended family and homies. Still others feel the need to hook up members of their local community or the larger African American community. Speaking of the obligations she felt toward her extended family, one respondent said:

> Like if there is someone coming into town who is an extended family member—I might not know them too well—I would feed them and let them stay at my house and help them get on their feet if they need it. My parents aren't really that giving but they would do something like that. They would take people in and try to help them get jobs.

Another respondent spoke of the general expectations that she felt African Americans have of each other. Feelings of obligation, expectations of mutual support run deep in the community. While blacks may not expect to receive help in any way from non-blacks, they often expect other African Americans to help out simply because they are African American. There is an expectation among blacks that people within the community will have higher standards, stricter values, and more shame than other Americans. Those who do not measure up to community expectations are censured by others. The labels "Uncle Tom" and "sellout" are commonly used to refer to those blacks who do not help uphold African American values, do not show an allegiance to African Americans, or do not give back to their community in some way. One respondent, speaking of the expectations of other blacks who work for nonprofit organizations, said: "The African American community as a whole expects more from its own people than from the larger white community . . . and when my friends work for AIDS organizations and such they expect me to give 'cause they know me. I always get stuff from them in the mail asking me to volunteer and stuff."

Hookin' up might include helping someone in a financial or emotional bind, taking care of someone's house or children, putting a word in for someone, giving a reference for a job, providing someone with a place to stay, connecting someone to a business network, or cosigning for a loan. It is also sometimes referred to as "having someone's back." The incentive ranges from a sense of responsibility to one's kin, community, or family, to a desire to help uplift the race. For example, some African Americans may hook up younger blacks with jobs or other opportunities as part of their efforts to uplift the race. As one college-educated respondent put it:

> Grabbing your brother or sister by the hand and pulling them with you too if they want to. We need it. So if I'm in a position where I had a job and there was an opening and I had a friend who needed a job then I would tell them, I'd say, "Come on, this is what you need to do." Or I'd tell my boss, "I know someone." That's what the expressions, "Don't forget where you came from," and "Don't forget to hook up your homies" mean to me.

Some respondents spoke of patronizing African American businesses as one way of giving back to the community. Black businesses often have trouble securing loans, connecting with distributors, and obtaining reasonable rents and insurance. Blacks feel they need to help out black businesses because discrimination sometimes prevents them from securing business from whites and other non-black Americans. Although it may require more travel time and might cost more, many African Americans will go out of their way to patronize an African American business:

> I give back to the black community by shopping in black stores and going to black businesses if I need something. Even though sometimes they can be hard to find 'cause there aren't that many black-owned stores out there. Even if the service isn't as good, or the prices more expensive than I want to pay, I do it 'cause you can be sure that white people aren't going to go to black businesses. Folks out there are trying to make something for themselves, so I try to help out.

In return, African Americans often expect to be hooked up by these businesses. They expect, first of all, to be treated with an intimacy and a kindness usually reserved for family. They may expect to get discounts, or to be able to make special payment arrangements, and to get exceptional service. One business owner from the South spoke of this tendency in her customers. Sometimes, she said, when she could not afford to give a discount, she had to raise the initial price of something when negotiating with blacks so that she could then lower it and appear to be giving them a break. She talked of how difficult it was to be expected always to give black people discounts even though her business was small and not yet profitable.

Respondents spoke of hookin' up other African Americans when in an unfriendly, all-white environment as a way of expressing solidarity. One middle-class respondent said:

> I grew up in a predominantly white community and even if we weren't really friends with the other black folks on the block you always knew the other people were there and you always spoke and there was that feeling that you could count on each other when somebody was sick in your family or if you needed a baby sitter, food or money, that you could really count on the black people to help you and to understand. I don't think you would necessarily have that level of giving without a close relationship in the dominant [white] community.

∞ GIVE BACK

A motivating factor voiced over and over by respondents was the obligation felt by many African Americans to give back to someone, some organization, or some group of people within the black community. The beneficiaries of this giving back often vary but the unifying theme is the desire on the part of an individual to help others because he or she has been helped at some point during his or her life. It also embodies the idea that someone who has a lot should help those who have only a little. The idea that poverty is connected to riches, that the lives of poor and well-to-do African Americans are inter-twined, and that African Americans who have made it owe their success in some part to those who have not is embodied in this give-back philosophy. In the words of one respondent:

> I think there are some conscious people out there who realize that they need to give back—that you can't just get yours and keep going like you came from nowhere. We are all connected to poverty in America. There's no such thing as old black money. It's going to take us a while to reorganize and begin to channel money back into the black community.

This idea of giving back, which is often abstract in its formulation, embod-ies a philosophy of reciprocity, fair play, equality, and graciousness. The ways in which African Americans give back and the persons, organizations, or com-munities to which they give back vary considerably; but many people expressed what they felt was a personal need to show gratitude for past gifts, whether tangible or abstract, with the giving of their own gifts. Sometimes the giving is direct. A respondent may choose to give to his or her alma mater, commu-nity center, old neighborhood, or scholarship fund from which the individual benefited personally. One informant, talking about her father, said:

> My stepdad gave to his fraternity and his alma mater. Even though he has a college degree, he didn't make much money. But somehow he still felt re-sponsible to the place that educated him. In a sense, that was making it—if you made it through high school, and especially if you made it through college. No one in his family had ever done that before, so that made it special, significant. He feels like he owes his institution and his fraternity. He feels like he can help give someone else a chance like he got.

Most respondents also reported learning about charity through the examples set by their parents. They were rarely told about charity specifically but were influenced by a philosophy of giving they heard voiced at home, in the church, and in the community.

Some people give more indirectly. They may give just to the black com-munity or to black organizations, recognizing that they owe something to all the African American people that helped them coming up. They may give to education in general as a way of repaying their teachers. Some people make a point of helping the elderly because they realize that when they were young, older people helped raise them. Others give to programs that benefit the poor because they were once poor.

The respect and care that African Americans give to their elderly is an-other aspect of the importance of reciprocity, gratitude, and the give-back philosophy: children should take care of the elders who took care of them. One respondent explained it this way:

> I think that for African American people our first thought is not to turn our back on people, especially elderly people. In general we have a unique rela-tionship with old people. White people are more likely to put their parents

in an old folks home instead of inviting them to live in their own homes and take care of them. It's still very taboo in the black community not to take care of your parents when they can't take care of themselves. We are just that way. People will look at you like you're the devil if you say you put your mama in an old folks home instead of letting her live with you.

Likewise, adults may contribute time or money to youth programs to help out the generation coming up because they feel that it is their responsibility just as it was the responsibility of their parents' generation to help them out. Some people feel that because so many African Americans lack resources, it is the responsibility of those who make it to help those who don't. One respondent explained the give-back principle in a blunt way when she said, "People who have their shit together need to set the example, need to influence the people who haven't had the fortune and the opportunities they have." One African American respondent reported that, without being told directly, she felt an obligation to give back:

> There was a very strong social message about giving, giving back to someone else. To give back, that means having an awareness of the food that was on your table, clothes on your back; don't take that for granted. . . . There was always the realization that your parents are working hard for you to have something and it's your responsibility to do and to extend yourself to help someone else because you were fortunate enough to be given what you have. . . . It's your obligation to give to the community, to do for other people.

One way in which many professional middle-class African Americans give back to the community is by sharing their skills, mentoring, or offering goods or services at discount prices to those who could not otherwise afford them. One respondent said:

> My parents definitely taught by example, and their teaching was: "You serve the black community." My father and both grandparents were attorneys and they served the black community where I grew up and I know they took cases *pro bono*. That's just what you do, and you don't say no to people 'cause they don't have money and you don't say no to people 'cause you want to make more money and you give by being leaders in the community and speaking in the community for or against different things that are going on and also if at all possible you put your kids through school. That's giving back.

Some respondents believe that self-help or the concentration of African American money in black community programs, black businesses, and black organizations is the only solution to the present plight of African Americans. One elderly middle-class man spoke about the importance of giving back:

> I would say you need to give back to the community in which you live in order to enjoy how the community thrives. It's the same principle that a farmer has to give back a little bit of what he reaps to the soil in order for it

to harvest again. You can't just take and take and take—it becomes bereft of minerals and everything else and it won't produce anymore. You have to give back in all situations, in all situations.

One respondent talked of how his parents had always given back to the community by volunteering to help flood victims, help with programs for the poor, help out neighbors in times of crisis, and participate in organizations. The main lessons he learned from his parents were from their examples. He talked of how people would give of themselves when they did not have money to give. He then went on to describe his own giving practices:

> I give back to my community through service. I don't give a lot of money. I don't have a lot of money to give back. . . . My main way of giving back is through community service programs. I involve myself with providing my time, my energy, my skills to community service programs. . . . I've been actively involved in the Urban League for several years and my involvement there has been in program development for training programs for kids in the ghetto, job training. I've been involved in a number of volunteer efforts which are kind of sporadic, helping homeless people in Phoenix, spending two Christmas days feeding the homeless. It's not a big deal but I've done it twice, helping and packaging and providing meals for homeless people throughout the year at various times and physically going to the sites, to the homeless shelters and feeding the people. . . . I've been involved on a number of boards. The Scottsdale League I'm involved in right now. That league provides monies for education and the arts. . . .

A young, college-educated respondent, speaking of the expectations she feels as someone who has made it, observed the following:

> A lot of people say that [you have to give back]. Some people say, "OK, yeah, when you teachin' and you makin' all that money, and you writin' your books and all that, and clockin' your dollars, I just know you gonna come back and kick some dollars down in your community." Or they mean you have to come back, while you're in school *and* once you're out and lead and take the community by the hand and lead them to . . . whatever people think you may be able to offer them. Just somehow just return. That goes along with [the expression] "don't forget where you came from," meaning, "Oh, you know, don't go up there and get you a plush house in the hills and a nice car and forget about where you came from." When you have the money they want you to bring it back. They almost expect you to do nothing, to sort of leave the community and never come back but then again they say they expect you to come back and do things like mentoring, talkin' to black folks at organizations or just people in your community, lettin' them know what you went through and how you got there and how they can do the same, stuff like that.

There's an expectation that the educated and the professionals will use their skills, knowledge, and money to benefit the class they come from, the neighborhood, the family, and the rest of their extended family. One respondent who grew up in an upper-middle-class home talked about how she felt when she had to help out other African Americans and poor people who had less than she did. She talked of how she learned about giving through the examples of her father and mother. Her mother donated time at a nursing center for several years and her father gave through his job choice: "That's like my father. He grew up poor. He made it. He was successful in his career and he didn't try to move into some area where he wouldn't be helping poorer blacks. He was a dentist. He worked in a black area. Most of his clients were black and he tried to give it back by not charging outrageous [fees]."

Job choice for African Americans is sometimes influenced by a person's need to give back. A person may choose to go into a service-oriented field and then practice that profession in the black community. Social workers, teachers, doctors, lawyers, and other service workers often specifically choose their clients in the African American community. They may also choose a position with low pay over a higher paying job because of obligations they feel to give back to the community. There is an expectation in the black community that a person will pick a job that is going to benefit blacks. Those who pick jobs that are lucrative but not service-oriented will be expected to give back with their time, mentoring, and money. One respondent said:

> If you have a job and you're living in this community, you are expected to contribute and give back to this community whether you want to or not; and there are ways that different organizations go about getting you to contribute. Sometimes it's your job choice. If you work for an organization that is doing something in the community and you're working for little pay, inadvertently you're giving them both money and time. There are all kinds of ways.

The expression "don't forget where you came from" is frequently used in the black community and has a literal, metaphorical, and historical meaning. In part it underscores the reality that almost all African Americans come from poverty, from slavery, from hard times, that no matter how much you achieve you can usually trace your family history back to desperate beginnings. One respondent defined the meaning of the phrase as follows:

> Remember what challenges and things you had to give up to get to where you are now, meaning remember times where you couldn't go out for two weeks 'cause you didn't have any money, or just if you get all this stuff don't take it for granted 'cause you may not always have it, so don't forget where you came from means remember the struggles and everything else that it took for you to get where you are, and then who's still struggling—I think you should always keep that in mind.

The sense of debt that African Americans feel to ancestors, elders, and the less fortunate is expressed in a number of ways. One man from a low-income background who had risen to an upper-class income level stated:

> I've managed to reach as much success as I have at this point and will continue to be as successful as I am on the shoulders of other people. It's

important for me, for my sense of kinship continuity and community, that I realize that I'm only one generation. . . . I'd like to preserve, I want my community, my kin to be preserved and to develop and grow and I can contribute to that directly by my own actions of doing different things.

∽ UPLIFTING THE RACE

Many respondents said that getting out of poverty and achieving success was not enough: it was necessary to help others do the same. Respondents exhibited a sense of racial and cultural group cohesion and feelings of mutual responsibility. One young respondent explained this sense of mutual concern she was taught by her elders:

It's something that a lot of older black people say. And now some of the younger people are on that tip 'cause they've gotten back to their roots . . . so you're sittin' there and you hear somebody say, "What can you be doin' to uplift the race, you as a person personally you know in whatever area of life, whatever profession you choose?" Basically you should be looking at a way you're gonna make some pertinent contribution to help the whole Afro-American experience of the United States of America. It's something that you hear a lot from older black people.

Uplifting the race involves a sense of racial cohesion. One respondent said:

There are some expectations among the people that I know and have known that black people will take care of each other, just because they're black. It's like the perception we have about blood relatives. You never put a blood relative out on the street. It's extremely taboo. And if they are doing something that you just can't take anymore, and you're forced to get rid of them, it's still very difficult.

For some respondents, being politically active in efforts to fight racism, provide jobs, or increase social programs for the disadvantaged is an alternative to giving money to nonprofit organizations. African Americans are often judged by other blacks not by their individual successes but by their contributions to the community and people of color generally. One respondent said: "Things haven't really come to us, because of racism, because of the repression of our race. We all owe something to one another. It's a part of life. If I take two steps forward, I should bring someone else four steps forward."

Another respondent observed: "I think there's a different legacy for African Americans—that of oppression, so we're trying to give and we're still working our way out as a whole. So I think the giving for the African American community is an effort to raise ourselves out of poverty whereas giving from the white community seems to be a little bit about making yourself feel better."

While for some respondents, being politically active was an alternative to giving money to nonprofit organizations, others gave to and volunteered for organizations such as the NAACP, the National Urban League, the National Council of Negro Women, and the National Equal Rights League, which have both political and philanthropic agendas:

> A lot of work I've done has been in the churches, and active participation in civil rights organizations. I've always been involved since I was a child. I was involved with the NAACP at ten years old. I was president of my local chapter when I was 14 and I did work with state organizations with the NAACP when I was a young teenager and a young adult. That was kind of more political as well as volunteer community things.

⌒ WOMEN'S WORK

Informal giving, or giving that occurs without the assistance of organizations (such as preparing and donating food and shelter and caring for children), was described as largely the domain of African American women in the community and in the church. Within the church, women are often responsible for helping the sick and preparing food for funerals, church socials, and other events. Most respondents talked of such effort as an integral part of African American culture but few characterized it as "giving." Many respondents talked about the amount of time their mothers and grandmothers give to the community, the church, the family and extended family. One respondent, describing her mother's and other mothers' roles in the community, stated:

> My mom did stuff for the community. It's kind of relatively a small community. Helping out this person or that person, it's not like we threw rent parties or anything but it was like . . . people around would make food, take a bag of groceries to somebody, loan somebody some money knowing it wasn't a loan. . . . Loaning out stuff, a lawn mower or something, loaning out her children to do stuff, like go clean Miss Polite's house, that kind of thing. She did a lot of free day care.

One respondent, when asked about the difference between the giving practices of women and men, replied: "My dad gives a lot of money to organizations. He's always giving money to things. My mother's a nurse. She gave her time but she never really gave money to causes." Another respondent said:

> I didn't see men do anything. . . . I always saw women helping out. They were always cooking for someone else if they were sick or they were old. I always saw them drive them to the store or do their laundry for them. I always saw them organizing trips for the kids. They were always involved with the church.

In the church, the division of labor is often along gender lines. Most members of black churches are women but most officers are men. One exception is the Mothers' Board or Women's Board found in many Baptist and AME churches:

Most [care of the sick and elderly] happened from the Mothers' Board. The women who were on the Women's Board of the Baptist church. Pretty much their role is to do, to be the caretakers. I remember the women, my aunts actually, who would visit other sisters and other women on the Mothers' Board. And they would take roses or what have you, offer money here and there to some. . . . Clearly I remember women being the forerunners, taking care of people in the house, in the church and making the phone calls and stuff like that, as well as the pastor's wife . . . the pastor's wife was always doing this or doing that, what I always hear or my aunt was doing this or that, all the women in the choir were doing this or that. It was always about the women.

Whether women give money at different rates than men in the black community, is difficult to determine. However, it does seem that women volunteer more often than men. Part of this is simply the result of the roles that have been assigned to men and women by the African American culture and the larger society. Women are expected to take care of others, to attend to household activities like cooking and cleaning, to be more helpful than men, and to care for the elderly and the children.

∞ TIMES OF CRISIS

Another form of informal giving found in the African American community is aid given to people in times of crisis. If a member of someone's family is ill, or if there is a death in the family, the family can usually count on extended family, neighbors, and friends to offer some form of support whether it be through cooking food, performing household chores, furnishing car rides, making phone calls, or giving money. The church is also usually quite helpful during these times. Many African Americans talked about giving to other people in their extended family or to the community during times of crisis. One respondent said: "People kind of shared time and their homes, and when they could [they gave] monetary gifts and support. I think it's one of the things that the black community does very well in times of crisis—people come together, come together in a very strong, solid way." Another, speaking of giving at crisis times, said: "When somebody dies, you bring food. . . . The bigger the tragedy, the more you let people know you care. You take care of them so they don't have to worry about a lot." Much giving in many forms goes on at funerals. In discussing what a person is expected to bring to a funeral, one respondent said:

You think of the person and you give what you think of. You give what you think they may need, what you think might replace some loss. Depending on what your relationship is with that person is what you end up giving. Usually money. Usually money is what comes before anything else 'cause people get a little embarrassed about their choices of gifts when someone has died. . . . Then it's food and it's support—offering support is a way of giving. "Is there anything I can do?" [you might ask.] Plus giving cards. And usually in a card comes money. . . . I think you'll see that more than an actual gift. It's food. It's a favorite meal. Something that gonna cheer the person up.

∞ THE CHURCH

The church has for years been a central political and social organizing tool for African Americans. One respondent referred to it as one of the last black-owned and operated businesses. Most respondents reported that either they give to the church or have family members who give to the church. Most of the time, offerings and time volunteered at the church are not seen by members as charity or philanthropy. One respondent, speaking about her family's involvement in the church, said:

> The church was often the focus and the center of socializing, at least for my neighborhood which was predominantly black. Our family supported programs that the church would sponsor [and had] a strong commitment to the church around tithing or whenever the church would ask [the congregation] to dig a little deeper in the pocket to help with community programs. I don't think we thought of it as philanthropy.

Many respondents over the age of 35 reported giving the majority of their donation dollars to the church. One respondent talks of her mother's giving patterns: "I think the largest amount of money [my mother] gave consistently was to the church, all the things that the church did, so there's a church building fund, there's a church school . . . you know the church this, the church that. My mom was forever giving time, money, etc., into those kind of things."

Black churches are involved in administering a number of community programs. Programs that respondents cited include care of the sick, the shut-in, the elderly, and families in mourning. Youth programs mentioned include tutoring, after-school activities, counseling, and recreation. Respondents noted that churches sponsor college scholarship programs, run homes for the elderly and day-care centers, and organize food and clothing drives for the poor and homeless. Speaking of the different programs her family participated in, one respondent said:

> I think everyone in my family—and I come from a large extended family—volunteered in the church in some way. We didn't consider it as volunteering. In terms of serving on the usher board, the choir, participating in Sunday school teaching, cooking meals if there was a death in someone's family, everyone was active in some way.

The black church and the giving behavior of black people are intimately connected. People financially support the church, and the church furnishes services and resources to the community. One older respondent, speaking of the role of the church in his community 35 years ago, described it as follows:

Blacks helped blacks in those days. . . . The community I lived in, many times when things would happen where there would be a need to provide for, you'd come to the church. You know, it'd be, "Sister Jones is sick and shut-in so therefore we'd like to have you take her a meal." You know, you didn't write checks for $15, no, you took meals over to someone's house or if someone got wiped out in a flood that happened in town. I remember my mother going and taking clothes. And there were a lot of people she would help. And it was mostly through the church. The church was the center of the community. That's where everything happened and was generated.

In the past, nonprofit organizations that have sought to get African American support for their various campaigns have gone to the church. Many blacks prefer to sponsor church programs because they are sometimes suspicious of other nonprofit organizations. While respondents reported being picky about what types of organizations they give to, many respondents reported giving large sums of money to the church without prior knowledge of how the money was to be spent. One middle-aged respondent said of her family's contributions to the church: "The major organization is the church. And the particular family that I was living with at the time [as a child] gave to the church in extension believing they were giving to the community. So that was one of their foremost committed ways of giving."

Many respondents reported tithing to the church. A tithe is a special collection which is calculated as a percentage of a person's yearly income, usually ten percent. Many African Americans, despite the fact that their incomes are low, feel it is part of their social and spiritual responsibility to give this amount to the church. One respondent describes his parents' participation in tithing as follows: "My parents had a little book of envelopes that the church gave you each month for your weekly contribution. The tray always came by twice on Sundays and you would put cash or checks in the first pot and your envelope in the second. I never saw the pot come around and my parents not give."

☙ GIVING TO ORGANIZATIONS

Most of the respondents mentioned giving money or time to nonprofit organizations. Respondents differed in both choice of organizations and reasons for giving. Some respondents preferred giving to local, visible organizations. Some give money; others prefer giving time. The church is the single most cited organization to which respondents reported giving. Some felt that giving directly to the homeless or to the needy in one's own neighborhood or community was the best way to help others. Some people felt that helping extended family, friends, and neighbors was better than giving to strangers. Some respondents give only to the church, but most also reported giving to other nonprofit organizations.

Typically, respondents reported giving money and time to a combination of national organizations, local and community programs, and the church. The following quote is representative of the comments made by many respondents:

> People in my family gave to the church. They gave money and volunteered time [in the choir], and they belonged to the mission society—they go out and they feed old people, clean their houses and stuff. . . . My parents also gave to the March of Dimes and sometimes when kids came by the house selling something so they could win a scholarship to college or something like that, my dad would buy whatever it was, even if he didn't need it, to help the kid out. My dad was always real skeptical, though; he would always ask twenty questions before he would give up any money. Sometimes my parents would give money to Jehovah Witnesses . . . they gave to the United Way too 'cause they knew some black folks who work there.

Some respondents expressed a preference for giving directly to people living in their community, whether friends or strangers. The respondents expressed a desire to see the results of their work, to know who was benefiting from their giving. Others gave to the community for the purpose of giving back, uplifting the race, or simply because they feel kinship ties with neighbors, homies, fellow church members, and other African Americans:

> I think my parents gave a lot to the people around them, their community. I don't think they really gave much money because they were always struggling just to get by. I have five sisters and brothers so it wasn't at all easy for them. As far as giving to organizations, they gave money to the church. The church provided a lot of services for the community right around our neighborhood so there wasn't really a need for other organizations.

Some respondents focus the majority of their resources on one way of giving. Those who were skeptical of large nonprofit organizations give only to local organizations. Some mentioned their inability to trust many organizations with their donations and others just need to be able to scrutinize the actions and activities of the organizations they give to, wanting to know the people running them and to be able to see tangible results. Some say they give only to local organizations because that way they can readily see the results of their giving and can check up on the organization. Quite a few respondents mentioned giving money to local youth and others who came to the door collecting. Trust is an important issue and being able to question the person collecting money seems to be an important part of the process of choosing organizations to which to give. One respondent said: "My mom gave money to different organizations like . . . when people were selling light bulbs for United Handicapped Workers or that kinda thing. I don't remember her giving money to NAACP or anything like that. . . . "

In making decisions about which organizations to give money to, many respondents cited familiarity with the organization, evidence of the effects of the organization's work, and relevance to the giver's life. Also, they wanted to know that the money was really getting to the people who needed it. The person who was soliciting the funds had to have conviction and be someone who could talk persuasively about the programs being funded.

Several respondents expressed a preference for personal, direct giving. One person said, "Black people are more hands-on-type givers. In general we'd rather give directly to the people in need."

- The family and extended family serve as an extensive and complex framework for sharing and helping.
- A system of ritual godparenthood is used to help pay for specific celebrations and to expand the support network of one's family.
- Money, goods, and clothing are often taken or sent back to Mexico to be distributed in one's hometown.
- The church is an important center of philanthropic activity.
- Housing is frequently shared with relatives and friends.
- Little giving or volunteering is directed toward non-Mexican, non-church organizations.

More than other immigrant groups, Mexicans have followed an ebb-and-flow immigration pattern. While much of the Southwest—where the bulk of Mexican immigration occurs—belonged to Mexico prior to 1848, the region was not heavily populated by Mexicans until after it became part of the United States. At the time of the Mexican War (1846–48) there were approximately 60,000 Mexicans in New Mexico, 20,000 in California, and 5,000 in Texas. Shortly after the turn of the century, nearly 10 percent of Mexico's total population had emigrated to the southwestern United States. Between 1900 and 1910, the Mexican populations of Texas and New Mexico nearly doubled, the Mexican population of Arizona more than doubled, and that of California quadrupled. A combination of forces led to this massive surge in the Mexican population of the Southwest. Primary among these forces was the development of railroads in Mexico and the United States. Railroads provided transportation north and a plenitude of jobs. Mexicans who came to the United States prior to World War I worked on the railroads, in agriculture, or in the copper and coal mines of the Southwest. By 1930 there were about a million Mexicans in the United States. Legislation following World War I had stopped the flow of European workers coming to the United States, resulting in many more potential jobs for Mexicans. The Depression of the 1930s reversed the inflow of Mexicans to the United States. Just over 30,000 Mexicans entered the United States during the entire decade of the 1930s. Meanwhile, about 500,000 Mexicans were forcibly repatriated as many Americans blamed their lack of jobs on cheap Mexican labor. Mexicans lost agricultural jobs to "Okies" and other American migrants who moved west. Often Mexicans who were citizens of the United States were expelled when they sought governmental relief. Shipping someone back to Mexico was cheaper than supplying them with one week's worth of relief, so when people applied for relief they were often sent to Mexico instead. Many other Mexicans left the country voluntarily as jobs dried up in the United States. By 1940 there may have been as few as 400,000 Mexicans living in the United States.

The bracero farm labor program was initiated in 1942. This was a program designed by the federal government to bring contract laborers into the United States from Mexico. The program supposedly set guidelines for living and working conditions, but these guidelines were often not met. In 1945 there were about 50,000 braceros in the United States; this number rose to nearly 450,000 in 1959. The program was formally terminated in 1964.

During the post–World War II era, with less need for foreign labor in the United States, deportations were begun again. This time citizenship was used as the determinant. During the 1950s about four million people were sent back to Mexico. Meanwhile, however, legal immigration was increasing. During the 1940s nearly 60,000 Mexicans entered the United States as resident aliens with permanent status. This increased to nearly 275,000 during the 1950s, over 440,000 in the 1960s, and almost 640,000 during the 1970s. The U.S. Census Bureau estimated that of the 22.4 million Hispanics residing in the United States in 1990, 13.5 million were of Mexican birth or ancestry.

There is, literally, an ocean of difference between Mexican immigration into the United States and immigration from China, Japan, Korea, the Philippines, or European and other nations across the Atlantic or Pacific oceans. Mexico and the United States share an 1,800-mile border. Also, unlike Canada, Mexico has long been a much poorer country than the United States. The desire for a better life, and the proximity of the United States, have long been major forces behind Mexican emigration to its northern neighbor.

Mexican traditions surrounding family, kinship, community, and religious life have created many practices relevant to philanthropic behavior. These customs are illustrated by the following excerpts from interviews with 40 individuals from the Mexican community.

⚭ KINSHIP AND COMMUNITY

In his book *The Buried Mirror* (1992), Carlos Fuentes called the Mexican family "the hearth, the sustaining warmth . . . and the security net in times of trouble." This statement was echoed time and again by the people interviewed for this study. Their responses indicated that the concept of *familia*, or family, is central to understanding Mexican giving patterns. This was true for most of the respondents, both recent immigrants and those whose families had been here many generations.

One's *familia* provides food and lodging, care in times of sickness, money and goods in times of need, and a variety of other services. The *familia* normally extends beyond the nuclear family to include grandparents, cousins, aunts and uncles, and a variety of other relatives. Additionally, the *familia* often embraces people other than biological relations; ritual kin and community members may also be included. Among Mexicans in the United States, the concept of *familia* is often extended to include all Mexicans or all Hispanics. No matter how inclusive one's *familia*, the primary obligation of the *fa-*

milia is the same: to give aid and support to *familia* members throughout life. The constant message is: It is as a tightly knit group that you will survive and eventually prosper. One woman explained:

> Obviously, not everyone gives, but, among those that do, it is the sense of *familia* that proves to be the primary difference from mainstream American culture. There is more giving done within the community and the family. The focal point of the culture is less on me, myself, and I. You help the group versus the individual. Even if you don't have anything, you give, just because someone is worse off than you are.

Traditional patterns of communal and familial support have continued to influence the giving patterns of Mexicans in this country. Due to the proximity of Mexico, Mexicans living in the United States have been able to maintain their traditional culture to a higher degree than other ethnic groups. Contact between friends and relatives in the two countries is frequent. Mexicans living in this country often return to Mexico for holidays, family vacations, schooling, and a variety of other purposes (Daniels, 1990; Portes and Bach, 1985; and Sowell, 1981).

Facing varying degrees of discrimination, language barriers, and often limited financial resources, Mexicans naturally turn to their *familia* for support. It is quite common for more traditional Mexican Americans to take in and care for their parents when they are older. Many families expect this to happen as a matter of course, as part of *el deber de los hijos*, the debt or duty of the children, or of *respeto*, the care and respect one shows one's elders. These expressions sum up the expectation many Mexicans have that children will take care of their parents when they are older. Housing parents is only one way to repay parents for all they have done for their children. While this presents a significant financial burden to the children in terms of free rent, food, transportation, laundry, and other services they offer to their parents, it is a custom followed by many of the respondents in this study.

A few respondents, though well educated, well paid, middle-aged professionals, indicated that they had no significant retirement savings. Their extra money went to support their parents and other family members, and they expected the same from their children when they were older. Although there is a large variety of government programs that could assist the Mexican elderly, pride, lack of language skills, and other factors keep them from making use of those benefits. Instead, they turn to the one source of aid they know they can always count on, their family.

One man said: "I moved in with my parents so I could move my parents to a better neighborhood." Another man said that as a people Mexicans tend to "take care of our parents in lieu of sending them to a nursing home." Most traditional Mexicans do not see a need for senior housing or nursing homes. One man reported that "in Mexico there are old folks homes but they are frowned upon." A woman expressed confusion with government housing policy in the United States. "The government will pay a convalescent hospital thousands of dollars per month but will only give the family $200 per month to take care of your parents within the family. You can't afford to do it." Another woman said that her mother was fairly free about lending her money out to relatives who needed it with no stipulations on being paid back. When asked what her mother intended to do for retirement, she responded that her mother felt that it was the responsibility of her sons to assist her if she needed help.

Children in many Mexican families are welcome to live at home as long as they wish. One woman said, "A Mexican family is very knit. If one falls, you try to pick them up. You do not get kicked out at 18. It's okay if you are 30 and still living at home." Many respondents could not understand the prevailing attitudes in the United States toward children living at home. One respondent said, "With most Americans, if the children get 18 then it is goodbye. The obligation is to feed them until then and then goodbye." One respondent, a woman in her mid-thirties, returned home after her divorce to live with her parents. While she misses some of her old freedom, she does not feel it is unusual that she has returned to live at home.

Mexicans do not provide housing solely for parents or children. They also take in brothers and sisters. One person said, "We came here because of family. My aunts took us in and helped get us on our feet." A man said that his "mother's sisters lived with us until they got married. One aunt was with us for ten years." Another person commented that her "uncle came and lived with us when I was 17." A young woman said, "My sister has a deformed child. His legs and arms are not normal, his torso is very small, and he has to drag himself with his arms. We were poor at the time but we took them in for about three months until they returned to Mexico." Many of those interviewed felt that Mexican families give aid in the form of housing beyond what is considered common in the United States. This is a great drain on the finances of those supplying meals and various services for other family members as well as care for elderly parents. This open-door policy is advanced to the extended family as well. One man spoke about relatives his parents took in: "[They were] my great-grandmother and three or four cousins who didn't get along with their parents over trouble with the law. The young guys stayed six months to a year, my great grandmother for about two years. Then she got cancer and all the relatives wanted to see her and say goodbye, so she rotated between houses." "An aunt was having trouble," another respondent said, "so I bought her a mobile home and now she lives with me for free." A young woman said, "Oh yeah, if a family member needed help, my parents would discuss it and both my father's and my mother's relatives would stay with us when they needed to." Another respondent's parents took in "a cousin from Mexico who wanted to learn English." Extended family are often as welcome as nuclear family members.

Extended family members also share food, money, services, and jobs with their relatives whether their relatives live in this country or in Mexico. Much of the giving that occurs within families flows from the United States to relatives who have remained in Mexico. Many respondents spoke about sharing goods and services other than housing within their extended families. A female university student said: "My relatives were basically all in Mexico, although one of my mom's sisters was in L.A. on our block. We were always giving her sugar, food, baby-sitting for her if she needed it, taking her to the doctor, and other similar things." Another respondent said that she sends many of her own clothes to her relatives in Mexico.

Another woman said that her aunts relied on her father's help in times of need: "My dad is the oldest of ten, so he is a very strong figure. Anytime you get in trouble you call Arturo, but it's weird to me because, like, what do [my aunts'] husbands do? Why call your brother?" This woman's father and uncles "got together and built a home in Vaya del Guadalupe for their parents. They made it with five rooms so the children could visit frequently and comfortably." She said that her parents expect her "to always help the family, even if I have to go out of my way." Another respondent said that he feels this emphasis on the family is typical of Mexican Americans, even to the point that "many kids are dropping out of school to support their families, and many families work together in the fields." He said that he sees "the community as being the second area of concern for Mexican Americans, but if, and only if, they have enough time and/or money."

A woman reported that her father has been sending money to her grandfather and other relatives since 1947. She said, "He just sends money and my granddad uses it as he needs it. He also sends presents because in Mexico they are a lot more expensive than they are here." In addition to monetary aid, many families send clothes to younger relatives living in Mexico once the children in the United States have outgrown them. One young woman said she would consistently "send clothes to my cousins in Mexico."

Giving to one's family in Mexico often exacts a high price in addition to the cost associated with the money and goods sent back. Coming to this country initially is expensive and sometimes dangerous even for those entering legally. Many of those who cross must pay a *mordida* (bribe) in order to assure that they are able to cross at the border and will be able to find work when they get across the border. So desperate are these workers to send money back home to their families and communities, and so great is their responsibility, that the majority of them work for less than minimum wage and resort to living in cars or buses, under bridges, and even in packing crates or the infamous coffin-size "caves" dug into hillsides in Monterey and San Diego counties. Despite these hardships, most continue to work in the fields for many years, returning cyclically to their villages in Mexico to visit families, attend important religious celebrations, or fulfill obligatory shifts on village councils.

Transportation and postal costs associated with sending money and goods back to Mexico can often be significant. One woman related an extreme example of the costs associated with such giving. A friend of hers returns to Mexico frequently, both for her work and in order to visit her 25 godchildren. She often travels by train and bus to reach her destination and there are frequent police and customs inspections along the way. Should passengers be carrying anything of value, portions of it will disappear at each customs stop. In order to beat this system, the woman took 100 left-footed shoes, and had a friend travel separately with the right-footed shoes, to give to her godchildren and members of their families.

Despite the emphasis on giving within the family, sharing within the ethnic community is quite common. This is true whether people direct their giving to their old community in Mexico, their new community in the United States, or both. For some respondents, especially recent immigrants, the community functioned as a substitute family.

What is perhaps most surprising about giving patterns within the ethnic community is the extent to which Mexicans will open up their homes to friends and even strangers. One man recalled that his "dad adopted a down-and-out cabbie and he lived with them for 10 years." He then spoke about other people that his parents helped: "Eight of my buddies and one girl were given homes, until they joined the service or got married, when they ran away from their homes. We still put up people—my wife's brother [who is ill], a friend's son, many others of my son's friends. We give them room and board."

"My mother always took in neighborhood kids, mostly my brother's friends," recalled another respondent. "Mom always had the door open." Many of those taken in are recent arrivals from Mexico. "Dad always had people coming from Mexico and he would put them up," said one woman. Another woman replied, "Yeah, about five years ago a friend's son was moving here from Mexico and he stayed with us about one month." One respondent said: "In a Mexican family or neighborhood, the doors are always open. It's just accepted." Another respondent said: "There are no homeless Hispanics because you will take someone in and help." Despite the financial burden, many Mexicans are willing to make this sacrifice. As one woman said, "Mom was always helping someone. We were a refugee center. I couldn't believe how many people lived with us. Someone was always living with us. We didn't have much but we shared what we had." Sharing involves not only family and friends but anyone in need. A woman respondent said:

> My parents would give food to people who came to the door [begging]. There was once one man outside the church, he was rummaging for cans through the trash, he was poor and hungry. My dad took him home, gave him some food, gave him our cans that we had been saving, and then gave him some money [about three dollars].

One respondent added, "It seems the richer people give less than the poorer people. I don't know why, maybe when you're poor you know what it's like and you give up your money easier. It's like survival, everyone helps everyone else. You always borrow sugar and stuff from neighbors."

Recent immigrants both participated in such sharing and benefited from it. One respondent said that her "father came up here first and got a job in the steel mill. When we came up, Hispanics . . . opened up their doors to us.

They gave us pots and pans and everything to set up a house. They also helped my mother get around and get used to the way things worked here." She commented that this sort of "sharing within the community wasn't thought of as giving, it was helping my mother adapt to a new environment." Another woman said that when she first moved to this country, her grandmother became well known throughout the county's Mexican community. "She did for everyone. She was especially active in Guadalupana, cooking for the church and the downtrodden, and getting clothing for recent immigrants and others in need." One person said: "Mexicans help Mexicans. I've heard of United Way but I have never been interested in helping them out." A man said:

> One thing a lot of people gave was their old, grown-out-of children's clothes to neighbors, and someone was always bringing us food, or my mom was always making food for someone. I don't know if it was that someone needed it or if it was just friendship. I never thought about it at the time, it was just natural. Sometimes I think people needed it because it would be grocery bags, and not cooked. Especially when children were involved the idea was that someone could use the old clothes and toys and things.

⑤ CELEBRATIONS

One is born into a *familia* and later expands one's *familia* through marriage. Joyous celebrations mark these events. They are also used as a means of reaffirming family bonds. A great amount of giving occurs at these events, primarily in the form of gifts from relatives and friends. Central to this form of Mexican philanthropy is the Latin American Catholic tradition of *compadrazgo*.

Compadrazgo, or copaternity, is an example of what anthropologists call fictive kinship. Fictive kinship strengthens and expands the safety net of *la familia* through the recruitment of new members into the family or by further securing existing family bonds when cousins, aunts, uncles or other relatives become *padrinos* (godparents). It is important to choose *padrinos* well because they are required to play an important role in the lives of their *ahijado*, or godchild. *Compadres* (co-parents) are expected to help provide for their *ahijado's* sacred and secular needs throughout his or her life, including accepting responsibility for the child should the parents die. Ideally, *compadrazgo* is a relation that engenders eternal ties of loyalty, trust, affection, respect, and mutual assistance. Several Protestant respondents reported that they practice this Catholic tradition.

One receives *padrinos* for many occasions, most typically when one receives the sacraments of baptism, first communion, confirmation, and marriage. In addition to the lifelong spiritual and financial obligations they assume, obligations that help assure the long-term security of some family members, *padrinos* are expected to help pay for the celebration and the subsequent party or parties. They are also officially recognized by the Catholic church. Some *padrinos* do not have the long-term obligations of the primary *padrinos*, nor are they officially recognized by the church. They may serve a supplementary role in a sacramental occasion (a monetary contribution or preparing food) or may be chosen for non-religious occasions, such as a child's first haircut, a graduation, or the purchase of a house or car.

The most important *padrinos* are those one receives at baptism. The ceremony and party for a baptism are usually not as large as those for other occasions. The *padrinos* are responsible for buying the dress, paying the church fee for the ceremony, and pouring the baptismal water over the child. By participating in the ceremony the *padrinos* demonstrate their life-long obligation to assist in the spiritual formation of the child. In addition to paying for the ceremony and party, *padrinos* often commission a photographer to preserve the special day for the family and friends. Often the *madrina* (godmother) sponsors an *aguacero*, or shower. The *aguacero*, in the words of one respondent, "is a big, big deal."

There is much variation in godparent customs. Among more traditional families the *padrinos* are responsible for giving the parents a *batea*, a tray filled with symbolic gifts. The *padrino* has an additional responsibility in some families; he and the father of the child give *bolos*, coins of various denominations, to children in attendance. The two men gather change and throw it to the children. One woman described this custom as "a gift of sharing the joy of the occasion with the kids." This custom also symbolizes good fortune for the child. Another woman said she had seen children receive *bolos* only a couple of times, once in old home movies. The first time she saw *bolos* thrown was "at my godchild's baptism seven years ago. The godfather did it and the kids and I didn't know what was happening until we were told, because our family doesn't do that. Once the kids were told, they scrambled for the coins. It was done at the house afterwards, whoever had change all pulled it together."

For first communion and confirmation there is usually only one *padrino*. Some families add one or two *padrinos*. For first communion the *padrino/madrina* buys the boy's suit or girl's dress, purchases a Bible as a gift, and helps throw a party for the child. For confirmation the *padrino/madrina* helps pay any fees, purchases a present for the *ahijado*, and sponsors a party or meal. *Padrinos* for a wedding (two or more) usually have larger financial responsibilities. They help pay for the bridal gown, the church fees, and the party. The *madrina* sponsors an *aguacero* for the bride. Extra *padrinos* might include *padrinos de ramo* (to buy the bouquet), *padrinos de lazo* (to purchase a white silk cord used to symbolically bind the couple, a rosary, and a Bible), and *padrinos de arras* (to give the couple thirteen pieces of silver money and the three wedding rings). Other *padrinos* may be chosen to help pay for an even larger party, the band, beer, the limousine, and whatever else is deemed necessary to the celebration. At the wedding reception the primary *padrinos* donate the largest sum of money to the couple during the money dance (with the exception of the couple's immediate family). During the money dance, the newly-weds are given money as guests take turns dancing with them.

The wedding party is usually quite large, which is why it is necessary for *padrinos* to help offset the cost. These parties are more than mere celebrations of an event. Largely, they exist to bind everyone together. As one woman said, "not all the attention is on the child; much of it is on just being together as a family."

Though a large portion of a *padrino's* responsibility is financial, such service is considered an honor and is often important in cementing friendships and family ties. Nelson (1971, pp. 78–79) describes the relationships as "a mutually contingent exchange system that also involves sentiments that emphasize the moral propriety of repayment—the idea of contract. Repayment is not exchanging equivalent items, but the feeling of a sense of moral obligation to another individual." While not everyone feels bound by this moral obligation, and often *padrinos* do not remain close to their *ahijados,* many respondents reported lifelong ties with their *padrinos.* One woman said: "My *madrina* from communion is a friend and I used her when I renewed my confirmation vows. She took care of me for six months when I was younger. She is kind of like a second mom. We are still in touch." Another woman said that she is very close with two of her *padrinos,* "one from baptism, he's a priest in Mexico and I see him when I go there. The other is from first communion, my aunt in Sacramento." Another woman stated that she is still quite close with two of her *madrinas.* One is "my aunt from Mexico who confirmed me [one day after my baptism], we stay with her when we go to Mexico and vice versa, and one aunt here when I was reconfirmed in eighth grade." A *padrino* reported: "I give money to my godchildren, loose change, whenever I see them." Another states that "a lot of security is given to kids knowing this [that they have *padrinos* who will help support them]. I think it is done quite a bit still [choosing *padrinos*] and helps form ties and nurture relationships."

Christmas is an important time for many Mexicans because of their traditional Catholic faith. Much of the giving that occurs at this time of the year is either devotional or directed toward various celebrations. Most giving is centered around religious symbols and occurs among family and close friends. Additionally, many celebrations at this time of the year, such as Las Posadas, occur within one's nuclear community and serve to reaffirm the community's sense of *familia.* In this ceremony, families go to others' homes pretending they are Joseph and Mary seeking shelter at an inn (*posada*). The ceremony is accompanied by candles, songs, and refreshments. The Christmas season generally lasts from the beginning of Las Posadas on December 16 to Dia de Los Reyes on January 6.

The celebration of Las Posadas is an important religious and cultural custom. Although it is on the increase in the United States, there are many communities in which a formal Posada is not available. Many respondents who did not have access to a Posada expressed considerable regret over this. Most of these respondents had participated in these celebrations at least once in their lives, and missed this link with their culture as well as the community spirit engendered by Posadas. The importance of Posadas in fostering communal values was illustrated by one man's story of the role they played in his parish:

> My mother helps the church put on a Posada every year. We used to have Posadas every weekend before Christmas [for one month]. People would get together and exchange and help each other; it would bind the community. They grew larger and larger. Each year people would volunteer their houses. The last week the party would be held at the church and there would be *folkloricos* [Mexican folk dances], food, drinks, and piñatas [10 or so]. The people were excited and the priest organizing this was exemplary of what one should do in the community. . . . The new priests wanted to cut out Posadas from going house to house and the people complained and made them keep them.

The giving that occurs at Posadas is primarily devotional in nature. Increasingly in the United States, however, Mexicans expend their time and, occasionally, money participating in Posadas because it is a link to their culture and an effective means of maintaining community.

A young girl's family and her *padrinos* celebrate her fifteenth birthday with a *quinceañera*, a traditional coming-out party. It is a cross between a confirmation and a debutante ball or, as one respondent put it, "a wedding without the bride." Traditionally, this is the time a young woman is presented as an adult member of the community and after which she is allowed to date. A *quinceañera* greatly resembles a wedding. The girl is dressed all in white and is escorted by a boy fairly close to her age. The boy is usually a brother or cousin since the girl is not yet supposed to be dating. There are fourteen other couples, all dressed formally as well. The celebration begins with a mass at which the young woman participates in the sacrament of confession so she can begin her new life free of sin. Afterwards there is a large dance party during which the young woman waltzes to a song that has been passed down by generations of women in her family.

On this occasion the young woman receives gifts from friends and family, and the celebration is paid for at least in part by the *padrinos*. The degree of financial involvement by the *padrinos* depends upon the girl's family and how lavish a *quinceañera* they wish to hold. At one extreme, a girl's parents will pay for the entire mass and accompanying celebration with the *padrinos* giving only small gifts; at the other extreme, the *padrinos* will pay for the entire ceremony and buy her dress, jewelry, and elaborate gifts.

Cinco de Mayo, May 5, is a national holiday in Mexico. Cinco de Mayo celebrates a Mexican victory in a battle against overwhelming French odds. Within the United States Cinco de Mayo is celebrated primarily as a cultural affair; in some cities this includes the culture of all of Latin America and not just Mexico. The nuclear community is the primary benefactor of giving on Cinco de Mayo. People invest their time and money primarily in fairs, festivals, and dances that promote Mexican and Latino culture.

The respondents reported a variety of giving activities occurring on Cinco de Mayo. Some volunteered their time as participants. One person stated that he

> was involved with a Mexican American association in Oakland, the Center Cultural Mexicano. We were involved with cultural activities for Cinco de Mayo and other events. We would rent out an Oakland auditorium for social gatherings and cultural activities. I was a dancer. I danced for two years, from '68 to '70. We were so wrapped up in this stuff that Vietnam almost didn't exist. We were in our own world; 80 percent of our associations were immigrant-related.

Some respondents reported week-long celebrations. "There is one week of comedy, art displays, concerts, and on Friday of the week there is a concert and a dance," reported one woman. "We would dance with the flag pole. We wouldn't do much in Los Angeles. Here [in San Francisco] there is more. For Cinco de Mayo there is a week-long celebration; there are piñatas and mariachis," stated another. The concerts, dances, and other such activities are staged by volunteers. Church groups participate as well. "The Guadalupanas have meals on Cinco de Mayo to raise money," reported one woman. That they choose that day to raise funds is a good indicator of the amount of involvement people have with Cinco de Mayo. Another person reported a celebration for Cinco de Mayo at church.

Cinco de Mayo has evolved in the United States into a celebration of Mexican culture with an emphasis on food and dance. Where the emphasis of many festivals celebrated by Mexicans is on the nuclear community, Cinco de Mayo emphasizes cultural pride and involvement throughout the extended community. One woman, testifying to the unifying power of this celebration, reported that she "joined the Hispanic Business Club and it feels good. At the last Cinco de Mayo I finally felt like I belonged, not just out in the wind anymore."

∞ SICKNESS AND DEATH

The interdependence of Mexican family and community life is evident when someone becomes sick or dies. Mexicans, especially women, give their time to help the person who is sick or the family of the person who died. Relatives and friends prepare food, clean the house, watch the children, make funeral arrangements, and pay for a coffin and a mass. If someone wishes to be buried in Mexico, family and friends help the immediate family bear this expense.

Although none of our respondents said they belonged to funeral associations, there are many such organizations. Members pay modest dues. When someone dies, the funeral association pays for the funeral and burial. In some cases a small sum of money is given to the deceased's family. Two respondents spoke of belonging to a small religious group that venerated Maria Auxiliodora and that offered a similar service. Members would donate small amounts of money throughout the year to assist with funeral expenses for other members.

Most often, however, the sick and the families of those who have died are provided for by family and friends. One woman said that when someone died, "everyone would come; the whole family would come out of the woodwork. Everyone would bring food and drinks and they would do the cleaning and take care of the children so that the immediate family does nothing." Another woman reported that her

> mother stayed home most of the time and took care of us. One of the few times she would go out was if someone was sick or if someone had died. [If someone was sick or had died] my mother would bake and do whatever else was needed; my father would help with the funeral arrangements and stuff, like notifying friends and relatives in Mexico.

Another woman replied that "with funerals you will help if needed. There will be coffee and *pan dulce* [sweet bread] and heavier pastries. You will be up all night with the mourners. Everyone who comes to the funeral will bring flowers."

After a funeral a novena is held at either the home of the person who died or at a family member's home. During a novena, family and close friends pray the rosary together for nine days. At the end of prayers evening snacks are served, usually provided by an extended family member. Some people mark the first anniversary of a friend or family member's death by reconvening the whole family for a memorial mass. Everyone brings food and occasionally memorial gifts. The gathering is usually a fairly happy one, standing in sharp contrast to the post-funeral reception. Members of the close extended family gather yearly on the anniversary of the death, pray the rosary, and share snacks or a small meal.

Caring for the sick and for those who have died is, like almost everything else in traditional Mexican life, a family affair. As one man put it when comparing Mexican and Filipino family life: "At a Filipino or Hispanic wedding you'll see kids and families. Funerals are the same."

⏰ RELIGIOUS CUSTOMS

For many Mexicans, the church, most often the Catholic church, is the prime beneficiary of giving outside the family and extended family. One woman said that giving was the entire purpose for going to church: "At church you are there to give." Another respondent said that his "family gave, and gives, mainly through church." Large portions of time and money are given to the church for the upkeep of the church structure, the maintenance of various parish programs, charitable drives, the weekly collection, the preparation and celebration of various religious holidays and festivals, and other efforts. This giving is devotionally important and also serves to foster and maintain communal values. Even people who do not attend mass regularly give to the church.

Respondents gave many examples of church-related giving. The most common was the weekly collection. Most respondents who reported giving within the church said they gave money to the weekly collection. Many also reported giving money to the second as well as the first collection. (In the typical American Catholic parish, the first collection benefits parish programs and the second collection benefits charities and programs outside the parish.)

One woman's comment was typical: "At church my parents always give money." Her family also gave to the second collection which was often used to raise money for Mexico. "If there was ever a disaster in Mexico they would ask for money at the second collection." Some respondents, however, did not want their money to leave the parish. One woman said, "Most of our money goes for upkeep of the church. It would bother us if the money was going outside of the community."

Monetary donations to the church begin at a very young age. A man told of the importance his family placed on giving to the church when he was a child:

> Growing, you always gave to the church. My father made sure the whole family put money into the basket. Now it is only my children who put money in. My wife's family still puts in fifteen to twenty percent of their income and repairs the church, etc. My family went to church because of guilt, they "had to." My wife's family because of gratitude and duty. In poor families all the kids will go to parochial school. In my family church was the only place you gave consistently and at holidays. Hispanics will give much of their extra money to the church even if they hardly ever go to church.

Despite the often significant expense, many Mexican families send their children to Catholic schools. In addition to tuition, many of these schools require that the parents and the children invest a considerable amount of volunteer time. This is seen both as moral training for the children and a way of easing some of the financial burden of the school. Additionally, the children are often encouraged, or sometimes required, to participate in charitable endeavors within the community as part of their education. One woman said that being a Catholic had a definite effect on her philanthropic habits. She said: "It probably started in junior high school when I started Catholic school. They teach you human values of giving. At first it was a prerequisite that you have to give to St. Jude or something every month. My dad has always given to the church and he has been a big influence." Another woman said that she

> went to Catholic school when I was in grammar school and my parents always had to help with donations, help out at carnival, and help with serving lunches. My dad didn't make much money and he preferred to work with the community (volunteer). My dad would also help beyond this with various carnivals and fiestas.

Another respondent reported that she "did the readings at mass in elementary school. I taught catechism to first and second graders. I was also involved in a program called L.I.F.E. in which we prepared the school masses and liturgy for the masses, and we led the school retreats." One woman told us that her daughter "has to volunteer so many hours before being confirmed."

Religious festivals offer perhaps the best example of how religious giving merges the devotional and communal aspects of the Catholic faith. Festivals are held in celebration of a holy day and participants are reminded through prayers and rituals of the religious significance of their fiesta. Staging and paying for the celebration is a communal effort and serves both to reinforce communal bonds and provide a day of relaxation and joy. Many respondents reported participating in various festivals at their churches. One woman said that her parish would have "fiestas and carnivals and food drives during Thanksgiving for the homeless. Another woman said, "We used to have a festival with rides and games, and *folklórico* performers as a fundraiser for the church and the school." Another woman added that "the church would have dinners and I would help. I also gave clothing and helped with food drives." A college student said:

> I was an altar boy and in Youth Stars. We would watch films and discuss religious issues and all; also we would play games revolving around religious issues and go on field trips. I was a member and helped organize and later coordinate the club. We had car washes for fundraisers, canned food drives, collected newspapers. We gave [clothes] to the church or needy and to different organizations such as St. Vincent de Paul. I was also a CCD [religious education] aide and eventually taught.

A man listed some of the forms of giving in his family's church: "the collection, volunteering in organizations like the Guadalupanas, fundraising, St. Vincent de Paul, CYO [Catholic Youth Organization], Holy Names, ushers, and visiting the poor. Within the neighborhood growing up, it was mainly the church." Others would help physically maintain the church. One respondent said that a "lot of physical plant services and washing and cooking are done by church members. Coaching CYO and stuff also." Another said that her "parents gave mainly within the church, helping to build the church, helping with cleaning the church. Father delivered for St. Vincent de Paul, mother helped with CCD."

One respondent stated that she does "volunteer work through campus ministry. I read bedtime stories to the kids; we do work with the homeless; we take dessert and coffee to women in a shelter in the Tenderloin." Another said: "My parents were pretty active in the community. Whenever the church or the [Catholic] school needed help, they were there. They would help with food and clothes drives, but always through the church and the Mexican community." A man, speaking of his parents, said: "He also was a eucharistic minister and my mother was involved with cleaning the altar cloths and keeping the church up. She taught CCD and became one of the first women eucharistic ministers at our church."

Some of the women told of their involvement in *Cursillos de Cristiandad.* One woman said:

> A *cursillo* is a three-day retreat. Some parishes are active in the movement; some are not. You go once through the course but then you can return as kitchen help, or a counselor, or something. Many people go back and help, although many don't do it every year. Men and women go to separate retreats. As a child I knew I would do this because my mom and my grandmother had done this. "*De Colores*" was the theme song for the group and my grandmother was buried in her "*De Colores*" dress. It had many colors, because she liked the group so much. *Cursillos* are run through many parishes and the camps have mixed ethnic groups there. There is a reunion for the group one week after the end of the program. It was a big deal. My mother, my grandmother, my cousins, and my grandmother's sister all came to pick me up when I came home. Afterwards there was a party for all the families at a church in Concord.

This woman would not relate the specifics of the *cursillo* she attended because she wanted the interviewer to experience it and did not want to tell him what to expect. The amount of time participants donate to attend the *cursillo* and then to help staff the *cursillos* in future years is considerable, in addition to whatever role charity plays in the retreat itself.

Several respondents said that some parishes and other church structures are not very responsive to the needs of Mexicans in the United States. One woman said, "The church does not seem to help anywhere near as much as they could." One man said that his "mom gave a lot to the church, almost to the point of being exploited." Another said that his mother would help the church by taking

> the clothes and wash them and get them ready. She would hang up clothes and sell them. She would help people with lice and stuff. They didn't have *La Clinica* and stuff so they improvised. When I became a student activist I used to bring this up with my mom; she would give and give and we were very poor and needed her more ourselves. The church wasn't very helpful; in fact, they were exploitative. All the clothes, etc., were from us. Nothing was from the church despite its being wealthy. Our perception of the church has changed. We see it as not giving back and we've stopped giving. I've seen my parents give nickels and dimes every week to the church when we need it tenfold. The same thing is happening with United Way.

One man said that his father

> was part of a church group, St. Vincent de Paul, I think. They would give money and clothes to people who needed it. Once a migrant worker came down from Salinas to Oxnard and his car broke down; he couldn't get any work right away and he had a wife and kids. He needed about $150 just to get through the next few days. The monsignor only approved $30. This pissed off my dad. They might as well have done nothing.

This man's father and his friends then raised the money themselves for this man and his family.

The same respondent told a story that illustrates the difference a priest can make within a community:

> The priest organizing this was exemplary of what one should do in the community. He started an organization like St. Vincent de Paul to help families with money and he held a big carnival every year for a fundraiser for St. Vincent, youth organizations, CCD, and other needs. He would teach self-empowerment as opposed to simply doling out money.

When this priest left the parish, the priests who replaced him lacked the same sensitivity to the community's needs and desires:

> With the new guys, much of the community spirit is gone. We used to have a Spanish mass on Saturdays and there would be films and dinners afterwards for new immigrants and others. The new guys have cut out much of this and now many [Mexicans] don't come to church anymore. The new priests aren't teaching people skills to help themselves; they aren't even teaching religion right because they've lost members and money so they don't have enough money for books and programs. Father Louie [the former priest] also had job placement and English-training programs that don't exist anymore.

Some parishes are more responsive to the needs of the community. These parishes in turn engender a greater degree of giving from their members. One woman said that she believes her

> church helps the community a lot. I give to the church money and clothing because Father Jim uses it. He gives them to prisoners and farm workers. I'm not Catholic, I just go to my church and I really like my church and what it stands for, social commitment. Father Jim's involved. I started going to the church because of my boyfriend. Father Jim visits people in jail, gets them pen pals, gives them presents from the congregation, works with halfway houses and single mothers. Several of his ex-prisoners come to mass now.

Another woman told us that she and her husband are involved in the church

> mainly through the kids. We want them to have this tradition [Catholicism]. They are involved in the children's mass and other activities and we help. St. Bonaventure's is a true Christian community. The people are very giving. My husband was not a Catholic and didn't like Catholics, but he converted because this is such a good community. The children's mass is organized entirely by the kids; they do plays and have a choir. The parents are eucharistic ministers and all the priest does is say what he has to. . . . If anybody needs something you just say so and you will be helped. At Christmas we have a giving tree. You put a star with your request/need on the tree and everybody gets one or so and gets what is on the star [not always mate-

rial goods] and puts it on the altar. It is so neat to see the altar filled with presents. It is impressive that everyone gives and the children take a very active role in all of this. Also we have continuous collections of food, clothes, and things for distribution. It is an actual working, giving community.

She then told us about the effort her parish was making to reach out to the local Hispanic community. "There is a weekly Spanish mass even though there is not really a large Spanish-speaking population within the parish [people come from throughout the county to go to this mass]. It is a very open church."

A wide variety of giving customs are associated with *santos*, all dependent on one's degree of devotion. People donate large amounts of time and money celebrating *Dia Santos*, or saints' feast days. These celebrations are usually centered around a church. *Dia Santos* are also celebrated within the extended family as one would a birthday party. People also venerate *santos* in small groups and at home.

Many respondents had been involved in festivals for different *santos*. One person said: "[My] mother helps out with the feast of the Immaculate Conception and various saints' feast days." A woman responded that her family "helped with feast days, fiestas, etc., at St. Peter's." Some prepare or provide food and entertainment for the festival. Others give or raise money to finance it. These festivals are also a time when believers make *mandas* (commands); that is, they commit themselves to some form of devotional behavior that can range from prayer to donating money or time to a cause with which the saint is associated. A person who made a *manda* to Saint Francis of Assisi, for example, might volunteer at an animal shelter.

Believers also make *promesas* (promises) to a *santo*. One who makes a *promesa* usually pledges to make a pilgrimage to the shrine of a specific *santo* in exchange for the *santo*'s intercession. Upon arrival at the shrine the pilgrim offers prayers, donates money, and leaves behind *milagros* (miracles), small plaques representing body parts one wants healed, pictures, and other items related to the intercession they seek. For example, if the request is that a loved one be cured, a picture of that person is left. One woman said that she "went to Mexico City with my mother on a *promesa*," journeying to the Shrine of Our Lady of Guadalupe. Another woman said that her mother made a *promesa* to

> go from the stairs of the church to the altar on her knees, if her son came home from Vietnam. She went to the church of San Juan in Texas. There is a whole display case of diplomas, certificates, pictures, etc., of *promesas* that have been left. There are only certain churches that you can pay your *promesas* in, a limited few.

In Mexico, *Mayordomías* consist of men who collect funds, look after the saints' robes and the church decorations, order fireworks and engage bands for the fiesta, and supply food for musicians and dancers at the fiesta. Women help the men prepare the food and dress the female saints. A few respondents recognized the term *mayordomías*, although only two used the term with regularity. Women play a much greater, often almost exclusive, role in the care of *santos* in the United States.

Guadalupanas are groups organized at the parish level whose primary responsibility is the maintenance and care of statues and symbols dedicated to the Virgin of Guadalupe and the sponsorship of a mass and festival in her honor every December 12. Members donate time and money in order to fulfill these obligations. The Guadalupanas promulgate religious and popular culture as well as a sense of community through their yearly celebrations. Guadalupana members are almost exclusively women. A few parishes end the day with the conclusion of the mass. In other parishes the Guadalupanas sponsor "receptions with *pan dulce*" and other refreshments. Another woman reported that her parish held "a big party with a king and a queen and then a dance" and also served "*menudo* [hominy, juice, and tripe] or *pozole* [hominy and juice]." Another woman responded that "in December, the first Sunday of the month, there would be a mass and a meal for the Virgin of Guadalupe sponsored by the Guadalupanas. Afterwards there would be dances and raffles." The raffles are held as a fundraiser for the furtherance of the Guadalupanas' activities.

In addition to their activities on December 12, many Guadalupana groups are busy throughout the year with other church activities such as cleaning, maintenance, and the sponsorship of other festivals and *santos*. One woman reported that in her parish the Guadalupanas "sponsored different saints. Every day for several months you pray for the saints. This is done in the months other than December." In addition to devotions to various *santos*, the Guadalupanas prepare and serve food at festivals honoring different *santos* and also hold fundraisers throughout the year. "They provide meals on Cinco de Mayo, father's day, etc., to raise money. They have an annual dance to raise money to help with the church upkeep," said one respondent. The Sociedad Guadalupana in his community also sponsors fiestas throughout the year and charges members modest dues to defray funeral costs if a member should die. The Sociedad has thus begun to take on the duties of a *mutualista* (mutual benefit society) in addition to its normal mission (Pitti, Castaneda, and Cortes, 1988, pp. 228–29).

While Our Lady of Guadalupe is the most important of the Marian *santos*, indeed of all *santos* in Mexico, there are many other Marian *santos* of importance to Mexican Americans. Two women told of groups devoted to Maria Auxiliodora. One described a celebration

> in March or May. I think she [Maria Auxiliodora] appeared in France. Her veil is blue and she helps with illnesses. They have a dance and a raffle, and they sell Mexican food. All the members of the Guadalupanas and Maria Auxiliodora make and donate food at the parties. They have 15–20 members. They have a box with a picture of the Virgin and a collection slot. The members put spare change in the box when they have it. Each member keeps the box for a week at a time. They say a rosary before she leaves their house.

If someone [a member] gets sick, they [other members] bring food to the family and help take care of them with money they take from the Virgin's collection box.

The other woman reported that her aunt's group followed an almost identical set of practices. She said that if she goes to visit her aunt and the box is there, she puts money in the box. Whoever visits her also does this. The money is then used to help cover expenses for the funerals of former members and is also used to sponsor dinners.

✂ GIVING TO ORGANIZATIONS

The role of the *compadrazgo* system was examined by anthropologist George Foster as part of his research into the social life of villagers in Western Mexico. According to Foster, *compadrazgo* exists in the gap "between the absolute, formal rigidity of the family and the absolute flexibility of friendship. . . . In other societies this gap is filled by such institutions as voluntary associations" (Foster, 1967, pp. 75–77). *Compadrazgo* enables people to expand their support network beyond the family, thereby increasing the family's chances for survival by increasing the number of people an individual family member can rely on in times of need.

This expanding network can be seen in the significant grants of time and money that are made by Mexicans living in the United States to churches, communities, and organizations in Mexico. Most of this giving involves money, clothes, food, and consumer goods sent back to one's former place of residence or church. Many of these grants are sent to Mexico in more general and anonymous donations. People send money in response to natural disasters such as earthquakes and they give to various charitable organizations that operate within Mexico.

Many respondents reported that they send money and goods to the communities in Mexico whence they came. Much of the giving is done by individuals when they return to Mexico. One woman said: "There are cases where families here go back to their town and provide music and toys and fundraisers for the town. They have seen the changes that are possible here and feel that they can help make changes there."

Another said that her family doesn't "like giving to Salvation Army because we give to the people in my grandmother's town Guadalupe, outside of Ensenada. We give whole bags of clothes at a time." Another woman's family consistently gives clothing to people living in Mexico. "Every time my aunt goes to Mexico, she takes the clothes we give her and gives them to my grandmother to distribute to relatives and the poor in the town. When I go down to Mexico I will often recognize my clothes on kids I see." Some of the giving is of a more whimsical nature. "I remember one year my dad bought baseball bats and gloves and distributed them to the kids in Jimenez," one woman reported.

People also give to their town and to Mexico in general through organizations in the United States. Churches are a common means of transmitting such help. A parish priest of one of the respondents "was from a village in southern Mexico [he was an Indian] and once a year clothes would be collected [in the parish] especially for this village and sent down. Though he is gone now, the church still does this." One young woman always gave to the second collection at mass if they were collecting money for a disaster in Mexico. Additionally, her "parents would send clothes to Mexico or give them to a *comadre* who would deliver them to poor people in Tijuana. In high school I would give money to causes like earthquake relief [in Mexico and Latin America]."

People also send money and goods to Mexico via various organizations located in Mexico. One woman's father sends money regularly to Nuestros Pequeños Hermanos y Hermanas, an orphanage in Mexico. When asked why he sends money to this orphanage, she replied that "he just believes in taking care of his people." She went on to say, "He asked if I wanted to, so I decided to help them," thus joining her father in aiding his home country. A popular form of organizational giving is to sponsor a child in Mexico through the Christian Children's Fund (CCF). Advertisements for CCF can be seen frequently on Spanish language television. Frequently there are half-hour and hour shows devoted to generating support for CCF, as well as telethons. Several respondents either supported a child already or expressed a desire to support a child when they were financially able. One respondent reported working for the fund while living in Mexico City with her husband. Individuals have also formed their own organizations that are designed to send aid to Mexico. The father of one respondent "developed a club with people in Los Angeles and got together clothes and things and gave them to the kids in town [in Mexico]." His hometown was called Vaya de Guadalupe; it is "a little dirt road town" outside Ensenada. The organization he founded "also held dances and raised money and gave baseball mitts and other items to the kids in town."

Giving back to Mexico is an important form of sharing for many Mexicans in this country. Fuentes commented that "whole communities in Mexico are supported by the *remesas*, or remittances, of their migrant workers in the United States, and that these *remesas* add up to $4 billion a year and are Mexico's second largest source of foreign income (after oil)" (Fuentes, 1992, p. 346). Fuentes' number would include the *remesas* sent home by illegal workers and by American citizens of Mexican descent.

Many respondents also said that while it is important to give money and material goods such as clothing and food, it is equally important to share oneself. One woman said:

> Charity is an important role in my life. From the beginning, I was taught by my parents to give. They would give me all they could and I was expected to do the same for others. The most important thing in charity is to give of yourself. Maybe you can't give money but just listening, or anything. This is important because you will feel good and you will help someone else.

Others reiterated this view, saying that sharing one's emotional self is just as important as sharing materially. A woman said: "There are many ways of giving: physically, spiritually, and emotionally. They are all very important. If you can give somebody confidence, especially to those younger than you, this is also important." She later said that "by sharing a little piece of yourself, or sharing what someone else has to offer, you can expand your philosophical outlook. You take them with you and vice-versa." Another woman said that, when giving, "you should try to give love and help. You should be able to feel good about giving. You should try to do it every day."

CHAPTER THREE ∽ *Guatemalans*

- •Guatemalan giving occurs primarily within the extended family.
- •Guatemalans send a large amount of money and goods to relatives, friends, and local communities in the home country.
- •Many respondents spoke of people returning to Guatemala for family gatherings, religious holidays, festivals, and pilgrimages.
- •Churches, primarily Catholic, are focal points of giving within the Guatemalan community.
- •Guatemalans in the Bay Area make use of volunteers in "radio clubs" to send messages back and forth to Guatemala via ham radios.
- •Many Guatemalans provide food and lodging to new immigrants.
- •Little giving or volunteering is directed at charitable organizations outside the Guatemalan community. Guatemalans have a generally low opinion of mainstream American philanthropic institutions and practices.

Over the last half century, U.S. corporations such as the United Fruit Company and Del Monte have largely forged United States–Guatemalan relations. These relations cooled considerably during the Arbenz and Arévalo socialist administrations (1944–1954). After the United States aided the anti-Arbenz military force that placed Colonel Carlos Armas in power in 1954, middle-class Guatemalans began emigrating to the United States in the 1950s and 1960s. These middle-class Guatemalans constitute the core of the Guatemalan community in the United States today (Vlach, 1992).

As a consequence of Guatemala's population explosion and a recent economic downturn, a new wave of Guatemalan immigrants and refugees has arrived in the San Francisco Bay Area since 1980. In her study of six Guatemalan families, Vlach (1992) cites three primary factors that preceded this most recent stream of immigrants: (1) inflation, unemployment, and low wages; (2) political tensions, repression, rebellion, and massacres throughout the homeland; and (3) the 1976 earthquake and its aftermath. According to U.S. Census figures, 13,000 Guatemalans lived in the San Francisco Bay Area in 1990.

The following statements on philanthropic practices in the Guatemalan community are excerpted from interviews with 40 individuals.

∽ KINSHIP

Many traditional giving patterns are maintained because of the large number of Guatemalans who are relatively new to the United States. These patterns emphasize tight, interdependent networks of family and friends. One young man spoke of some of the feelings that drive Guatemalan giving patterns:

> To me, traditional giving practices relate back to the Indian Mayan way of life. Spanish people do not give something for nothing. Giving is usually mutual, which is not to say equal, but generally reciprocal. If I help you, I expect that when the time comes, you will help me. If we are friends, I will help you in any way I can and hope that when the time comes you will have the *voluntad* [good will] to help me—not as a return or payback, but because you care for me. We have many ways of spreading the wealth around, but when we just want to give something away we donate underhandedly, anonymously, so the person's pride is intact. We would rarely do anything like this for a stranger; how would you know they needed it? It is, however, very common with friends.

Another man said, "No, it is not that we expected to be paid back, but it would have been unheard of to assist and care for someone and not have it returned when we in turn needed help." And from another respondent, "It's part of our values not to hoard, to be generous, not to own, but to share, not to waste or to take for granted what we have; and we assume everyone else feels the same."

Sharing within the family is of prime importance to Guatemalans. One respondent put it this way: "My family gave because it was proper and necessary to function as an integrated unit to preserve our lifestyles. By sharing we had a place to live, food to eat, a television, even a ratty old car." Several respondents felt that the definition and role of family were very different for mainstream Americans and Guatemalans. As a 69-year-old woman pointed out, "Family is family, kin by marriage or blood. This immediate and extended family idea is a silly American notion." The families of many respondents were large, self-sufficient networks that often fully took care of the needs of their members. So efficient and comprehensive were the family support networks of some of the respondents that giving outside their families rarely occurred, even to other Guatemalans. One woman said, "The best always goes back to the family, where our strongest ties are, and there isn't much left for anyone else. Giving to friends is discouraged because then there is less left for the family. Giving to strangers is laughable." Another person said, "My family in fact discouraged us from associating with other children, children outside the family circle of influence. My cousins were my best friends going through school." Restrictions on giving outside the family ensure that all available resources and emotional energy are directed inward, toward the family. Thus, the likelihood that the family and its individual members will be successful is greatly enhanced. Success is the result of a concerted group effort.

While few respondents narrowed their giving to this extent, most spoke of the importance of familial giving. "Unless [Guatemalans] have a relationship with American friends, they follow what they used to do. If they do not, they follow the old ways of helping. Relatives living in the same house, even if they are not close, a lot of money sent to [relatives in] the homeland. I wish you worked for Pac Bell because you would see the huge bills from calls to Guatemala." The extent of family giving is well illustrated by one young man who had recently moved from home and found that, thanks to his family, sustenance was not a problem. "Everyone [in the extended family] still sends me food. I haven't gone grocery shopping in over a year and a half, except for stuff like beer and potato chips, but they send me everything else. . . . they even send stuff to the mother of my two sons, just because she's their mother."

Even impoverished, an individual is obligated to support his or her parents. "My family in Guatemala was very poor, they never had anything to spare or give away, not even to their brothers and sisters or their families," said a respondent. "[Nevertheless] my parents gave to my grandparents because they were obligated as their children to support them. My uncles and my aunts did the same." Another respondent remarked: "I do not give money to anyone but my family, my parents and my father-in-law, and my wife and children [in Guatemala], not because they needed it, but because it is my obligation. I need the money more than they do; if I had the money, I could live in an apartment." Guatemalan customs of supporting parents do not always mesh with the support systems of the dominant society in the United States. As one woman said:

> I live with my mother and I support her. She has no income, no social security [she is 62] and no medical insurance. That takes up a lot of my giving. I pay rent, food, and medical expenses. I also have a brother who is always asking for money, but he has kids and a wife so I must help them. I have all kinds of insurance for myself, but I can't insure my mother in my policy. Can you believe that? I can't insure her. They say she is not my dependent. Can you believe that? I take care of her.

While many Guatemalans maintain this custom over several generations, it is also apparent that many other than first-generation Guatemalans prefer the manner of the dominant society which places the responsibility on the individual's shoulders. A second-generation respondent complained about the demands the extended family places on an individual:

> Our families, they're too damn large and too damn frequent. They're always somewhere nearby waiting to tax your wallet. They're always lying in your bed, reading your books, eating your food. *Mi casa, tu casa*, they're not just kidding. They're always in your business and under your foot. They always need money or a place to stay. Don't even get me started on the out-of-towners—"Mr. and Mrs. Quetzaltenango will be visiting you this year, and their fifty children." And the old people, they're like a weight, a noose around your neck, barking around the house, promising to die but never doing it. They're terrors, those old people, preying on the smallest, weakest children in the house. Family, I'd say, is the number one drain on an individual's expenses. I already told my parents to set up a retirement fund

so they can go to a nice retirement home. I'm not footing the bill. I consider it an unnecessary expense for me to bear. I'm telling them now so there won't be any surprises later. Old people are a tremendous drain.

Shared housing affords more family members the chance to live in the United States, thus swelling the size of one's family in this country and increasing the chances of success for all its members. There is, of course, a price for this increased chance of success. The family that provides the housing generally does so free of charge and is often faced with considerable expense because of this generosity. As one middle-aged refugee told us, "Giving shelter is very important because families usually accommodate extended family. Plus obligations come with shelter like food, clothing, transportation, and communication."

The cost of these obligations is significant in families who open their homes to one or two people. However, several respondents' families house many people at once. The costs to these families is obviously much greater and it is a cycle of giving that will probably continue for many years. A teenage boy gave an example of the large numbers of extended family that could be living in a relative's home at the same time:

> I live with my mom and dad, my two grammas and my grampa, my brother Tomas, my brother Mike and his wife Shaundra and my two nephews, Chris and Matt, and my niece Mia and my sister Channelle and my sister Beatriz and her husband Donald. My cousins Mark and Celeste also stay with us and Tio Joaquin, who's not really my uncle, one of my dad's old buds.

Not surprisingly, much of the housing provided to extended family members was offered to recent immigrants. Many respondents spoke of such activity. "My mother came here when my dad died in Guatemala and stayed with my sister while I was there. . . . She has been living with me for about three years," one woman said. Another woman reported:

> I tried to help my brother and sister live here because I was lonely. It's hard because once you live here it is hard to go back, because there are no jobs in Guatemala. My brother came here to visit, and then he went back to Guatemala, and then he got a permanent visa to stay here. He stayed with me and I helped him with food and things. People remember how hard it was when they came and they always bring relatives and help them.

Most of those who received housing assistance from a family member would eventually be able to afford housing of their own. These families would then offer housing to other Guatemalans, thus perpetuating and expanding this giving custom. One man responded, "I came on my own, but I had family living here and I stayed with my sister for five months." When asked if he had ever done the same he replied that he had taken in his younger brother for a year and a half. "I grew up with my grandmother, my aunts and uncles, my older cousins, even some of my mother's friends, but it was never for very long, just until my mom got back on her feet from whatever was happening," said another respondent. This person went on to say that after his family was able to obtain a house the roles were reversed:

> The first thing we did was take in three of my cousins, my aunt and uncle, then a couple of years later we took in my mother's cousins and husbands who came from Guatemala and two years after that their kids. Me and my sons lived there for a while; so did my sister and her husband, but before I left there were thirty people living in that house and more coming.

Housing assistance in the United States often comes from nonprofit organizations and the government through subsidies. The provision of housing to other family members bypasses this system and, as indicated in the response of one gentleman, can supplant other social services as well. "We always had relatives with us at home, especially women who had left their husbands or been beat up by them," he said. "We always provided shelter for family members. We are very supportive for family."

Another common form of assistance found among Guatemalans in the United States is financial support sent home to relatives in Guatemala. One respondent noted that "there are patterns of economic connection between [Guatemalan] families here and in the homeland," and that they are economically significant. One man who claimed that 50 to 60 percent of El Salvador's GNP is attributable to transfer payments from relatives in the United States was asked if he believed this was also true for Guatemala. He replied: "I assume so. When you have a conversation with a Guatemalan, they say, 'I can't do this because I have to send $100 to my family' and this and that. They are always counting on money that has to be sent to the family."

The importance of transfer payments to individual families was illustrated by the remarks of the same interviewee: "We [family members in the United States] all send money back, and it has helped our family in Guatemala. Most are now middle-class, most have homes, and most of the children can go to school. At one time my father offered to bring them here but they refused, so my father has helped them do better there."

These transfer payments were often referred to as *despachos* (packages of gifts or necessities). Packages containing clothing and sundry goods that were sent to extended family members living in Guatemala were also referred to as *despachos*. One teenager said that, other than his nuclear family,

> I don't have any family in the United States. Everyone was back home and [my parents] have always sent money back every month. Sometimes we send things, too, like appliances. We sent back a microwave to my aunt two weeks ago. We usually send objects like clothes or presents back with someone or we know it will never reach them. We know a lot of Guatemalans who travel back and forth. Some go back every year for Semana Santa [Holy Week], and we ask them if they could please take this *despacho* or whatever to our relative such and such. It is supposed to be an honor to be asked. People don't usually refuse, but it can be a pain in the butt. Sometimes we pay their expenses, too. It's polite if they have to go out of their way to another town or something—you may give them some money to get there.

"We sent money and gifts and anything of value back to our relatives. One time we sent over a hundred calculators to them which was only enough for about half of them, because my father really hated mathematics," one woman said. "We still send money to my mother's family and care packages full of American candy and chocolate," said another woman. "What they don't eat they can sell, American chocolate sells well. We also send clothes and toys." "My father always sent about half his pay back home to the rest of the family, the village, and the church for the care of the *santos* [icons of Jesus, Mary, and the saints]," said another respondent.

Money and goods sent by Guatemalans in the United States to their nuclear and extended families in Guatemala are significant pieces in the mosaic of Guatemalan giving patterns. These *despachos* are also good indicators of the solidarity of Guatemalan families, as seen in the comments of one woman who said that her family sends

> money and gifts on a consistent basis to ease the burdens of the people they left behind. Frequent visits are quite popular. Americans always think it is guilt with us; but it is love, love and respect. Though the miles separate us, we are still a part of them and they of us. Barely a day goes by that I don't think of my great aunts and uncles, the second cousins, and the friends that I grew up with. We are removed but we cannot forget what we have been nor what we have left.

The importance of family obligations and ties was also evident in the comments of a man who said: "I was brought up with a sense of responsibility toward all those I'd left behind. They weren't memories but living people and even while I was in this country, they were still my family and my obligation. I sent home money."

For its members, the extended family is a form of insurance against a multiplicity of maladies. It gives support for the elderly and housing, food, and transportation to family members in need. The importance of these family networks is underscored by Guatemalans' maintenance of the system of *compadrazgo*, the Latin American Catholic tradition of ritual kinship, in the United States. *Compadrazgo* affords Guatemalans a chance to expand their family networks by accepting fictive kin into their families. The custom of *compadrazgo* also allows existing kin to become *padrinos* (godparents or *compadres*) which serves to reaffirm and solidify existing family ties.

One may receive *padrinos* on a variety of occasions, most of which are related to Catholic rituals and sacraments such as confirmation and marriage. One may also receive *padrinos* for more secular events such as a girl's *quince primaveras*. A *quince primaveras* is essentially a girl's debut on her fifteenth birthday. The most important *padrinos* are usually the *padrinos de bautismo* (baptismal godparents). *Padrinos de bautismo* are required to give more time, money and goods to their *ahijado* (godchild) than other *padrinos*. Like all *padrinos*, *padrinos de bautismo* normally help pay for the ceremony in which they will be involved and give their godchild presents and money. *Padrinos* help pay the church fees, sponsor an *aguacero* (shower) for the child, and purchase a dress and small gift for the child. Giving continues as the child gets older. Children receive birthday and *Dia Santo* (saint's day) presents as well as other forms of material support from their *padrinos*. These forms of giving resemble those of the dominant society but differ in that *padrinos* have been brought into the family network for life and are now an important link in that chain of support.

One woman spoke about the importance of choosing *padrinos* who could be counted on for support:

> Godparents very often are family members, for many reasons. Often if there are family problems the new mother will make [an in-law] the godmother of the child to ease tensions and to make the ties between [the wife's] family and [the husband's] family more binding. Also, most families rely on themselves and close friends for support, especially when it comes to entrusting the future of the children to another. Picking godparents is rarely random. It is usually thoroughly discussed among the family, especially for baptismal godparents because those are the child's second parents. Usually the honor goes to family because it is the circle of primary loyalty and the [likeliest] group to provide well for the child.

Other parents seek successful *padrinos* in the hopes that their children's lives will be changed as a result. This occurs primarily when choosing baptismal godparents and, to a lesser degree, when choosing *padrinos* for one's wedding. Choosing godparents wisely can be an important part of the support network:

> I did not live with my parents long. I went to live with my *padrino* when I was eleven. . . . When I came to live with my godfather it was hard at first because I had no family and he worked me hard. I was only one of many servants in the house. He had sent for me, offered to take care of me because I was the same age as one of his sons and I could be his son's playmate. . . . I did well; my grades were higher than all but the eldest and my godfather did reward me; he sent me to medical school in Guatemala City when I was of age, to return when I finished into his employ. I did return to work for him and eventually he gave me one of his daughters to marry. He is now my father-in-law. He is the one who sent me to the United States a year ago.

Some of those who are well off or well respected are inundated with *abijados*. One person said that when his grandfather died, he had over three hundred godchildren from baptism, seventy-five from confirmation, ninety from weddings, and countless others from various ceremonies.

∞ COMMUNITY

Several respondents said that the primary difference between Guatemalan giving patterns and those found among the dominant society in the United States is that giving is a more personalized activity among Guatemalans. These interviewees expressed the belief that one does not give to organizations but rather to the needy that one directly encounters. One woman said that in Guatemala,

> Philanthropy is more of a working than a giving-money thing; it is community work. . . . Guatemalan people are very hospitable and kind; they want you to eat with them and so on. People are poor and can't really give money. There is not really an infrastructure for formal giving. People are very caring and giving.

Another woman said that she was very happy growing up in Guatemala as a child: "People gave each other many things, food, clothes, [and] made toys and candies to give to each other, especially during religious days, all without expecting to be rewarded." Another woman said that her mother would never give away food because to do so "would have been to take it from the mouths of her own seven children, to give away clothes would have left them all bare." She went on to say, however, that her mother fed many hungry children on a daily basis and would mend and alter clothes for people in their village. Similarly, a man spoke of his mother, who had been a street peddler in Guatemala:

> In the evening, when it started to get late, she would give beggars and street children what was left of the vegetables and hot rice and tamales. Sometimes she would feed the children near our home as well soup and cheese, tortillas, avocado, and beans. My father did not share as much of anything— mostly, I think, because he was saddled with the responsibility of providing for all of us.

His father did share his skills, however. "He would often go and work with his friends when they needed it, harvesting, planting. He always helped without having to be asked."

A woman said that in her community in Guatemala, the wealthy families in the area, after large parties or dinners, would often share their leftovers with the small communities around them. These families also gave clothing. She explained that since the poorer people were usually thinner than their wealthy patrons, they could alter the second-hand clothes by stitching and hemming them or by using a length of rope to take them in. Many of her meals, and most of her toys, came from the *sobras* (leftovers) of a wealthy family who lived nearby. She also received many of her clothes from the family's six daughters.

One man spoke of this custom from the perspective of a landowner. He said that his grandfather, who owned a moderate-sized farm, told him that

> things worked themselves out if you practiced *buen negocio*, good business. He did not believe in giving anything away, nothing was ever "free" with him, and he certainly never believed in charity, but when I look back he was a very charitable, generous man; he just called it something else, good business. He felt fairness and goodness were everyone's responsibility. My grandfather knew he would need help, people who were loyal and hard work-

ing, who were willing to work for him. . . . He got the local prison to turn over half their population; he succeeded in winning their [ex-prisoners'] support by paying off their debts and offering them a share of the profits when things took off. To many people he offered sanctuary . . . when men came with their families, he not only provided them with a place to live and a percentage of the crop, he guaranteed them meat and eggs and milk, schooling for their children, and clothing, and material with which to make clothes and even alcohol and cigars.

An 84-year-old woman who had spent much of her life in Guatemala echoed this description of interdependent, reciprocal relationships: "Among the people, peasants, there was a lot of sharing and cooperation and trade but not much giving without return." A man who had grown up in Guatemala concurred: "In our small community, each person was an important part of the whole and every person had their own piece to add; it was both necessary and expected that people take part. People are all different, some are more generous, some more stingy within our community, but everyone gives, everyone reciprocates."

One man said that from the time he was at Berkeley working on his Master's degree "I was involved in the community through most of my [architecture] classes. I took most of my classes with the community in mind and did work in the community. I did projects in the Mission and helped spruce up neighborhood businesses." Another man said:

If someone needs help, and you can afford to give it, and you know this person will not be wasteful, you can invest the money in their well-being. It should never be a forced thing. People are only bitter and resentful when they are forced to share what they have. It is always random, you give when there is need.

Aiding others can involve the provision of services as well as goods and money. In this vein another respondent gave an example of what he felt was charity:

Last year I "delivered" a ten-year-old girl to her mother in Huehuetenango. Her father had enough only for the girl's airline ticket but found out I was going. I consented to escort the child to her home. He gave me $20 so I could ride on the bus with the girl to her home in Huehuetenango. [This was beyond his destination of Guatemala City.] As it turned out, I got a ride from a friend in Guatemala and didn't need to use his money, so when I got back I gave it back to him. See, the favor is that I took her with me, that I had us picked up at the airport, took her to my aunt's house to wash and eat and sleep and finally that I made sure she got to her mother. . . . This is charity to Spanish people; you do something for someone without demeaning and breaking them [monetarily], but you are not expected to play the fool and take onto yourself debts you cannot pay. It was nice for me and the father of the girl, I provided what I knew I could, food, lodging, time, and he gave me what he could [$20] to ensure safe arrival. Neither of our prides were damaged in the transaction.

Another important form of giving within the Guatemalan community, one that mirrors what occurs within the family, is the provision of housing to other Guatemalans. It is common among Guatemalans to house friends of the family who need it. They come *recomendada* (recommended) by other friends or family members. This custom is practiced frequently, in some cases almost constantly by several respondents. One person said that whenever possible, he has someone stay with him at his house.

This practice is especially important among new immigrants and refugees. One man said that while he does not often have to house relatives, he frequently houses refugees:

> This whole house has been filled with people or friends, many of whom dropped by out of the blue. We would have 10 or 15 people at a time in addition to our family. [My wife] took some getting used to it. We have a good support group. Three men called from Tijuana once saying that the *coyotes* [middlemen, smugglers] wanted $500 for each of them [to bring them to the San Francisco Bay Area]. By calling friends in our group we were able to raise the money that night. . . . We are known as "The Hotel." There are always a lot of musicians, cultural workers, poets, writers, printers, musicians, theater groups, community leaders, and representatives of the revolutionary movement. We are trying to help redistribute the land to the peasants and to make them the managers of the forest.

Sharing one's house with other Guatemalans affords many people housing who might otherwise not be able to afford shelter and allows people the chance to secure a foothold in the United States. Several respondents could not understand that Americans typically do not help one another in this way. One woman said:

> I can't believe what happens to some people in this country, the old people who eat dog food. I can't believe all the homeless you have either. We come from Guatemala and we have homes and we don't speak English. . . . I can't understand, if we who are not from this country are working, I think these people can be working, too.

∞ DEATH

Sharing within the community extends to funerals as well. One respondent gave a representative view of the help families receive when someone dies:

> When my grandfather died, everyone came. Many brought food: beans, rice, bread, coffee, sugar, and candy for us; and others brought flowers, candles, incense, curtains, mats [for the guests to sit on]. Others came and helped prepare his body, clean his clothes, help my mother feed the guests, or told tales, stories to entertain the guests, all of which joined in to pray for my grandfather's eternal rest. It takes many days when properly done, nine. Imagine how it would be if all those people forsook us and left us to do it all

alone. Why, my father and my two uncles did not even have enough money to buy nails for the coffin wood. Rather, the old shopkeeper two miles away made a special trip to bring us nails the day before so that the coffin would be ready for the first day of the rite. He pulled them out of his own chairs, to spare us embarrassment, so we would not look poor in front of everyone, even though everyone knew. It was a small thing but my father never forgot and when the shopkeeper's wife died my father paid to honor her in a proper church, and he and my uncles and me and my brothers and cousins carried her body nine miles in the rain to the church with my mother and aunts behind us singing. And ever after, my mother, every Sunday, in honor of the memory of the woman, left food on the grave, because she was Indian.

Another man said that it was commonplace for his grandfather to give money to others to help them cope financially with someone's death. He said his grandfather "would give a sizable amount of money, usually equivalent to a month's pay, money *para sivirle* [to serve you], and that was for any member of the family."

While these examples occurred in Guatemala, many Guatemalans are first-generation and are very likely to repeat these patterns in the United States. The interviews indicated that Guatemalans in the United States donate a great deal of time and effort to assist families who need help funding a funeral. Close friends and family donate time to help the bereaved family maintain their household by doing chores, and help accommodate guests who have arrived for the funeral. Additionally, in the United States the monetary costs of funerals are much greater, especially for those who wish to be buried in Guatemala. Funding in such cases often came from a larger portion of the community than was normal in the other examples of communal giving mentioned here. As an example, one respondent's friends took a "body to the funeral parlor but there was no money to ship it back home, but a reporter from El Grande 1010 got on the radio and told everyone what had happened and we all donated so they could ship his body back. No one complained and everyone gave even if they didn't have a job. It was expected."

Other respondents reported that they used local and short-wave radio to help raise money for funerals: "In my group, if someone dies and needs money to send back to Guatemala, we go on the radio and ask for money."

∽ RELIGIOUS CUSTOMS

Churches in the United States (primarily Catholic among the respondents) also serve as focal points for giving within the Guatemalan community. One woman said that in her parish they "have baskets for the poor and the sick" and that "parishioners will help renovate the homes of other parishioners." Another respondent stated, "These days, during Lent, the parish gets together and makes a 'humble meal,' soup and bread. There is a different group each week, and the money we would have spent we give to Oxfam and similar groups." Respondents did not feel that all churches encouraged community giving, however. According to one woman, "priests would rather renovate the church than feed the poor."

Several respondents spoke of communal giving through their local church, such as feeding and clothing newly arrived immigrants. One woman explained that she works for the church as a housekeeper because she remembers "how hard it was when I came to this country and how the church helps the poor and the new immigrants." She said the churches help with "food and clothes, they help with education [scholarships to Catholic schools], they provide shelter." She went on to say that "people knock on the [church] door and ask for help" and help is given. In an effort to meet an ever-increasing need, the church has begun asking its parishioners to "give more money, explaining to the members how [the new immigrants] are poor" and in great need of assistance.

Several respondents talked about another form of communal giving that occurs within the church; gifts and donations in honor of *santos*. *Santos* are religious icons, images of saints, especially those of a town's or church's patron saint. *Santos* also include images of the Virgin Mary and the Christ Child. Most members of the dominant society in the United States, and many Guatemalans, would probably not consider this in a discussion of philanthropy; however, those Guatemalans who are believers view *santos* as an integral part of their community. In exchange for caring for the statue, gifts of money and other goods and prayers, the *santo* will use its power to help. One man spoke of the interdependence of the saint and its worshippers:

> There is no such thing as charity in religion. No one gives away something for nothing, certainly no poor *milpero* [farmer, peasant] is going to give away his hard-earned, hard-won money to the church for nothing in return. You must stop treating it like that. People give their money to a saint firmly believing that the saint will benefit or will repay them in some [prayed for] way, usually by guaranteeing the health of the family and their friends, or success in a business venture, blessings for children or some other desire. The person and the saint are actually conducting business, exchanging service for money.

One man spoke at great length about the importance of *santos* to many Guatemalans. He said that with the *santos,*

> there is a lot involved. It is where most of the monetary support is given, one of the only times that people donate money and jewelry and gold and jade and *guipiles* is in support of the holy articles. Statues and crosses have a great deal of importance, just in themselves, in Guatemala. . . . They are almost like sacred [beacons] with the actual saint or the Virgin able to intercede on the asker's behalf with God. That is not entirely all. The saints, they have powers, each of them has their own, and people reward their saints accordingly for a good year, or the prosperity of the upcoming year. If a *milagro* [miracle] is necessary, people may give to the Virgin in the hopes

that she will discuss it with her son on their behalf. Few ask God directly. Fear and piety and prestige motivate people. When the festivals come, people give all they have to the street procession, to their best, most favored statues. They have nothing like it in the United States. That is why the churches here don't make as much money, no Semana Santa. Many people in the United States, too, journey back to Guatemala, not always annually, but when they return they often go to certain churches, Esquipulas, home of the Black Christ, Santo Tomas in Chichicastenango and Pocojil Peak and many others because of the value of the statues. Any statue will not do, that would be to say that all were the same, it is like trying to place a call to someone on a child's play phone. The statue has its own value and ability, certain statues are considered closer to God, like the Black Christ in Esquipulas.

The giving surrounding *santos* is done more personally in the United States both because of differing Catholic traditions and because some parishes frown on the veneration of *santos* in this manner. Our informant said that in San Francisco he

> saw a woman last week crying bitterly in front of the church. Well, she had given money, donated it expressly to the *santo* of El Señor de Esquipulas so that they would buy the painting a new frame, but church officials told her God did not want the money used in that way and that the old frame was just fine. She was distraught because she had been promising the *santo* that she would bring the money soon in her prayers.

Since the church officials would not use her money for the frame the woman "intended to try to find some way to borrow money so that she could go out and buy a frame herself." Another respondent, a teenage boy, related an instance in which his family sought help from a *santo*:

> My family prays to all these gods and saints and stuff, some are Catholic saints like San Francisco, and when our pets get sick we pray to him and set him candles and incense, we give money to the church to fix his statue up; my aunt leaves him fresh fruit and water like he's Santa Claus or something. My gramma says we do it because the SPCA is too expensive and the saints will help instead if we do everything right. Sometimes it works, sometimes it doesn't. But it never hurts to try, even my dad says that.

In addition to those who devote time and money to venerate particular *santos* in this country, several people reported sending money back to Guatemala in order to maintain favorite *santos* there. "My father always sent about half his pay back home to the rest of the family, the village and the church for the care of the *santos*," said one respondent. Another said that "we help and donate to the *Mayordomo* and the church here and in Guatemala for upkeep of the *santos*." One woman said that "every year since 1968, after the death of my brother, we [the whole family] go to Esquipulas for Semana Santa to pray for his soul, especially in the most holy place we know. We pray to the Black

Christ in Esquipulas at the most holy time of the year, for the security and eternal rest of my dead brothers and the continued existence of our own family." She continued:

> Yes, saints are big money in this country, too. Not only do many of the Guatemalans in this country [make a pilgrimage] every year to Guatemala in January, but people often invest a great deal of money in these statues and pictures because they are representations of the true God and his followers and they are said to be [beacons] to the ears of God. There is less reverence for these things, but even those who say they don't believe are superstitious and give.

For most Guatemalans, the most important of the *santos* is the Christo de Esquipulas (the Christ of Esquipulas), also known as the Black Christ or El Señor de Esquipulas. On January 15, Guatemalans in the United States celebrate this feast. The Christo de Esquipulas plays a strong role in the religious life of many Guatemalans. One person said that certain parishes hold a "fiesta on the 15th of January for Señor Esquipulas, complete with food and music. Funds raised will be used to present the following year's party and anything extra will be sent to Guatemala for humanitarian relief." A woman said that "many years ago, at St. James, a couple would sponsor a mass and afterwards they would invite us to their home and they would have free food and drinks. For many years the couple paid all the expenses. Now we who go will give them some money. Mexicans and Salvadorans will also take part. About three hundred or so people will go." One man said that he is involved with a group that is seeking to unite the Guatemalan community in San Francisco. He said that they are trying "to organize religious and social events using a statue of Señor Esquipulas they received from Guatemala as their drawing card."

∽ GIVING TO ORGANIZATIONS

Fewer than half of the respondents reported giving to formal organizations other than the church. Those who did were very active, saying that they gave time and/or money to many different organizations. By a margin of two to one, the organizational giving that was reported was directed toward Guatemalan organizations. Giving to these organizations is split between organizations whose primary beneficiaries are in Guatemala and those whose primary beneficiaries are in the United States.

A handful of respondents reported that they gave money to American-style philanthropic organizations—mostly social service—such as United Way, the March of Dimes, Easter Seals, soup kitchens, and homeless groups. Also mentioned were organizations with strong communal roots such as the Boy and Girl Scouts and children's sports teams. This concern with the provision of social services and with communal organizations mirrors the general giving patterns of Guatemalans.

Many respondents expressed a fundamental distrust of philanthropic organizations and mechanisms within the United States:

> You want to know why people do not donate to American charities? Because they think it is a trick to separate them from their money. As the large institutions grow to become more like corporations, resembling businesses, they will get less because people are afraid to feed into greed. . . . They feign interest in [Hispanics] to get our money, but their efforts are feeble and poorly disguised for what they are. Trust, respect, and long-standing commitments are investments in the future that people make together. My part should not end after I've signed the check if they ever want me to sign another, and I will not be solicited by machines or faceless, nameless people who disrespect me, nor will I be any more motivated to give by someone sent to me because they mimic my kind by having a Latin surname and appearance. We may be ignorant but we are not stupid, and when we feel that our contributions don't matter we will not give, and the more our own institutions change to be like the American institutions, the more support they too will lose in the community.

Similarly, a 67-year-old man felt that American-style giving was deficient. "Someday [Guatemalan children] will need to embrace American charity because they no longer remember any other reason to be charitable and kind. They will not know how to be sociable or how to share." Likewise, an 87-year-old woman spoke of her children, "We, Arturo and I, pushed them to succeed, to compete, to be educated, but when they were, we their parents no longer had a place in their lives. Their values changed, more and more motivated by money and greed. They left us behind when our ignorance proved shameful. The goodness, the charity toward others we thought firmly ingrained, was suddenly gone."

One man related that even before he came to the United States he had a negative view of American-style philanthropy:

> [Americans] wanted to show us, their backward, wayward southern cousins, how to be charitable. Like the missionaries before them, they displaced the systems before their coming and left us with less than when we began. They pooh-poohed patronage in all its forms and left us with vague concepts of goodness. My parents gave large donations to the church and orphanages, threw large, Western-style parties, and supported the embassies. These were considered socially acceptable giving forms by the American and European groups in Guatemala prior to the thirties. Prior to their coming, our main companionship was the lower class; we worked cooperatively to stay in business, so to speak. There were class differences, of course, but wealth was a matter of luck and learning. I always felt that a landholder was like the chief of a tribe, the leader because he was the smartest, the most able, the luckiest, but with his position came the responsibility of looking after the rest of the tribe.

Echoing these sentiments, a woman said:

> When you are fortunate and receive something extra, it is luck and luck should be shared and enjoyed. [My parents] were generous when they could be and sometimes when they could not. I don't remember many times when they gave something for nothing. [Guatemalans] are not Americans and our manner of giving things is not comparable. To give something for nothing in our culture is only to be gullible, to have been tricked. My parents gave to our family and friends willingly and easily but much of it was repaid eventually in one way or another.

The acceptable giving in these last two examples, like much of the giving presented in this report, was directed toward people known to the person doing the giving. A young, second-generation respondent believed that this was a primary difference between Guatemalan and American giving. She said, "Latins do not follow the American model of charity; we do not give to strangers. On rare occasions of great need we might, but not generally so, and we do not give unless there is a reason, we give when there is need."

Direct experiences with American philanthropic institutions left several respondents with negative impressions of giving in the United States. One person commented:

> I'll tell you what really turned me away from American charity institutions, and the Goodwill in particular. After my old friend Mateo died, we [his friends and companions] went in to clean up his room. He had no family and we took his things, clothing and such, to the Goodwill on the corner. He had left us everything, but we could not use it all and it made us sad. When we got there one of the workers, volunteers, whatever, picked up Mateo's uniform and told us they wouldn't take any of this garbage, this was not a dump. I have never taken them anything else.

This person and his friends sought to recreate a form of giving that was familiar to them, the sharing of clothes that a person no longer needed. Goodwill insulted them by refusing the gift.

Other respondents felt that the very process of charitable giving is demeaning. One woman said:

> I don't give much money because it's like charity. Charity is not a good thing from a Guatemalan point of view; it is a means of belittling others, demeaning people. Do you know what *rodillar* means? *Rodillar* [literally, to knee someone] means that you make someone go down on their knees, make them kneel before you, humble them. You must never do this to people, they will hate you for it. Being humbled is its own payment for any favor, any gift, any amount of money given.

A second-generation woman also spoke of the indignity of receiving aid. "Money given out of *voluntad* [good will] is always anonymous. You must never brag or you cheapen the gift. When people are on welfare or they get food stamps they must endure the indignity of their humiliation before unfeeling strangers and the debt is paid right there. The loss of dignity is payment in itself and people feel no sense of gratitude or indebtedness."

This loss of dignity makes charity unpopular among many Guatemalans. One woman said:

> I do not know any Latins on welfare probably because most of my friends are middle-class like myself, but I can see where it might happen for a while— Latin America being largely illiterate, compounded with the difficulty of learning a new language, learning a new job, adjusting to a new way of life deprived of old family contacts. But I can't imagine it lasting, because in Guatemala, my mother says work is seen as necessary to achieve happiness and people who have to rely on others without being able to offer anything in return, like welfare, are seen as absolute failures. That is part of the reason charity is so unpopular and why you would only insult someone by offering charity when they are struggling to make it. It is a total lack of respect for the person. It's much better for the person to ask or just to slip some to him without his noticing.

In that vein, one man commented:

> [The older kids in my neighborhood] don't work, or if they do, they blow it on fancy cars and boom boxes, and that is life. You can cry wolf for so long and then it is up to you. Hispanic families come here as immigrants with no education and then five years later they are moving up. Dependency is horrible and many international relief organizations come [to Guatemala] with the same attitude. Don't just give people money, everyone has to work to help themselves, even if they are receiving aid.

Several people found it useful to give to American-style philanthropic organizations in addition to sharing within the community, though their focus is still on giving within the Guatemalan community. Respondents reported supporting organizations such as CARECEN, which gives legal aid to Central American refugees, and CRECE, a social-services group for Central American refugees, through donations of time and money.

Other fledgling organizations were attempting "to build up a base of support, especially among the most progressive, open, and sensitive organizations," or were seeking to establish a better sense of community among Guatemalans in the United States by sponsoring social, cultural, and religious activities designed to unite the community. A few respondents felt that this was a major challenge facing Guatemalan community-based organizations.

"We don't have the tradition of social cooperation like the Salvadorans. The Indian segment of Guatemala seems close knit, the non-Indian segment does not," responded one person. Said another, a second-generation Guatemalan: "What we need to do is to start channelling all of our money into ourselves so we can start achieving as rapidly as the blacks in reaching Anglo status. Stinginess, necessary stinginess, is the key. Later for all the 'back home' stuff. I'm American, I live in America and I want American success."

One respondent felt that there was a good communal network supported through local churches. She said that her mother is "involved with the church community. She developed a lot of community outreach programs." She added that, for her, Catholic high school helped develop community involvement. While in this high school she became involved in campus ministry and Peace and Justice, a social action group. The school would also bring in the Sisters of Mercy, St. Vincent de Paul, and Amnesty International to speak to the students about the importance of helping others and to educate them about what these organizations were doing. She also said that the students would volunteer at soup kitchens. While all of the groups mentioned above support others besides Guatemalans, they all are involved in giving within the Guatemalan community, both within this country and in Guatemala.

As already mentioned, several of those interviewed gave to organizations that were active in Guatemala. One man even felt that organizational giving among Guatemalans should only be directed toward aiding Guatemala. "My idea is not to support Guatemalans here because that just reinforces the idea of the land of milk and honey. My idea is to develop the infrastructure within Guatemala and to build a strong community there and a good country."

Other respondents reflected this emphasis, directing much, sometimes all, of their institutional giving to organizations in Guatemala. They also give to organizations in the United States if the emphasis of their activities is to improve conditions in Guatemala. Respondents give money to Guatemalan guerrilla organizations, refugee camps in Mexico, and organizations in the United States that seek to disseminate political information, aid refugees, or lobby the American government for changes in Guatemalan foreign policy.

Several respondents reported that establishing a sense of community among Guatemalans in the United States was difficult. One woman, who is involved in an organization whose goal is to make available information on Guatemalan political events and also to attempt to promote political reform in Guatemala, said that she believes Guatemalans have difficulty establishing a sense of community in this country

> because it is very expensive to get together and to share food with each other. And if you try to organize them, like we are trying to do, it is very hard because we are a political group. We are not trying to change their views, just tell them what is going on, but they want to forget, leave it behind them. Guatemalans are fighters, so they don't have time after school and work, after all that they just want to be with their family.

Cost was mentioned as a prohibitive factor in community organization by several other respondents. Food is often shared in a potluck manner at gatherings of people, or served by the host. This is especially true at holidays. The cost of food in the United States is often too high for people to purchase enough to share with large groups of people. Additionally, finding some traditional foods is often difficult and even more expensive. Thus many social occasions that used to be communal events are now only celebrated within the family, if at all.

The geographical distribution of Guatemalans also affects communal development. One respondent said, "In the Bay Area a great number of Guatemalans are in Marin and Sonoma counties where there is a small presence of Hispanics." There are few existing networks in such communities because many Guatemalans are first-generation and are still fighting to get a foothold in this country.

Another impediment to the formation of communal ties among Guatemalans in the United States is that many people maintain close ties with family and friends who remain in Guatemala. A large portion of the support, in money and goods, given by many Guatemalans is sent back to Guatemala rather than being given within the Guatemalan community in the United States. Several people indicated that they view the Guatemalan community in the United States as merely a temporary agglomeration, and their loyalties (as well as their donations of money and goods) are directed toward their families and communities in Guatemala. These respondents plan on returning to Guatemala as soon as the political situation there becomes stable. Additionally, the importance of giving to people in Guatemala is highlighted during times of crisis there. One woman said that after the large earthquake of 1976, she "sent a lot of money to Guatemala for the victims along private channels, people commuting back and forth between the United States and Guatemala."

One respondent told of an interesting form of volunteer work that serves to maintain links between Guatemalans in the United States and in Guatemala. He and other Guatemalans in the Bay Area use ham radios to transmit messages to and from Guatemala. Some of these men have formed groups, and members of these groups transmit information twenty-four hours a day at no charge. These operators help people stay in contact with relatives who live in the mountains and jungles, where there may be little or no phone contact. They also provide a free alternative to the phone company and, given the lack of phone service in Guatemala, a much quicker one in times of emergency. They transmit messages throughout Latin America concerning deaths, requests for burial expenses, accidents, weddings, births, general news, and other concerns to one's friends and family in Guatemala and Latin America (because Guatemalan refugees are scattered throughout the region). The Red Cross has given away radios to isolated areas of Guatemala in order to use these operators to help establish contact in emergencies. The operators donate large amounts of time to help maintain these links. The person who described these groups said that he devotes twelve to fourteen hours a day to this task.

One 44-year-old respondent said that he believes ethnic identity and tensions are also important in stifling communal development among Guatemalans, that Guatemalans on occasion "try to dissociate themselves from other Guatemalans." He went on to say, "In part I think this is because we are lumped in with Mexicans and we try to remove ourselves from this because white society looks down on Mexicans." A few other respondents indicated that they did not want to be lumped in with Mexicans in organizations or in other people's perceptions, but they felt this was a positive factor in uniting the Guatemalan community. As one man stated, "Guatemalans have many identities, but one thing that draws us together is trying to dissociate ourselves from Mexicans."

CHAPTER FOUR   ❧ *Salvadorans*

- Most Salvadoran giving takes place within the extended family and ethnic community.
- Salvadorans send and bring large amounts of money and goods to family and friends in El Salvador.
- Salvadorans prefer to give directly to individuals and tend to distrust large charitable organizations.
- Salvadorans rarely relinquish the care of elderly parents to government or nonprofit organizations.
- Salvadorans commonly provide shelter to other Salvadorans for little or no money.
- Some Salvadorans give to and volunteer for mainstream nonprofit organizations.

While Salvadorans have been in the United States in moderately significant numbers since the 1930s, most Salvadoran immigrants to the United States have come during the last twenty years. Of the 565,081 Salvadorans reported in the 1990 United States Census, 106,405 were native-born and 458,676 were foreign-born. Like other groups before them, some of the Salvadorans in the United States have emigrated in order to seek improved economic conditions. El Salvador is a country in which a small, extremely wealthy elite rules over a tiny middle class and large lower class. But most Salvadorans who came to the United States did not come as immigrants seeking improved economic conditions. They came as refugees fleeing for their lives. It has been estimated that during the 1980s over 75,000 civilians were murdered by the Salvadoran government's death squads, at least another 8,000 disappeared, and over 1.5 million became refugees. Salvadorans who survived the arduous journey to the United States faced conditions that were little better, in economic terms. An estimated 70 percent of Salvadorans in this country are unemployed or underemployed. Most have no health insurance and live in substandard housing conditions. Many are homeless (Zografos, 1991).

The following comments on sharing and helping in the Salvadoran community are taken from interviews with 20 individuals.

❧ KINSHIP

A first-generation Salvadoran woman said that she believed the lack of institutional forms of support was a primary difference between Salvadoran culture and that of the United States: "Oh yes, Salvadoran people helped their own families, but they had no welfare or anything like that. You were expected to take care of your family. There are no retirement homes or anything like that; it is within the culture."

Respondents spoke of the importance of familial giving and the role it plays in their day-to-day lives. A 52-year-old woman who has been living in the United States for over twenty years said that Salvadorans "don't expect, but feel obligated" to give to their family. Salvadoran immigrants reveal a conscious effort to expand one's circle of support, especially in a society that cannot or does not rely on organizational forms of support. A young man said, "Our relatives don't ask us for help. We just do it. We have to care for our own. Giving is vital to expand your circle of family and friends." Those closest to you assure that you will be taken care of in times of need, therefore you must expand your circle of support whenever possible.

From the time they are able to work, children give money to their parents. People of all ages, including respondents in their twenties, said that they support one or both of their parents in some manner. "I always help people in need and I always give money to my parents," said one 22-year-old woman. "When I work I can do this." Another young respondent said, "Financially, I [send money to] my mother and 17-year-old niece in San Salvador."

Respondents said that they expect to support their parents for as long as they are alive. Aid to parents usually involves monetary support, food, and often shelter and care as well. One woman who had moved away from her parents spoke about how she would share her family's food with her mother, "Among family we shared a lot. I lived apart from my mother and father. So my husband would pick fruit and vegetables that I would share with my mother." Children often make personal sacrifices in order to care for their parents. For instance, a 30-year-old man said that he still lives at home in order to help his mother: "I take care of my mom by paying for half of the bills at home. I could live on my own. But I don't." He has told his mother that he "will not leave until she is well taken care of."

Some respondents felt that American-Salvadoran differences in caring for the elderly stem from different attitudes toward the elderly. As one woman said, there are "many nice Americans, but there is a lack of love. It's like fast-food relationships, not close relationships with parents. There is a lot of loneliness. In El Salvador, even if people are very poor, they share their food and their thoughts." But, as with other groups in this study, these attitudes often change over time. The longer Salvadorans have been in the United States, the more independent they become. One man who is half Salvadoran and half Mexican said:

> Mexicans and Salvadoreños think similarly. Once you come here, you are once or twice removed from your country. The sense of family is lost. But when I visit relatives in Mexico, or Salvadoran relatives come here, they stress family, dedication to mother and father, never turning your back on family, and dedication to sisters and aunts. It may not be spoken, but when something goes wrong, you have to be there for them. When my grandma comes here, we talk about these things.

Some of the responses indicated that this change in attitude can occur before the second or third generation. A 50-year-old respondent born and raised in El Salvador but a resident of the United States since she was a young woman said that her attitudes toward supporting her parents have definitely changed: "Now I wouldn't have my mother live with me because it is such a different life and I don't have the time to take care of her and my attitude has changed in this country and I am so far away from my family that I have become independent."

Giving to one's parents often includes the provision of housing. This form of giving is offered to extended family members as well. The provision of shelter to extended family members was one of the most frequently mentioned forms of giving within the family. Respondents said that in many instances they would not have been able to come to the United States had relatives not opened their homes to them:

> During the late seventies and the early eighties many Salvadoreños were offered a chance to come to the U.S. by Salvadoreños here, even if they were not family or friends. I got the offer from both friends and family. My friends from my hometown were living in California and my family was living in Texas. They would send me letters saying, "We can help you. You can come live with us." This is just one case. But there are thousands and thousands of cases like this. Immediately in the early eighties thousands of Salvadoreños came to the United States because they had doors opened.

A 31-year-old woman said, "When I first came to the United States I was living with some relatives" while she got established. Another woman said, "I lived rent free in my uncle's house for four and a half years." Another respondent's uncle was able to provide his family with a house that enabled them to escape the war. "In 1978 we were escaping the civil war. We got a chance to leave because of my family. My uncle helped us come legally. He had been here since the fifties." Said another respondent, "We always had an open-door policy for relatives from El Salvador and Puerto Rico. People also came from Nebraska. If they visited they knew where they had to stay. They never looked for a hotel. If they stayed at a hotel that would be absurd."

A woman said that her brother helped gather $2,000 for her to come to the United States. "Once I arrived I paid them back. It took me six months to pay back the $2,000, so I have lived with the same brother since my arrival." While the brother recouped the money he sent his sister for her journey, he will never be reimbursed for the lodging. Nor does he expect to be. Instead, he counts on the knowledge that should he need it, his sister will assist him in any way she can. The family's welfare is of primary importance because it is through the family first and foremost that one can ensure survival. The importance of family ties was demonstrated by a man who said, "My dad mostly took care of his family. My parents divorced. So he had two wives and nine kids. His *primo* [cousin] would come stay with us. Sometimes he would let him or other relatives come from El Salvador. They would stay for free at our house or at my step-mom's." Even in families divided by divorce, these customs prevail.

While those provided with housing typically do not pay rent, they help their relatives in other ways. One respondent said: "My mom had two cousins come stay with us. We had an open-door policy. Sometimes other relatives would come visit for a month. The doors were always open unless they didn't give any respect. My parents didn't want money. But they expected the people who stayed with us to buy bread or clean." Another respondent said:

> I have two roommates. My little sister just moved in until she can get on her own feet. My sister does not pay any rent. I help her and my mother out with money. I also help with my nephew and nieces. Even though she is living free in my house she will offer to pay a bill or clean up. She'll cook up a storm for a week whenever she has money. She also walks my dog.

Many families send some of their members to the United States in order to take advantage of relatively higher wages and increased job opportunities. This form of support both differs from what is commonly found in the United States and helps to explain how extra income (beyond what is needed for one's own support) is spent. Several respondents spoke of family members in the United States supporting family in El Salvador. "Yes, I help my mother send money. I'll add to whatever she sends to her brothers and sisters. She sends them money year 'round. We also send blenders and pots when my grandmother goes to San Salvador." Another man said that his mother also supports her brothers and sisters in El Salvador, "My mom also sends money to her brothers and sisters back home. She has always done this. She has never stopped." This need to provide a better life for one's family in El Salvador has even separated mothers from their young children. A 33-year-old woman said, "I send clothes for my kids. Since my children are in El Salvador I give them support by giving them an education there. So I have to send them clothes and money."

While family members remaining in El Salvador are often largely supported by those in the United States, they still remain part of the family's extended support network and are expected to come to the aid of other family members whenever necessary. Therefore, one will see token or ritualistic forms of giving occurring from family in El Salvador to family in the United States. This helps preserve the pride of those living in El Salvador, but more importantly serves to reaffirm familial support networks. One respondent said, "The last person I think my father gave money to was his father-in-law. He visited here a few months ago. This was the first time they really hung out. He gave him $500 to take back to El Salvador. He probably told him, 'Take me for a beer next time I see you.'"

Much of the assistance from Salvadorans goes to those trying to emigrate to the United States and to those who recently had done so. Some Salvadorans follow a pattern exhibited by groups of other nationalities who come to the United States seeking improved economic opportunities. Some families seek to improve their lot in their home country. Members in the United States are there for a finite period of time only and return after family goals have been met. Other families send small groups of men out together to establish a base in the United States. They secure jobs and housing and then supply the means for other family members to travel to the United States. A young woman in such a family said, "My father came to Berkeley to work with friends. Then he sent for us two years later."

☙ COMMUNITY

Lessons learned within the family regarding the importance of giving and sharing are easily translated into communal support systems. "If I know someone needs something, then I will try to help them no matter what. If I know my friend needs a pair of shoes, I will give her an extra pair of my sister's. We used to do this in my family," responded one young woman. That giving patterns common in families were recreated within the community was as essential for Salvadorans as it was for several of the other groups in this study, especially those comprised largely of recent immigrants. Many family members remain in El Salvador. For Salvadoran immigrants to the United States, communal support networks supplement or even supplant familial networks. Again, the difference from American support systems is striking. As one woman said:

> If someone needed help they would tell their neighbor. It's very different from here. Your neighbors know all your business. They will help you. Here your neighbor might run if you ask for help. Your neighbor probably won't offer you a drink of water. There your neighbors will help you pay rent. They will give you food. At the grocery stores you can get credit with no interest. You pay your debt when you get paid.

Similar in tone was the reply of a 26-year-old man who said that in the Salvadoran culture, "there is still a sense of community. This implies that you are with someone through the good and the bad. This is a collective experience. Here it is me, mine, my house. There is not a sense of community, there is fear. People do not even play in the streets." A middle-aged woman said: "We grew up with community. People gave to each other easily. If a neighbor needs tortillas or beans, then you give it to them. The poor in this country have a very poor spirit. In America, the more you have, the more jealous people are and the more miserly people are."

One result of the mutual support system practiced by many Salvadorans is that people within the community are more open and trusting with each other. "People in this country sometimes think it's weird of you to give, they don't trust why you give," said one woman. A first-generation 34-year-old woman said, "My mom also taught us we must offer things even if we don't have enough for ourselves. When people would visit we would feed them. Afterwards my mother may pay for their bus fare. The neighbors would make sure that your house is not lost because of overdue rent." While this sort of mutualism certainly occurs among the mainstream populace in the United States, most respondents in this study felt it was not the norm.

Several respondents indicated that the Salvadoran mutual support derives from the extensive institutional support system and the extreme concentration of wealth in El Salvador. One man said, "I always relate this to social justice. There are many resources in my country that are concentrated with rich people. Then there should be a way to give to those who have nothing. If I'm in the position to struggle for this, then I will do it no matter if I'm here or there." Another said, "When I was in need no one shared with me, so I learned that if there are many people in need, if you have, you should give to those in need. All my life I have distributed what I have."

Many said that they learned from their parents that giving was a social responsibility. One woman reported, "This is a family tradition, social responsibility, that has been carried on for two generations. The tradition must prevail. [My parents] expect me to use my knowledge for the collective benefit, for the betterment of society in general." Another woman indicated that she learned from her father that giving should be done equitably: "What I liked about my father was every time he bought things he distributed them equally among all his children. There were eight of us. The youngest child received just as much as the oldest. I learned from him to give equally to your friends. Give each person one or give each person two. But give equally."

A teenager said that her mother had not only emphasized the social justice aspects of giving but the psychic benefits as well. When asked what she learned from her mother, she said: "I learned that not everybody has the same ability to get things, not everybody has enough food, and not every single kid has a home to play in. She has taught me to be sensitive to other people; how to understand them, not be selfish. The more you try to help someone else, the better you feel."

Once in this country, Salvadoran giving focuses on items necessary for survival, such as food. "I offer food to my neighbors or friends who are in a tight bind. I do this all the time," one woman said. "If I had food, then if a neighbor or friend needed some, I would give them some of the things that I had," said another respondent. The same man said, "If I think that I have enough for us I will send my friends or neighbors food or invite friends and neighbors to my house to share with them." Another respondent said:

> If there is someone who needs clothes, I will give them clothes. But if I have money to buy them new clothes, then I will buy new ones. If I see a friend is lacking food, I will at least take them beans. What I like is that they are never without enough beans. Sometimes I see my friends don't even have enough for their child's shirts. If I have $20 then I will give it to them.

One respondent said that his mother did a lot with senior citizens. "She would take people food in my neighborhood. She also cleaned people's houses. When I had friends whose parents weren't good, she would feed them." Many times food was shared at social events. One respondent said:

My mom and dad always want us to be ready. We always have food and drinks. If anyone comes over they are welcome to come in. They can have any food or drink. When there is a big fight [on TV], my dad will have about 30 guys over. He'll invite the guys at his work, some of the car washers. My mom is the same way. Sometimes she'll have a little gathering. They always offer something.

Guests as well would bring food to their hosts. In the words of one informant, friends would "bring *unos chorales* [pans of food]," when they were invited to someone's house.

On the surface, this tradition mirrors the universal social nicety of serving refreshments to one's guests. But the meaning is deeper for many Salvadorans. The man who spoke about his father having food for friends who come over for the fights said that he believes this social grace is indicative of the belief in sharing that is prevalent among Salvadorans: "This is something that I think is common with all Latinos. Since we were kids we were taught to share." This social giving also serves to reinforce communal ties. One thing that Salvadorans and mainstream Americans have in common is that women do most of this work. As one man said, "Women seem more active than men. Women cook. If there is an event in the family the women would organize it. The men would be content with participating."

Like food and clothing, shelter is basic to survival. Many respondents reported that much of their giving involved the provision of housing. Usually there was no expectation of return. As one respondent said: "If I give a friend a place to stay I don't expect anything back from them." Sometimes there were expectations of remuneration. A 29-year-old said, "When I first moved to San Francisco I worked for free in exchange for room and board."

Shorris (1992) wrote of a 47-year-old Salvadoran man living with twenty-five other people in a one-bedroom apartment in Los Angeles. None of the respondents in the present study spoke of living with so many people, but many of them spoke of the monetary sacrifice involved in housing others. One person said:

> In some cases I would receive friends for whom I would provide my apartment for a few months. In 1984 there were three men who came to my apartment looking for me. I wasn't home at the time. I didn't know they were coming. When I arrived they were waiting for me at the door. They were my friends from my neighborhood [in El Salvador]. I couldn't tell them I didn't have enough space for everybody. So I let them in. They lived with me for six months. They couldn't work during that time so I had to share my food with the three of them.

Another respondent said:

> When someone needs a place to live, we will allow them to stay with us or we will find them a place to stay until they get a job. This is help because many of us don't have anyone here in this country. The church does this too. It is beautiful when someone offers a homeless person a place to stay, a hungry person something to eat.

In some instances basic needs such as food and housing were provided for individuals by families who would essentially adopt them. One young woman said:

> My parents took in two children. They were not related to us, or friends or anything. They just needed help. One lived with us for one year and the other for about five years. The children were from a really poor family who could not support them. Some friends of ours knew about this family and this is how we found out about the children. It was pretty customary that people would do things like this to help others.

Some respondents spoke of such informal adoptions occurring in El Salvador. Wealthier families with a sense of social consciousness would give aid to neighbors or servants. One woman said that her father, a doctor, would often provide free medical care to people in their community and always to their servants. Also, her mother "would bring in families of maids if they were sick [and] often take in servants' kids as well."

Another respondent said she was living in the United States as the direct result of such an informal adoption: "[My] grandmother worked as a housekeeper for an old woman. The old woman's children had grown up and left. The old woman wanted to have little children. So she decided my mother and aunt would be her children. She raised them in her house." The old woman told this woman's grandmother that she wanted to raise the two girls as her daughters, and her grandmother agreed.

This same respondent went on to say that she believed that helping other Salvadorans learn to read and write English is essential to their success in the United States. She spoke of her sister, who teaches English to other Salvadoran immigrants and refugees: "My sister buys up to fifty notepads to give away. When she holds classes in her house, she gives these notepads to her students. Her students are friends of ours. Both adults and children come for help. Most adults want help in writing. They can't complete applications or write addresses. She tells them, 'Come, I will help you read. Then you will complete your papers by yourself.'"

In addition to communal giving, Salvadorans provide specialized help to each other. One 24-year-old said:

> [My parents] would like me to help their friends with my accounting. I will also be able to help people when I finish law school. This is what I want to do. But they don't expect anything. They don't say it. Right now I don't feel like I am doing anything. My whole month/year is going by without accomplishing nothing. The only way I could see myself happy is by helping people. I might go teach grammar school or talk to Berkeley High about working with kids. Whatever the case, I feel the only time I am satisfied is when I help people. This has been instilled in me. I have seen all the help my father and mother have given. I feel if I'm not this way, I'm losing a part of myself.

He then spoke about his father:

I never saw him give many things to people. He gave more time and effort. He's a car salesman. So people from El Salvador and Mexico would come to him for financial help. He would get them financing to get started. Because he helped people they would give him gifts and presents. Ten years ago, a man from Mexico asked my dad to help him buy a car. My dad helped him with cash. Then he helped him get credit. With that the family opened up a little grocery store in the Mission district. Then they opened another store. Now they are millionaires. Whenever they see my dad they feel they owe him something. They always give him boxes of mangos and bananas. They bring him everything. He says no. But they still give it. They don't give money. Because that is just not the way things are done between families. It's more important to give things people will appreciate.

The young man went on to say that his father has helped many Salvadorans and Mexicans "get cars and [down payments for] houses. He doesn't ask for money. They just pay him back when they can."

Sending money and goods to El Salvador is a common form of giving. A Guatemalan respondent said that 50 to 60 percent of El Salvador's GNP was attributable to transfer payments from relatives in the United States. Salvadoran respondents agreed. They reported that family members in the United States send money, clothes, and utilitarian items such as pots and pans to extended family members in El Salvador. Often these items are personally delivered despite the cost involved. One person who lived with friends in order to share rent and food regularly sent money to El Salvador:

At the same time I was sending money to my family to help them. My cousins, brothers, and sisters needed the money to go to school or to buy basic things. I would send material things to them, clothes and appliances. But not just with family, but also with friends. They stayed in Salvador. But they needed some money in order to buy things because they lost their jobs.

Most Salvadorans still feel very connected to El Salvador. The Salvadoran community places great emphasis on supporting other Salvadorans within the United States but also on supporting those still in El Salvador. One respondent said his parents

would always take whatever [clothes] we weren't using [back to El Salvador to distribute]. Every year we would buy or rent a new van. Underneath we would carry about four boxes of clothes that we didn't need. . . . One time we stopped at a *mercado*. My dad bought some inexpensive gifts like balls and dolls. This only cost four or five dollars. Then he stopped at a park to give this away to kids we didn't know.

Another man talked about more organized forms of giving to El Salvador:

Now we are seeing the other way. Once we are here, there are many people organizing by themselves. If they are from the same hometown they are sending back aid: material and economic. For example, there is a community from a small town called Entupica, located in the eastern part of El

Salvador. In Washington, D.C., there are a lot of people from this small town. So these people organized by themselves in the early eighties. They were trying to build streets, parks, clinics, and libraries for the town. They also would send money for a specific family of the town or for children.

Speaking about those who get involved in such efforts, he said that "sometimes they are relatives or friends. But most importantly they are just from that town. Even if they do not plan to return, they are thinking how to improve or rebuild their hometown. This is not just the case with the Salvadoreño community, but we do have this expression coming from the Salvadoreños in the U.S." When asked if he believed this involvement was due to a concern to rebuild the country after the civil war, he replied that such efforts were

> not necessarily from the war. Those who came before the civil war would think about how they could do something for their town. The civil war accelerated the process. Most saw the need to immediately help those who stayed in those towns. They especially tried to build clinics and send medicine. In some cases they even sent ambulances to their hometown.

Several respondents indicated that their communal giving patterns, in regards to El Salvador, were primarily motivated by political considerations. One man, who is now the executive director of a refugee relief center, said, "Since 1982, when I came to the U.S., I became very involved with community projects that involve Central America. I've been working in the community, especially for promoting human and civil rights, as well as denouncing human rights violations in my country." Another man said, "[I have] a lot of contact with El Salvador. . . . I still support the popular movement, the revolutionary movement. Solidarity means you're supposed to give something. The war is related to sacrifice. We asked for equality and we got bullets."

Despite the cost, traveling to El Salvador to deliver goods to family and the wider community is desirable for two reasons. First, it is a way to ensure that the goods and/or money arrive at their destination. Second, seeing family members and friends solidifies and maintains supportive ties. Many respondents indicated that they traveled to El Salvador as often as possible in order to visit their families and to take them necessary goods. One woman said, "When we go to our country, we take clothes and money to our friends who don't have anything. We don't go very often. It takes years to save up." A man said, "My mother goes there at least once every two years. She takes a big army duffel bag packed with clothing, pots, and pans. People don't have a lot of this down there. She give this to her family." Another respondent said, "My dad takes clothes to give to people. He gets this from his church. When I go next summer I'm going to take clothes, books, and condoms." Some have decided that the risk associated in sending their relatives goods and money by mail are outweighed by the potential costs of traveling in a country beset by frequent civil wars and government crackdowns. One young man said: "Before the war, I visited. It was the last time I went because of the unstable circumstances. Then the earthquake hit. We sent money to repair some of our relatives' houses. After that we would just send pots, pans, and money." Other respondents indicated that they do not return to El Salvador any more because of the violence in that country.

One respondent spoke about the communal patterns of support that enable the Salvadoran guerrillas to continue their civil war against the government:

> The fact is that for many years the opposition has been growing because of the support everyone has been giving to others. This reflects the way we share, not just time, but also material things with those who will struggle for social justice. Even if people didn't participate directly by giving their time, they were participating by donating material things like food, clothes, or other things which sustained those directly involved in the war, and this has been for many who came [to the United States]. This is why many, including the U.S. government, did not understand how the guerrillas were surviving for many years in such a small country. Why? Because they were sustained by the people. Even though the majority didn't participate in other struggles, they sustained the military strength of the guerrillas. Maybe this happens in other countries, but this is how I would reflect on how people give in my culture.

☞ CELEBRATIONS AND CEREMONIES

Families use rituals to cement existing ties. Family giving at these events also helps to pay for them. As was true in the other groups with a Hispanic Catholic tradition, these occasions are centered primarily around life changes and religious events: baptisms, *quinceañeras*, weddings, moves, and funerals.

Like other groups in this study, Salvadorans commonly receive godparents at their baptism. Godparents help pay for the baptism and are responsible for the children's welfare should the parents die. This responsibility is taken very seriously, especially given the effect on families of the civil war. The giving surrounding this event is straightforward for most Salvadorans. "They baptize the kid. Then there is a dinner. The godparents give the clothes the child will wear. Then the mother cooks the food," said one young woman. The fact that the godparents have agreed to become ritual family members is of primary importance, the events surrounding the baptism are less so. Respondents indicated two possible reasons for this; cost is one of them: "The godparents promise to be second parents for the kid. Later the kid's family or the godparents will have a party. Some people don't make a big deal of it. Others do not get baptized because they don't have money. In my case, my mom, father, godfather, and godmother paid for it." Another young woman indicated that the absence of a celebration could be attributed to tradition as well as cost. She said, "In El Salvador they just baptize the baby. That's all. . . . Here they have a party at the family's house or in a hall. I think both the parents and the godparents pay for this."

Fewer respondents mentioned giving at *quinceañeras* and weddings. A *quinceañera* is a party given to a girl on her fifteenth birthday. As one respondent told us, it "represents the blossoming of a woman," when her parents present her to church and community. The giving that surrounds both *quinceañeras* and weddings is similar. Extended family members and, to a lesser extent, friends help pay for the wedding. Like baptisms, families often use *quinceañeras* and weddings as appropriate occasions to enlist fictive kin as godparents. While not as important as baptismal godparents, godparents at *quinceañeras* and weddings are expected to look out for the long-term welfare of their *ahijados*, or godchildren. They are also expected to help with some of the immediate costs of the ceremony and attendant parties. Sometimes these costs can be quite expensive, much more so than could be afforded by most Salvadorans in this country on their own. A 24-year-old man spoke about the expenses involved in sponsoring a *quinceañera*, "The price could range from $4,000 to $20,000. I think this is too much. I wouldn't want to spend that much on a wedding." Banding together, though, family members can raise significant sums of money for these occasions. One man said that at his cousin's wedding, "a lot of family gave donations for the wedding, the reception and the honeymoon. They raised so much money they went on a honeymoon."

Ritualistic giving also occurred at times of loss, when a family member was leaving for someplace distant or when a member had died. Parties (*despiedidas*) are held for family members who are preparing to move elsewhere. One man said, "At the *despiedida* family and friends attend. Everyone brings something for a *requierdo* to remind the person of where they left. Sometimes the gift will have the date of departure or a picture." This token will serve always to remind the recipient of where their family ties lie. Additionally, some respondents indicated that they used *despiedidas* as mechanisms for redistributing money and goods to other relatives in El Salvador when a family member is returning there. "They had a little good-bye dinner. People gave him clothes to take back. I just gave him $50. I thanked him for the time he spent with us here."

Much of the giving surrounding funerals, like that with *despiedidas*, serves to confirm the support network existing among surviving family members. Some of the giving, such as the *ofrendas* or altars that some families build and make donations of food to, is purely religious and spiritual. A large portion of the giving surrounding funerals is practical and serves as a demonstration of the importance of the family networks. Burying one's dead properly is an important obligation in most societies. Due to the costs associated with funeral and burial fees, both in El Salvador and even more so in the United States, many Salvadorans would not be able to afford an adequate and satisfying funeral for loved ones on their own. A 35-year-old woman explained the role family networks play in helping when there is a death. She said that in El Salvador all her family members saved money every month toward family funerals. During the war this custom became even more necessary. At the funeral, all the women in the family would make tamales and drinks in order to feed all the guests. The savings would be used to pay the church and the other expenses related to the funeral. Her family continues the custom today.

∞ RELIGION

Among institutions, the Catholic church and some Protestant churches play an important role in the communal giving patterns of Salvadorans. Several respondents traced their attitudes about giving within the community to the church. "The Salvadoran community does expect each of us to help, it is all part of our religious belief. In many ways our strong Catholic upbringing fosters the sense of community and helping out your neighbors. We do not have much money; however, we give and share," said one person.

Some Catholic churches within the United States serve as social outlets for their parishioners. The church gives members and non-members alike a focal point for activities that serve to bind members of the community to one another. A young man said:

> [My mother is] really involved in the church. She's not real religious but it's a social outlet. They will all get together on Sunday or after work for coffee. If it's the Salvadoran Independence Day then they will have a celebration. At the church they also help retired people. She'll take them to the hospital. She also donates clothing.

A woman said:

> [When I] got married the ceremony took place in the church where we worked. The community helped. People brought food. We invited all the people we worked with and community. A Salvadoran girl cooked turkey and bread. Some other friends brought a cake. We didn't spend anything. All the people contributed food and decorations for the hall.

Similarly, another woman said that sometimes her mother would make a communion dress for free for families who could not afford one.

As was true with several other groups in the study, Salvadorans reported that much of the time and money they committed to organizations went to religious organizations. Some respondents felt that it was better to give individually rather than giving through the church. "We love and we help friends. If my friend or neighbor needs help, I am there. I do not give money to the man in church," replied one. Said another, "I believe there is a God. But I don't agree with all the facts of the church. If you can help someone for an hour, I think that God, if there is a God, will be just as happy as if you went to church."

There were some differences in the patterns reported by Salvadorans when compared to the other Hispanic groups and including Filipinos, who share a Hispanic Catholic tradition with the Latin American countries. One significant difference is that many more Salvadorans are Protestant. Nearly 25 percent of the population of El Salvador is evangelical Protestant. One man said, "[My] mother donates money to the [Seventh-Day Adventist] church every weekend. Sometimes she helps with funerals and baptisms. She will decorate or bring food. She also calls people. Her church also houses new immigrants." Another said that his mother is still an active Jehovah's Witness who goes door to door promoting the church. Another difference is that few Salvadorans participate in what would be considered more traditional Catholic practices. Only one informant said that all of her giving to organizations is directed to the church.

More people reported that they were active in charitable pursuits commonly associated with the church in the United States. One young man said that his mother participates in a variety of activities through the church. Her group

> helps take old people to the hospital. They have a bus service which takes people to run errands. She'll also cook when they have fund-raisers for kids' education. They sell cake and *pan con chumpe* [bread with turkey] to raise funds. They also plan other events on Sundays. They get work done, but it is mostly social. They plan dances to raise scholarship funds. Then they give this money to kids who want to attend Riordan or other private high schools.

Another young man said that his mother "gives money to church and donates time to raise money for social programs, shelters for the homeless and youth gangs. There is also space for Guatemalan groups. The shelter is open to Latinos, including many Salvadorans." Another respondent said, "Through the church we were involved in community activities such as collecting food for the poor, clothes, and money in the collection. We [the church] also took in other children occasionally."

Several Salvadorans who reported that they were actively involved in giving through the church spoke of being involved with the liberation theology movement and the social activism that the Catholic parishes had begun. One respondent said:

> I attend church at least once a month. My own personal religion plays a big role in my life. There have always been two kinds of Catholics, people in the traditional church and the popular church. The popular church has always been for human rights; we have been working within to provide food. This sector has been playing a very important role in my country. And I've been very close to people in this sector. These are the people who have been promoting the liberation theology.

This woman believed that one must actively participate in bettering one's community and in helping others. Another respondent felt that the Catholic church in the United States did not follow this tradition and because of this he does not give the church any money. He told us: "In the U.S. I have not given money, as I did in El Salvador, to the Catholic church. The Salvadoran Catholic church [meaning those parishes practicing liberation theology] not the Roman Catholic. The Salvadoran is more horizontal, meaning human-to-human, more grounded in the here and now, not the afterlife." Similarly, a woman said:

> The organization that helps [the people] the most is the Catholic church. There are many priests who have a lot of land. They will give a family a house where they can plant food for sustenance. Many people live on these lands. But I don't know if the priest give away the land or not. There are many small houses. Every family from each house works in the same field. Then they divide the food. If they plant corn, they will sell half of it. Then they will divide the remaining food.

∞ GIVING TO ORGANIZATIONS

Respondents held differing views about the role organizational giving played among Salvadorans in the United States. Some felt that Salvadoran giving patterns were perfectly in sync with forms of giving common in the United States. "I volunteer because of the personal responsibility that I have with the community. They are extended members of my 'family,'" said one man. Another person said "Yes [I volunteer]. I want to be useful to society. It is the right thing to do as a responsibility to the human race. We have a moral responsibility to help others." Another respondent, though, felt that he had learned more formal giving patterns within the United States. He said, "At the university [Berkeley] a sense of civic duty was instilled in us. We were taught to believe that we must feel useful to your community; the city where you live. And I welcome this." He went on:

> I believe it is important to instill in young people a sense of obligation to their community because we need them. They need us. When I worked at Berkeley High School, I liked it. I knew I was making a difference in these youths' lives. I felt good about myself. When I worked at Horizons Unlimited [a youth program], it was very rewarding.

Several respondents said they did not participate in formal giving patterns for several reasons. Some either preferred, or were just used to, giving to individuals. "Giving to organizations is good, but I like helping people one-to-one best," one woman explained. Another woman said, "Among Salvadorans there is a suspicion of many [charitable] solicitors. If you help your neighbors and your friends, then you are doing well." Another woman stated:

> It is much different in my country because there is no support from the government or organizations. You help others or else people will die. There is a lot more personal involvement in the community. The church is also very involved in giving food staples to the poor. This is not always well distributed, though. Often these goods are sold on the black market or the wealthy keep them.

She went on to say that in El Salvador people must help each other in part because "there is no other choice. There is no welfare or anything. I won't accept welfare or any of that; I'd kill myself working first." The latter part of her statement here, and her remarks on the corruption in food distribution by the church in El Salvador, reflect a distrust of large institutions that was echoed by other respondents. "I give what I can give to the people who need help. I don't give money to organizations because you see corruption and you see them take advantage of a situation. The people who need it don't get the help that they need," stated one informant. In the same vein, another responded:

> [I give] clothes to the homeless. Instead of giving clothes to the Salvation Army, I got five friends together. I had old blankets, sleeping bags, and clothes. My friend brought her truck. We dropped that off right in the middle of city hall because they were freezing out there. I was cold in my own house. So I could imagine how cold they were.

This person expressed, through his actions, a preference for direct action and a lack of faith in the effectiveness of large, traditional, charitable organizations.

Others indicated that they did not give to organizations because they lacked the money or time to do so. They worried about day-to-day survival, and were working in poorly paying jobs until they become more solidly placed in the society of their new country. Instead, money and time are expended to help ensure the survival of one's family and community. When asked if he ever donated money, one respondent said, "I cannot afford to do that. But my uncle will be visiting for a month. I will help my mother take care of his visit. He will bring very little money if any." Another informant said that his mother would like to act as a volunteer in a nonprofit organization but wasn't able to. "She often mentions nonprofit organizations, but she never has [volunteered] because work won't let her. The same goes for my uncle." He then went on to say that his "brother and sister have time. They are very civic-minded. They like to volunteer for the city a lot." Those in his family who did have time gave it to the larger community.

Some respondents reported volunteering at their children's schools or at local hospitals. One woman said that she volunteers "at the hospital in order to share my experiences with other cancer victims." Another woman said that her husband "volunteers at the office of city planning. He works there two days a week. He works on computers there." Two respondents gave money to animal shelters, one to the disabled. One young woman said that her parents "helped handicapped and veterans' groups by giving them money and by buying light bulbs and flags from them [items sold as fundraisers]." Another respondent said, "[When I] was a kid I did walk-a-thons and the Jerry Lewis Telethon. I also attended the Raza Unida dances. They cost $20, which was pretty steep. But I did attend because it's for a good cause. In college it was rough because I didn't have money for myself. But now that I'm making some money I can help. I donate things here and there."

One man spoke of his support for youth programs, especially those revolving around sports. He said that he gives some of his time tutoring at his old junior high school and also

> here at the neighborhood center, at the playground, and at the projects. I did outreach to show off my program to people selling drugs. I offered to get them a job. But it's almost impossible. I've only helped a few kids. But that's enough. It's like a quick fix when you help someone. At the playground, I've done outreach there also. The kids there didn't want work. They wanted to play football. So I organized some games. I got a couple of kids enrolled in P.A.L. Football. Then I introduced them to the coach. I also help give wrestling clinics at my old high school. I wrestled for thirteen years, so it's fun. We spend a hour and a half showing the kids moves and techniques. My friend Carlos teaches the kids how to use the computers. I'm not computer-literate so I just give support. But these computers were donated. So we try to get the kids interested in computers.

Many respondents involved in organizational giving donated their time and money to organizations that directly helped Salvadoran immigrants or that were concerned with Salvadoran politics and war relief. Often, these people were continuing work they began in El Salvador. One young man said that he had volunteered for the student movement in El Salvador and was now working for immigrants' rights groups in the United States. Another respondent spoke in more detail about why he had become involved. He is active in organizations that seek human rights reform in El Salvador. He said that during his initial involvement with such groups in the United States, he donated his time because he did not have any money to give: "In this country I started participating in the social justice movement, in the middle of the '70s. We didn't donate money because we didn't have enough, but I donated my time to organizations working for social justice. The situation in my country made me feel the need. The injustice made me participate."

Respondents spoke of supporting a number of other organizations that focused specifically on Salvadoran political and immigration issues. A woman said that her mother works for AYANSA, a legal-assistance group, and WRAP, a youth counseling organization. One man replied that he volunteered for La Raza Centro Legal and MALDEF, groups which have worked on legal issues surrounding immigration. One respondent said that his wife "is very active on a committee, Las Vueltas, a grassroots organization that is helping to build up a town in El Salvador. The committee sends delegates with equipment, medical supplies, caravans, school supplies, toys, and volunteers." Another respondent spoke of being involved with two organizations that give aid to those who were involved in the war:

> Foundations like Bravo Fund help ex-soldiers of the FMLN make the transition back into civilian life. They mostly offer psychological help because these soldiers are under a lot of stress. Many of them have lost all their family. Remembering this can cause a lot of problems. So they receive help from professionals. Money can't help this. We need medics to give check-

ups. We need teachers. We need carpenters to rebuild the building. Bravo Fund does all this. SHARE also does this. But Bravo Fund specifically helps ex-soldiers. SHARE helps the whole community.

Two organizations, CARECEN (Central American Refugee Center) and CRECE (Central American Refugee Committee), were mentioned more than others by those who spoke of donating time and money to organizations that concerned themselves with Salvadoran political and immigrants' issues. CARECEN provides legal, health, and social services; conducts fact finding missions to Central America; and publishes reports documenting immigrant and refugee conditions. CRECE is a membership-driven community organization. Additionally, Salvadorans run EMPLEO, a job cooperative whose services are utilized by many Salvadoran refugees and immigrants. Pointing newly arrived Salvadorans to these and other such resources is viewed as a very important responsibility by many of those interviewed. One young woman said:

> I volunteer here [CARECEN] after school and on weekends from three to five. On Thursdays I come at three, then leave at five. Then I come back from six to nine. I keep coming back because I like the work they are doing here. My mother taught me when you do something for someone, never expect nothing back. You should do it because you want to do it. I also like the work because they are helping Salvadoreño people and I'm Salvadoreño. They also did my paperwork [immigrant legalization] here. So I help here.

Similarly, another respondent said, "When I first arrived in the U.S., CARECEN helped me. Now I help people answer the questionnaires when they come to this clinic. I also talk to a lot of people who say they want to work. I tell them to come to CARECEN." Another person stated, "Right now I just volunteer here [CARECEN]. Sometimes I come to help in the office during the day, but I always come to the clinic on Thursday evenings." Several other respondents said that they volunteered time to one or both organizations or that others in their family did so. One man said that his wife had been donating her time to CRECE for many years and another said that his parents volunteered for CRECE in addition to a few other organizations.
One man, speaking of his friend, said:

> I think the only way things will be good is if we all help each other. She helped me with money and showed me where to study. Then she showed me where I could go to feel comfortable. Because when one comes from a different country he feels terrible not being able to contribute. This system has different customs, cultures, and languages. The people are very different too. The Latin Americans here are very different too. They are very aggressive and opportunistic. That's why CRECE helps orientate one. It also helped me with my papers and food.

Another respondent said, "We must help our people get informed and involved. They need to know how to use available services. A lot of times people don't know how to succeed. So it's our fault if we don't help." A woman said that her friend gave her "a lot of support. She helped me enroll in school for a couple of months. Then she took me to CRECE." Another woman said,

> I know a lot of people who don't give food or money. But they give people an orientation to the United States. They tell them where they can get legal help. They recommend where one can get medical attention. This is helpful. I don't believe it is helpful to give money or food. It will help to adjust to the U.S. if you show them how to read and write. This will help this person in the long run.

•Much of Filipino giving is characterized by reciprocal obligation.
•The sharing of food, both in times of need and at ceremonial occasions, is very important to Filipinos.
•A system of ritual godparenthood is used to help pay for specific celebrations and to expand the support network of one's family.
•Filipinos send and take a large amount of money, material goods, and food to relatives living in the Philippines.
•Regional organizations, based on town or district of origin in the Philippines, are popular with Filipinos in the United States.
•Filipinos are very religious (Catholic) but give little to the church.

Before 1898, the United States had little contact with the Philippine islands. The islands, populated by a largely Malay people, had been colonized by the Spanish since the sixteenth century. Once the United States gained control of the islands, joint programs with the Philippine government were established in the early 1900s to send Filipino students to the United States to gain knowledge and acculturate them to American-style democracy. These immigrants (*pensionados* and *illustrados*) were students who had received territorial scholarships. *Pensionados* were required to return to the Philippines and serve in the public interest. The training they had received enabled many of them to rise to positions of national prominence, assuming leadership positions in government and business. *Pensionados* and *illustrados* who returned to the Philippines became zealous exponents of American democracy and social customs.

The *pensionados* and *illustrados* programs did not bring a large number of Filipinos into the United States. By 1912, only 209 Filipinos had received a college degree or advanced training under the auspices of these programs. However, these programs had the effect of encouraging independent Filipino students to enroll in American schools. Between 1910 and 1938 about 14,000 such students enrolled in schools in the United States. For a variety of reasons, many did not finish their schooling and instead settled in the United States. Many of these settlers were forced to find work in agriculture and domestic services.

These students constituted only part of the first wave of Filipino immigrants. Contract workers recruited to fill the void in cheap agricultural labor in Hawaii and California caused by laws restricting European and Asian (exclusive of Filipinos) immigrants made up the bulk of the rest of the wave. Some of these workers returned to the Philippines after their contracts expired; many stayed in the United States.

The second wave of Filipino immigrants, those who arrived during World War II and continued into the 1950s, were primarily "war brides" or those who had served in the United States Armed Forces. A third wave of immigrants began to arrive after the passage of the Immigration Act of 1965. Approximately two thirds of this wave were professionals, notably nurses and other medical personnel, people from the cities with extensive exposure to Western and especially American culture (Chan, 1991; Crouchett, 1982; and Daniels, 1990). One respondent said:

> We are the most Westernized [Spanish and American] of the Asian cultures, so that affects our giving patterns. Also, immigrants will give differently than second or third generations. The first generation gives to causes related to the Philippines and to the church—whatever reminds you of the Philippines. The second and third generations, we are Americans and we give to our community and to what concerns us.

A salient characteristic among the Filipinos interviewed was the great difference in giving patterns between the generations. Within one or two generations many of the more traditional Filipino giving customs were no longer practiced by respondents. Many interviews revealed a general lack of awareness on the part of younger Filipinos of the traditional names of the giving customs, although they recognized the customs when described. First-generation Filipinos bemoaned the rapidity of acculturation among second- and third-generation Filipinos.

The following comments on Filipino practices of giving are excerpts from interviews with 40 members of the Filipino community.

✆ THE FAMILY

The Philippines are a complex society made up of various strains of immigrant populations. People of Malay descent make up the majority of the population but are divided into numerous subgroups speaking many different dialects. Most of the respondents interviewed used the Tagalog dialect. Added to the mix are immigrants from China and India as well as descendants of Spanish and American colonizers. Regardless of background, most Filipinos consider family loyalty of paramount importance. Traditional Filipino life is based on firmly rooted group relationships that are begun within the family (Crouchett, 1982, p. 71). Within the nuclear and extended family a complex system of mutual obligation ensures that all family members will be fully supported (Meñez, 1980, pp. 30–31). These family values were in evidence in many of the interviews. One young woman said, "With Filipinos, the family is close, there is a much tighter bond. The family is first. If we had plans to go out and a family thing came up, then we would go with the family. We are very close." Another respondent stated: "When I was a teenager I wanted to go places in the summer but couldn't because I had to help my dad with carpentry and farming and my mom with cooking and cleaning. Family values and support were important. My son is starting to realize this now."

Culturally Filipinos are bound by a communal sensibility: "we" or "us," vs. "I" or "me" (Crouchett, 1982, p. 71). Though lifestyles and values are altered somewhat when Filipinos come to this country, there is a conscious effort on the part of many Filipinos to maintain traditional forms of giving and support. Filipino children, for example, are expected to show their parents gratitude when they are older. In the Philippines, children turn over part of their earnings to their parents to demonstrate this. In the United States, the obligation to support one's parents is relaxed somewhat because it is often not necessary as a survival mechanism due to the availability of pensions and social security. But Filipinos in the United States still feel an obligation to their parents and cannot understand why Americans send their parents to nursing homes. For Filipinos, not to support their parents would be a grave violation of cultural norms (Meñez, 1980, p. 46). One respondent said:

> I won't let go of the kids until college. I will support them. After college I will let them go if they want to, but I will always be here. I have already asked the boys if they will take care of us when we are older. My mother stays with my sister now because she has young kids. She stayed with us when we had young kids at home. The old people's war here is loneliness. They are not used to going to a senior citizens' home and playing bridge.

In the Philippines, as a second-generation Filipino explained: "It's relations, not organizations. Organizations are comparatively new, outside of the government. The family system is predominant. They don't have old-age homes, nor do you have places for the mentally ill and disabled, except for the very ill ones."

The American ideal of independence suggests that one does not have to rely on parents and friends for support. "This is America. You have to earn your own money," said one respondent. Despite a shift toward a more independent outlook on life when they come to this country, Filipinos still offer a great deal of support within the nuclear family. Filipino parents in this country are more than ready to offer their children support throughout their lives if they should need or want it, and many children live with their parents or receive some form of aid from them throughout their lives (Meñez, 1980, p. 48). One young woman responded that "it is important [that you can rely upon your family] because once you have a problem you can't always run to a friend. Your friends can't always help you but your family always can." Among some Filipinos, there is a sense of dissatisfaction with Filipinos who have become acculturated (*mayabang*) to such a degree that they no longer send money home to their families. This is considered a deviation from cultural norms (Meñez, 1980, p. 48).

The support structures begun in the nuclear family extend outward to the often large extended families of Filipinos. One woman put it like this:

> Another thing that happens is with day care with minors. Grandpa, uncles, aunts, etc., will baby-sit the family's kids instead of sending them to day

care. My husband does this two days a week. They [people concerned with quantifying giving] don't take into account many things minority communities do that were traditional when they came here as immigrants.

The Filipino family is so supportive that it often renders community ties superfluous. As one respondent stated, "My parents never really joined the community because we have a tight [extended] family and we spend all of our weekends with them." Like other immigrant groups before them, and currently, giving within the extended family begins with the journey to this country.

In order to ensure that they will have financial and emotional assistance, members of extended families settle in the United States in close proximity to one another. The location of one relative in the United States often determines where other relatives move. The money for such a move is often obtained by pooling the resources of various family members. Other considerations such as jobs or schooling are subordinated to family considerations. One woman said, "A cousin was sent to go to school at Berkeley to help my uncle if he ever needed it." That Berkeley is a good university was somewhat incidental; the primary motivation was to be available if direct aid to a family member was needed. Approximately 200 to 250 members of one man's hometown live in his community in the United States. Almost half of these are family members. "Thirty-one of our town mates here are family, my brothers and sisters, and their spouses and kids. The number on my wife's side is about the same, maybe a little more." He later said, "My father and ten others originally came over before World War II. They were to come and bring everyone over and then go back and forth and bring their wives over. They were interrupted by World War II and then they really started up after World War II. That was their main form of giving."

This unity is reinforced by a seemingly endless stream of family visitors that are entertained and given room and board. These family visitors came from the Philippines or from just around the block. One person said, "My father and my mother would often have people staying with us. Any time someone came from the Philippines they stayed with us. There was one time we had eight people staying with us." When discussing her aunts and uncles who live nearby, one girl stated that "during the weekend we are always visitors at one another's house. Once my cousins came from New York and we spent every day of the summer with them. We go to New York to see them occasionally." Another woman recalled that

> the Filipino Cannery Workers Union dispatched Filipinos to Alaska. Our relatives worked the fields and then in the off season they came to Seattle and lived with us and were dispatched to Alaska. All of these were extended relatives and they all stayed with us. . . . Our relatives would help with food [fruits and vegetables from California] and would bring back canned salmon from Alaska. Many times, though, they came back broke because they had a bad season or they lost their money gambling, but they always knew they had a place to stay.

When defining what giving means to them, Filipinos often include the family in their definition, "I see the Filipinos I know as givers. They donate money and energy to take care of their family and their extended family, and the community." This belief that one must give within the family affords many Filipinos, especially immigrants, a degree of security, comfort, and self-reliance they would not achieve otherwise in the United States. One respondent's entire family worked together to save money for a house and their success in doing so stood out in their neighborhood:

> In the community [neighborhood] someone will ask how come you've been here five years and have a house and I've been here twenty years and have only an apartment. Filipinos here work their butts off and work twenty-four hours a day to reach their goal. They work on their days off. Americans take their two or three days off. Filipinos, especially new immigrants, work seven days a week. They are hungry for what they don't have in the Philippines. . . . [I] bought a house for my brother. My brother repaid the down payment and I gave him the house. My brother was new to this country and just married and I had the money. All of [the children] are here in Martinez now and only two of us don't have houses and they are renting from our sisters. You give new family free or partial rent when they first come. If we have a birthday or something the brothers, sisters, nephews, kids, and everybody will come over and help. It's a good feeling to know if I ever get in a jam I will be helped and I don't need to worry.

This pattern is repeated within the families of other respondents. "One of my daughters lives in Seattle with her two kids. They live in one of the houses that my mom owns [next to her] and they pay only the taxes on the place."

This self-reliance (within the family) continues throughout a person's life and extends to all facets of living. While speaking of housing, one respondent stated:

> Another thing I can't comprehend is you work all your life and you finally own your own home and you have to sell it when you retire because you are on a fixed income and you can't afford the property taxes. That is why I say help the family first and then others. I don't want to be real high and have the rest of my family down low.

Such values decrease Filipinos' reliance on the charitable and philanthropic organizations that some other Americans use in times of need and may explain why Filipinos appear not as charitable as mainstream Americans. Their excess money and time are in good part turned inward to the family, toward self-support and mutual assistance.

☙ COMPADRAZGO

Many Filipinos in the United States continue to rely on the extended family for support. In order to expand this interdependent support structure, Filipinos enlarge their families by assimilating outsiders through the *compadrazgo* (ritual kinship) system. Important sponsors are sought out for baptisms, weddings, and confirmations. Traditionally, *ninongs* (godfathers) and *ninangs* (godmothers) serve to forge bonds of loyalty that now link a child to his or her godparents. In the past, these ties would serve as a form of life insurance and also occasionally as a means of upward social mobility (Steinberg, 1990). Today, in America, *compadres* (godparents) still often serve this same function, but decreasingly so. There is a drop-off over the generations in the number of sponsors or godparents that are chosen, and their traditional role of providing "insurance" is less necessary. Still, many Filipinos adhere to this custom and its attendant giving practices. In a functional sense, the godchild is a means of establishing a ritual kin relationship that the parents or grandparents desire. In the past it was customary for the grandparents of a child to choose the godparents for the infant.

The form and function of *compadrazgo* have changed for many Filipinos living in the United States. Traditionally, it is customary for the godparents to be a stable, successful couple. For much of the early and mid-20th century, however, this pattern was altered somewhat because of the dearth of Filipino women in this country. One respondent stated: "They are always part of the family. Because of the situation here [in the United States], godfathers were always single Filipino men and godmothers were always upstanding Filipino women, all married. My *ninong* always bought my school clothes. I was his daughter. When he became ill, I took care of him."

There have been other changes in the custom of *compadrazgo*. A 54-year-old man who has lived in the United States since 1972 said, "Relatives are the first ones chosen, best friends also. Baptism, you choose relatives first." This represents a shift from a person's status being the main criteria for choosing a godparent. Two respondents spoke about some of the ways in which these changes have affected godparent-godchild relationships. One person said, "Here the godparent is only responsible for spiritual support, there [in the Philippines] economic and also networking. . . . There is less support [in the United States], but you still use them, usually friends and close relatives." Another respondent, who was born in the Philippines and came to the United States at about six years of age, stated that her mother's sister and friend are her baptismal godparents. "I have five or more sets [of godparents] for baptism . . . but I don't really know them . . . but they give us gifts always when we see them."

⚭ SUSTENTO

Traditional Philippine society places great emphasis on interdependence in social relationships. This interdependence is still stressed within Filipino families and communities in the United States. However, while the cultural ideal for Filipinos in California is to maintain traditional Filipino values, living in this country has altered these values somewhat. One change is that financial independence is valued by Filipinos in this country (Meñez, 1980, pp. 45–48). While the financial obligation owed to family members in the United States has decreased for many Filipinos, the great disparity in relative incomes between the Philippines and the United States has increased the financial obligations owed to one's family in the Philippines. This ongoing, regular financial support is referred to as *sustento* (allowance or support). As one woman said, "Many of the people are very poor in the Philippines, so we must help them." Family members in the United States send money to family members in the Philippines, although these donations seem to drop off through successive generations. These monies are vital not only to the individuals receiving them but to the Philippine economy as well. The Philippine government actively solicits such monies.

Filipinos have accepted this challenge. In 1984 Filipino contract workers throughout the world sent $625 million home to the Philippines. This total was equal to 11.6 percent of merchandise exports from the Philippines and 2.2 percent of the Philippine gross national product. Legal Filipino contract workers in the United States alone sent $390 million home to the Philippines in 1988 (Eckhouse, 1991b). A 1984 study of physicians emigrating from the Philippines showed that, in monetary terms, the country actually gained from the loss of these doctors because of the large sums of money they sent home from their much greater salaries overseas (Eckhouse, 1991a).

Many respondents reported sending significant amounts of money back to the Philippines each year. One man said, "Filipinos do send money, even if they are only working minimum wage. But, foremost in their minds, [is] 'I have to because I have to send part of this to my family.'" Another person said: "[People with relatives in the Philippines] also continually send money for one thing or another, like if someone needs a pig or schooling." When questioned how frequently this occurs, she went on to say that because Filipinos in the United States are constantly being asked for support, "Some people will automatically decide to support just a specific child and no one else." Another woman said that she had "some relatives who are going to college in the Philippines, so whenever we have extra money we send it to them for tuition and things." One woman sends money regularly from each paycheck in an amount equal to her tithings in church. A man recalled his father sending *sustento* to his sons; and added, "I sent [*sustento*] to my father and brothers . . . they got lots of land in there [because of the money I sent]." Another man said it feels "very nice to reach out, because in this materialistic world, people are too materialistic. It takes time, money, and talent. People have money, but no time; time but not talent. We need an integration of people with all three." This same person sponsors the education of three children in the Philippines. A woman responded, "My parents' property, everything goes to me because that's the way it should be. [She is an only child.] My uncle administers the farm and half of the yearly profits go in the bank and half to my relatives in the Philippines." Another respondent described how a day-care facility is funded:

I give money every month [to the Philippines] . . . this is for helping the poor. I give money to a day-care center in Southern Luzon, the day care cares for the comparatively rich and vendors [children of salespeople], so what they do is charge the rich more and solicit donations from people to pay for the children who otherwise could not afford it.

Like many Filipino giving customs, *sustento* provides primarily for the family. The values of interdependence and self-supporting family units are clearly evident in this practice. As one man stated, "foremost in [my family's] minds, I have to send part of [my wages] to my family. It is hard to say it is an obligation, but I do it. I think it is a sense of responsibility, rather than an obligation to me." Though this man does not truly view *sustento* as an obligation, he recognizes that his family views it as such and that he is all but required to send it, just as they would if he were in need.

☡ BALIKBAYAN AND PASALUBONG

The custom of *balikbayan* (return to hometown or country) primarily involves people returning to the Philippines and bringing with them gifts of food and material goods. It is also expected that money will be given personally by a traveler to the Philippines to those that greet them upon their arrival. This practice is called *pasalubong*. *Balikbayan* also includes gifts of food, material goods, and occasionally money sent from Filipinos living outside the Philippines to their families and friends living in the Philippines.

First- and second-generation Filipinos return home frequently, often every two or three years; and many residents of the Philippines travel back and forth as well. A 19-year-old woman said, "Folks always want to bring something when they travel . . . as a welcoming gesture, now it seem more like within my family that people take back things." Another woman spoke of her grandmother, saying, "She comes three or four times a year from the Philippines. My uncle will get [re]married [in an official church ceremony] in the Philippines to please my grandmother."

While people look forward to returning to the Philippines, they do not always look forward to the financial burden *balikbayan* and *pasalubong* will place upon them. Since many foods and material goods are unavailable or relatively expensive in the Philippines, there is considerable pressure placed on relatives to come laden with gifts. Several informants suggested that one of the reasons that people come to greet travelers on their return is to receive the *balikbayan* and *pasalubong*. A first-generation 70-year-old, multilingual man put it this way: "When I went back [to the Philippines] in 1984, I gave $500 to my brother, $200 to each of his four kids. You are ashamed; they know that I have to give it to them. Even a shirt I have to give, I had two, and he took one. . . . They know it's ritual. . . . *Pasalubong*, that is why I don't go back so much." Similarly, another woman said:

Your relatives expect you to bring products from America like cereals, corned beef, perfumes like Opium, and designer clothes. Our wealthier relatives expect these things from us, while our poorer relatives just want something, anything. It was often more expensive to buy all the items they wanted than it was to fly over there.

A transfer of goods or service, whether requested or not, compels the recipient to show gratitude to ensure that the recipient does not remain indebted to the giver. The greeting of a returnee is viewed as a service, thus generating a sense of gratitude and indebtedness in the returnee. Since there is the expectation that something will be given, to withhold *balikbayan* or *pasalubong* creates a sense of *hiya* (shame) in the recipient. Filipinos try to repay this indebtedness as soon as possible to avoid the stigma (Lynch, 1970; Hollinsteiner, 1970). Another respondent stated, "It is kind of a thank you for not forgetting me. . . . It is expected that you give, or they will change how they think of you." Through largesse, one changes others' perceptions in a positive manner. One woman stated that "*balikbayan* is when you go to the U.S. to become a surgeon, lawyer, or whatever, and you go back to the Philippines as a 'big' person and you spread the wealth around. You are a patron, you help them and then they owe you allegiance." The role of the patron provides a strong social reward and helps ensure the success of the community.

The Philippine government under Ferdinand Marcos saw *balikbayan* as a lucrative means of support and actively encouraged this behavior in order to generate revenue. To this end, the government instituted a "*balikbayan* program." The program offered Philippine expatriates a number of benefits that made it even more attractive for them to return to the Philippines and visit their relatives, bringing with them gifts to help sustain their family and spending their money once they arrived (Necesito, 1977, p. 60).

The custom of *balikbayan* and the money and goods that flow back to the Philippines have been beneficial for those living in the United States as well. Certain industries have profited greatly from these transactions. *The Filipino Guide to San Francisco* states that "many business-minded Filipinos have tried their luck—and succeeded—in car dealerships, real estate, and insurance. But one business into which they have put their hearts and mind is the travel industry" (Necesito, 1977, p. 9). Many Filipino-owned agencies cater primarily to other Filipinos returning to the Philippines.

In addition to travel agencies, businesses that ship goods and transfer money are also prospering. These businesses serve the Philippines exclusively or almost exclusively. One respondent stated, "That is why there is a proliferation of money changers." Other companies make boxes available for those who want to send goods back to the Philippines. "They even have boxes prestamped with *balikbayan* on them," reported one woman. These boxes are also used when goods are personally delivered. The same woman said, "My dad just came back [from the Philippines]; he took a *balikbayan* box. I filled it up with candy and toys. Mom will take a box when she goes soon."

✆ TULONG AND UTANG NA LOOB

Tulong means help or aid given to those in need. This aid can take many forms, from money to lodging to food. The custom of *tulong* is practiced most often within the family and the nuclear community and seems to occur only when someone is in immediate need or is sick. Filipino social values emphasize interdependence: if one's relatives or friends are in need, they should be helped. Many respondents adhered to these values and practiced *tulong* whether they termed their behavior as such or not. One woman felt that the primary value, in terms of giving, in Filipino culture is to "help those who do not have enough in life." This definition perfectly conveys the spirit of *tulong*.

Tulong encompasses many forms of giving, the only constant being that the need is both immediate and temporary. One woman responded: "For the very sick, widowed, death in the family, that is the time that they really need the money. These are the times that they really need the help. You can't just give money all the time to people who don't really need help." She also indicated that *tulong* is the only form of giving that she practices. One man remembered that relatives would often come to his grandmother's house looking for food and money. Another man said that one of his relatives was in the service and that this man stayed with his family after an accident. His mother "provided food and at times *tulong* [in the form of money]" to this man.

Tulong, in the forms of food, lodging, and money, is also offered to relatives who have just arrived from the Philippines. One woman stated that "the third stage [of Filipino giving] usually included newcomers; relatives coming from the Philippines to live or visit in the United States. Assistance was usually in the form of (1) money to help them get settled and (2) a place to live until they could afford to move into their own place." Many respondents said they had either helped relatives who were new to this country or were recipients of such help, suggesting that this form of *tulong* will be practiced as long as there are people coming to this country from the Philippines.

Tulong also includes various forms of giving outside the nuclear and extended family. Speaking of his father, one man said that he "had an open hand. Neighbors, relatives always came to him for money and time. It was never returned. I think he felt very lucky, so he shared." Another man remembered his grandmother and aunt who ran a market together. He recalled that "beggars usually came to their area on weekends and were given mainly rice and sometimes money." One woman remembered her family aiding one of her neighbors:

> There was an elderly man who lived in the house behind our house who was actually sick quite a bit of the time. So my mother would send us to his house with food and she was essentially providing his meals to him, and I don't know if they ever gave him any cash. . . . They also brought groceries for him and never accepted money.

The notion of *utang na loob*, a debt of gratitude or a reciprocal obligation due another, is central to Filipinos. Filipinos are aware that they must practice *puhunan*, returning of favors done for them by others. This assures that the person who helped you will have aid when it is needed and so will you in the future.

∞ CELEBRATIONS

A first-generation Filipino who has lived intermittently in the United States for 22 years said, "Godparents give 98 percent [of the] money [for a wedding]." While this proportion varies from family to family, godparents are often responsible for a significant portion of the expenses associated with the various ceremonies and parties that occur at baptisms, confirmations, and weddings. One example of their largesse is called *pakimkim*, a custom by which the godparents contribute jewelry, clothing, money, and food. The *pakimkim* monies are nominally for the godchild but really for the parents. One respondent said, "My recollection would tell me that cash is easily given during weddings and baptisms. It is really funny, because I know that it really goes to the parents."

Anima (1978) relates several other forms of giving practiced by the godparents at the baptismal reception, including the custom of *pahinaw*, in which godparents throw coins to the guests, who scramble for them. This custom expresses a symbolic desire for the child to grow in plenty. The second custom is called *pabuisit* (good will money), which is given to a visiting infant who is brought to the house of kin in the Philippines. These are terms of the Ilocanos dialect. An additional baptismal custom is the practice of *pabandeha*, "a reciprocal gift from the infant's parents to the godparents in appreciation of their graciousness to sponsor the baptism" (Anima, 1978, p. 3).

The parties and other forms of giving surrounding a confirmation are typically small and gift-giving is limited to money, clothing, and religious items. An 18-year-old woman born in Manila spoke of her confirmation godparent: "She gives me presents. She's more like a sponsor, but she is also like a *ninang* [godmother]." Another respondent said that she had two sets of sponsors for her confirmation. Together the sponsors "were responsible for giving us [siblings] our parties."

Godparents also play an important financial role in weddings. Since weddings cost more than baptisms and confirmations, there is a corresponding increase in the number of godparents chosen for weddings. One respondent described her godparents' responsibilities at her wedding:

> Three [couples/sets of sponsors] at my wedding. They were responsible for the parties and cooking. . . . There were parties before the wedding, there was a breakfast after the mass, and there was a dinner later. Each sponsor also had a responsibility at the wedding like tying the cord or putting on the

veil. [My parents] chose couples who were upstanding citizens in the community. The sponsors' names go on the wedding invitations. It is a status thing, the sponsors you are able to get. My mom and dad had six sets of sponsors for their 50th wedding anniversary. They were given a rope of silver dollars [containing 50 coins] as part of the ceremony.

In addition to giving money, godparents have other roles at weddings and other ceremonies. For example, when large-scale cooking is required for a wedding or funeral, one's *compadres* will often contribute food and/or help prepare and serve the meal.

ॐ RELIGIOUS CUSTOMS

Most Filipinos are Catholic and very religious. The term *abuloy* is used for two Filipino giving customs: general religious donations and donations to the family of someone who has died. Linguistic analysis suggests that *abuloy* as a death custom was practiced by the indigenous people of the Philippines before Catholicism took hold. *Abuloy* later came to encompass church donations because of its connection with funeral services. One respondent, speaking of religious donations, said, "No, no expectation of return, because it's going to the person [God] who gives it to you anyway."

The Catholic church in the Philippines is a missionary church and as such relies on outside support to fund many of its activities. While much of this financial support comes from the Vatican, a large portion of it comes from Filipino organizations in other countries, primarily the United States and Japan. As a result, Filipinos do not contribute as much to the general collection as Catholics do in other countries. When Filipinos migrate to America, they continue to donate a relatively small amount to the general collection and spend more lavishly on religious rituals. This can lead to funding problems for parishes that have large immigrant Filipino populations and also can contribute to the impression that Filipinos are not generous. Some respondents addressed this issue. One person, who has been in America less than five years, said:

> I like to share what I have. . . . I think the only change is that here [in the United States], it is more structured. Like in my church where I am actively doing volunteer work, you have to register, just as you regularly commit, you use this envelope, and there has been a lot of comments about parishes having money, I think, that they need for the operation of the parish. Because many Filipinos are moving in, and they are not into using the envelope, they do give, but they are not into the dollar mentality. . . . I tend to be protective, I understand. I try to tell them that in the Philippines we are not expected to contribute on a regular basis, I mean whenever we can, if we can. And this is because the churches in the Philippines are being subsidized by the archdiocese, and here it is the reverse, the churches give money to

the archdiocese. That is why they have to [be structured]. In the Philippines they don't really force you to. You have to educate the Filipinos [in the United States] about it. I had to be educated; I used to be a dollar person [someone who donates one token dollar] also, but I did realize, and maybe it's part of my own spiritual growth. I realize that I do have to give time, talent, and treasure, my own spiritual belief. I had to get used to using the envelopes by committing a certain amount of money every month. It is really very funny, I still don't understand, because it really does not have anything to do with your income level. I realize there are so many who are well paid, but do not commit.

This person believes that unwillingness to commit may stem from fears that later one may not be able to uphold the commitment, resulting in feelings of *hiya* (shame and embarrassment). A second-generation Filipino woman also spoke on this subject:

I went to an institute this summer to learn about the Philippines. . . . The Catholic church says Filipinos are the "dollar givers." The people running the institute say that is the way it is in the Philippines because the church is a mission church and it doesn't have to pay for itself. People pay for services, weddings, baptisms, house blessings, and they pay through the nose [in the Philippines]. Here there is less outreach; priests are much busier in the Philippines blessing houses and cars and such and blessing animals for St. Francis day. The idea of envelopes and registration and such is foreign in the Philippines. Why doesn't the church charge these people through the nose here since they aren't going to get money in church from Filipinos. I give to the collection every week.

Another woman who has donated a great deal of money and time to the church stated, "The way things are done in the Philippines is very different from the way things are here."

Though some Filipinos are "dollar givers," others give greater amounts. A 45-year-old man who has been in America for 22 years still goes to church each Sunday. Even when he is on a business trip, he takes time to find the closest church. "I still go to church every Sunday and give *abuloy*. I would like to do more. Last year, I gave $2,500 to the church back home for a new marble floor for the chapel." This same man mentioned that his grandmother went to a chapel weekly and gave *abuloy*. There are many small chapels throughout the Philippines, and when people cannot travel the distance to a church, they often go to chapels.

One woman respondent saw no difference in Filipino and American orientation to giving. She said that in the Philippines her family "also gave to the church. Sometimes the parish priest would come and ask us to donate a pillar, doors, or a chalice for a new church. But there was no set percentage; we gave what we wanted to. There is no difference between Filipinos and the Americans."

While many Filipinos do not give large donations to the church because of their cultural background, the Catholic church has certainly shaped Filipino giving patterns. Many respondents cited religion as a reason for their giving behavior. A first-generation Filipino American stated, "For me giving is very important because of my religious background [Catholic]." One man said: "If we did any giving as a cultural kind of thing, then it was based around the church. In the Philippines the Catholic church is part of the culture. You cannot separate the church from the culture of the Philippines, so from that standpoint, if you gave money at a funeral or a wedding, it was more of a religious kind of thing."

Many informants shared their families' experiences of giving to beggars in the Philippines. Much of this giving revolved around Catholic festivals. The beggars would come on certain days of the week. It was like a tradition, "[My grandmother and aunt] tried to help them. . . . Not a donation, like a helping hand." There was usually a heavier concentration of beggars just before festivals, because of the generous giving atmosphere shared by the community. A first-generation male remembered that as a child, Igorots (a mountain tribe) came prior to religious festivals like Santa Rita Day (saint for the town of Pampango): "There was a general atmosphere of giving. They came and danced three and four at a time. Once they finished dancing in their native dress, which was . . . loin cloth, then they go from house to house for food, rice, and money. . . . They did not even speak our language, but people gave."

Religion continues to inspire Filipino giving in the United States. In addition to creating a generally philanthropic attitude, religion stimulates specific devotional forms of giving that are not widely practiced in the United States, such as house blessings performed by the local priest. During the ceremony—because it is considered propitious for the house to be full of money—the home owner may litter the floor with quarters and dimes which guests scramble to retrieve. This custom is termed *sabog*. Picking up any of the thrown money is supposed to bring good luck. At these occasions, the guest may bring *regalos* (gifts) and there may be a banquet.

∞ DEATH

When someone dies, Filipinos give *abuloy* to help defray the funeral costs. In the Philippines, the money may also be used to provide food for those who attended the survivors and who came to pray for the dead person. During the novena refreshments are served each night, with a banquet on the final night. Often guests also bring food. A Filipino who has lived in the United States intermittently for 22 years said, "You have to give something. The people are poor, and it costs to pay for the coffee and food for nine days of mourning."

When the father of one respondent died in 1976, he took ten family members and his father's body back to the Philippines. *Abuloy* was used to pay for the trip. When they arrived, he was surprised and pleased at the well-attended memorial service. The experience of his father's death, and seeing the many people who had come to pay their respects, changed his impression of his father. He remembered that in the course of his father's life there had been many arguments between his mother and father about the latter's generosity, and now realized that that generosity had not been in vain.

A first-generation Filipino man who has lived in the United States for 42 years gives *abuloy* not only to people he knows directly but also to many organizations that he belongs to, including the American Legion, Disabled American Veterans, First and Second Regiments, and the Filipino Senior Citizens.

Traditionally, *abuloy* was a quasi-contractual obligation. The bereaved kept a record of the names of the donors and the amounts contributed. Then when someone in a donor's family died, the *abuloy* would be given in return. However, none of the Filipino respondents mentioned anything about a record being kept. This may be another situation where one's cultural customs are taken for granted by those within the culture.

A distinction is made between *abuloy* given to one's social equal and *abuloy* given by a family of higher status to a lower-status family. In the latter case, *abuloy* may be returned in the form of a service like preparing food or saying prayers after a death in the family of the higher-status donor (Hollinsteiner, 1970).

As is true in the other groups studied, Filipinos gather together to help the bereaved by doing various chores and tasks around the house, or by means of *ambag* (partial financial aid). A young woman commented:

> The people just give monetary aid for the family of somebody. It is given to the family directly. It is expected especially with immediate family members. . . . Voluntary, whatever you can afford. . . . Maybe indirectly [amount given related to donor's status], but there is not a written rule or it is just that if you can give more, some people do give more. And I think Filipinos are good at that. If they can give more, they will give without any structure.

A good deal of the *ambag* (smaller donations) received by the family is used to pay for activities surrounding the traditional nine days of mourning (Lardizabal and Tensuan-Leogardo, 1976, p. 109; Meñez, 1980, p. 45).

☯ GIVING TO ORGANIZATIONS

Sharing among Filipinos does not occur solely within family networks. The interdependent values Filipinos learn within the family are often transferred to the Filipino community. As one man stated,

> I think there is a strong sense of family. . . . We grew up with that sense of family within the Filipino community, knowing only Filipinos and anything outside of the community was untested territory. . . . A lot of ethnic communities give a lot within the community and that is seen as an aberration by the outside society and that is giving in a way that is different. We may not build multimillion dollar homes for the aged, but we will stay home and

take care of our parents. People see that and say, "Why are Asian adults staying at home instead of going out on their own?" These institutions have no personal connections with us. They are not in touch with the people.

Most contributions to and affiliations with organizations are specific to Asians or Filipinos.

The differences between traditional Filipino and mainstream giving and sharing practices have, accordingly, caused difficulties for some Filipinos. One respondent joked that he gave up his law practice in America because of the emphasis many Filipinos place upon following tradition. "When I got my law degree, immediately it was free legal help." Others believe they have problems because Filipinos have a reputation as givers. A first-generation male stated: "Filipino [issues] have a special ring where you get touched a lot. I get a lot of calls and mail; I guess they have me on their lists, but there is less meaning."

Many Filipino American mutual benefit groups have been organized along geographical lines, usually according to *barangay* (neighborhood or barrio), the lowest political subdivision in the Philippines. These organizations are composed almost exclusively of people from the same region of the Philippines. When responding to a question on the different types of Filipino organizations in the Bay Area, one woman replied, "It often breaks down into the regionalism that happens within the Philippines, where there is very heavy regionalism. In 1986 there were almost 500 Filipino organizations in Northern California; they were organized even down to the barrio." Another woman said, "Filipinos have associations, like the Tongs, that are based on what town you came from."

Some Filipinos are troubled by the large number of organizations that revolve exclusively around *barangay* ties. They feel that while *barangay* provides a solid base of mutual support and charity for those members truly in need, it also fosters parochial attitudes that block overall Filipino unity and political influence. One respondent stated: "In California there are many more separate pockets of Filipino American clubs than there are in Seattle. There is a group for Pittsburg [California], and one for Berkeley, and one for San Francisco, and so on. In Seattle there was much more unity; there was one club for the entire Seattle area." Several male respondents said that Filipinos should form cohesive groups as the Chinese and the Japanese in this country have done.

Many respondents spoke of belonging to their town or province associations. One woman stated, "I think that [Filipinos] give very generously to their regional organizations or that organization of other people from the same part of the Philippines as they." Members of these associations give money to their organization to support anyone within the *barangay* that is in need. One respondent said she belonged to Cabalen, a provincial association that acted as a service organization. One woman stated, "[My association] did provide support if someone was ill, this was very important." Another gave much of her money to Calabyan, a town-mate association whose main goals were to pay burial expenses for single immigrants with no family and to serve as a support network for its members.

The *barangay* also assists organizations within the Philippines. "Many organizations that have ties to the Philippines send money back there for the church, health, etc.," one woman said. "Every year there is a fundraiser," another commented, "a private banquet for people from the same province to come together and give money to send back to their province in the Philippines. They donate all the proceeds to a particular church in the province to use it for the betterment of the community, in this case Visayan."

These *barangay* organizations also serve to perpetuate traditional Filipino cultural practices by sponsoring and continuing festivals and celebrations for their members. "In the summer," one woman said, "the [village associations] have their little fiestas, each has their own name, they are mainly social and cultural." One man said, "In fact on June 24 we [the village association] celebrate the town festival, the feast of St. John the Baptist." One respondent stated that many of these organizations "send money to the villages [of origin] and set up scholarship funds." These associations also help maintain more tangible ties with the Philippines. "People from our barrio [from the Philippines who live in the United States now] sent my sister back to our town in the Philippines for the town festival on Rizal Day," said one woman. When queried as to her responsibilities, she replied, "She acted as a goodwill ambassador to bridge the generation gap, to help maintain unity between here and the Philippines." Other associations give money to improve the infrastructure of their village, town, or province or send material goods not easily or cheaply obtainable in the Philippines. The associations in the United States also respond to emergencies. "We did stuff for the earthquake victims and we will do something for Mt. Pinatubo," one man said.

CHAPTER SIX ⬿ *Chinese*

- Clans and mutual benefit associations are important centers of Chinese philanthropy.
- Money is given more easily than time, but time given has a higher value.
- Chinese give to mainstream charitable organizations as well as to Chinese organizations.
- There is a strong sense of reciprocity in Chinese sharing and helping.
- Chinese often make donations to charitable organizations as part of ceremonial events such as births, weddings, and funerals.
- Confucian and Buddhist traditions have some influence on Chinese philanthropy.

The Chinese have the longest history in America of any Asian group. They arrived shortly after the signing of the Declaration of Independence. The Chinese population remained sparse until the mid to late 1800s, when gold was discovered in California. The main impetus for migration was the increasingly difficult situation created in China by flood, famine, and social and political unrest. The Chinese immigrants, mainly from the southern part of China, came as sojourners intending to stay only long enough to get rich. California had a labor shortage and the influx of Chinese immigrants was tolerated only to the extent that their labor was needed in mining, railroad construction, reclamation, agriculture, and other endeavors (Low, 1982).

Employers in the West regarded Chinese immigrants as a necessary but undesirable source of cheap labor. The anti-alien climate among European Americans and racial intolerance of Asians led to the passing of discriminatory legislation. The California Foreign Miner's Tax (1853), for example, was aimed primarily at the Chinese. From 1853 to 1870, California collected $5 million, a sum representing 25 to 50 percent of all state revenue, from taxes levied against the Chinese laborers (Takaki, 1993). This and other forms of legalized discrimination against the Chinese continued for many decades (Takaki, 1993; Yu, 1993; Lyman, 1986; and Low, 1982). Harassment and violence against the Chinese were common and frequent.

The culmination of these events was the enactment of the 1882 Exclusion Act. This was the first immigration law to bar the entry of members of a specific ethnic or cultural group to America, and resulted in a dramatic decrease in the number of Chinese immigrating into the United States for 60 years afterwards. One result of this law was that by 1883, Japanese had replaced Chinese as the major source of cheap labor.

Over time, restrictions on Chinese immigration were lifted. The Magnuson Act of 1943 had the effect of repealing the Exclusion Act of 1882, and the McCarran-Walter Act of 1952 made Chinese immigrants eligible for citizenship (Lyman, 1986). Nevertheless, the racially intolerant environment in American society held back Chinese economic development. Chinese immigrants and their descendants were essentially pushed into small business niches, because they were excluded from mainstream unions and other economic opportunities. Their success in business was due in part to the existence, in their communities, of institutionalized quasi-kin clan relationships that were the basis of trust upon which enduring economic relationships were built (Fugita and O'Brien, 1991).

Prior to 1942 most Chinese immigrants were Cantonese; from 1942 to 1949 most came from north and central China; and from 1949 to the present most were from Taiwan. There have also been a large number of immigrants (mostly students) from the People's Republic of China (PRC) since 1979, and from 1990 to the present, a new wave of immigrants from Hong Kong.

The following comments on Chinese sharing and helping are excerpted from interviews with 40 members of the Chinese community.

⌀ KINSHIP AND COMMUNITY

Kinship patterns have been important in the development of giving practices in the Chinese American community. These patterns have changed over time, determined in large part by the exigencies of immigration, cultural adaptation, and survival. Kinship is a principle of social organization for traditional Chinese. The Chinese traditionally establish social organization around kinship and clan networks (Hsu, 1981). This tradition is still evident in contemporary society, especially so in Chinese communities outside the PRC (Baker, 1979).

For Chinese Americans, kinship networks have been fluid and have changed over time. As sojourners, Chinese immigrants left their wives and families behind to await their return. In the early days, there were very few Chinese women in America. For example, by 1852, there were only seven women out of 11,794 Chinese in California (Takaki, 1993). These pioneers became known as the "Bachelor Society." The absence of women and family networks required the creation of new networks. The original immigrants soon established mutual benefit associations to replace kin networks lost through this fragmentation. Subsequent immigrants were required by earlier immigrants to be members of these associations.

Kinship often plays an important role in determining informal modes of giving. In the dominant culture the focal social relationship is conjugal, husband and wife. The definition of family for Chinese is one based on the relationship between father and son (Hsu, 1981). Thus, one finds in Chinese culture values and practices that emphasize the importance of intergenerational relations. Children learn respect for their elders within the home, and the importance of these values is reinforced in Confucian education in schools. Chinese Confucian philosophy supports the authority of all elders. Obligation to the family, which often extends to cousins, and to elders, is ritually reinforced in a number of informal giving practices.

Hierarchy and respect for parents were so strong that care of parents traditionally came before all other obligations (Hsu, 1981). The Chinese system of patrilineal descent prescribed the equal division of a family's land among all adult sons, as well as the sharing of responsibility for their elderly parents (Takaki, 1993). Chinese children are also included in adult matters and activities from early childhood. If there is a problem in the family, the children are not sheltered. This results in a sense of responsibility at an early age and a sense that everyone must do his or her share to help the family (Hsu, 1981). Elders are perceived as knowing better. By observing their parents caring for their grandparents, the children are influenced and this results in continued respect and caring from generation to generation. Caring for parents and elders is a way Chinese Americans pay back those who have given to them. One 79-year-old respondent stated: "Looking after the old elders, that is why we have large families. Before we had social security, they expected the boys to care for the family. They expected the kids to support. In the Chinese, it is more family-oriented than the dominant culture." Another respondent said it is "important to maintain because it is a built-in resilience for the family."

In addition to family obligation there is an obligation to the clan. The clan is a much larger aggregate of individuals, often based on a locality and distant relation identified by a surname. Kinship and clan have historically provided a sense of solidarity and security for the Chinese and have shaped informal giving practices. Traditionally, members of a clan would lend money to fellow clan members so they could bring other members of their families to the United States. Once the families become established, ties with the lenders were maintained through gift exchanges. The large influx of new families also necessitated the provision of other services. The clan organization was instrumental in helping out new immigrants in a number of ways. They were involved in community development on a number of levels, especially the founding of schools for children. Some terms related to giving among kin and clan are discussed below. The terms given are Cantonese because all of our respondents came from or were descended from people from South China.

Yéuhng ga is an old custom based on a shared responsibility for the maintenance of the family. Chinese men first came to America to help their families do better. Even with their meager financial pay as immigrants, they sent what they could to their families and community back home in China.

Heung yàuh gàm and *Chìh sihn gàm* can also be money donated back to the hometown or village by those who have settled permanently in the United States. Many of the respondents said they and their families sent money back to China to help build schools in the villages. An international cargo shipping businessman mentioned supporting a school in his home village entirely from his own funds. An executive director of a community organization spoke of funds sent to China: "Since normalization with the United States, the money is used to provide schools and education for the young."

A first-generation respondent from Hong Kong stated that it was expected of him to "financially support the family and other siblings [in Hong Kong and Hawaii]." He and his wife care for their parents because of the guilt of separation and because their financial situation is better. A 17-year-old respondent said that her grandparents continue to send money to Hong Kong and China. However, she does not know exactly to whom or for what reasons the money is sent. Another respondent, of Chinese descent from Malaysia, is helping support his family in Malaysia. The family is very important to him, and he sends money home to make what he says is "a better life for his parents." He feels this is an obligation.

A 69-year-old woman said she continues to send money home twice a year to close relatives, and has sent money home to help build a school: "You just do it like you are supposed to do, as a rule to give out things. You can't be so selfish not to give out anything, right? If I did not do it, I don't think I would feel good. . . . Just to follow the people, whatever they have to do, I have to do it, I guess."

An 18-year-old woman related that her family supports a large network of relatives and friends, which she refers to as "family." When first asked about relatives in China, she replied that they sent money "to the family." Further questioning revealed that the family sent money to several people in the community in China, not just relatives but anyone living in the village who was in need. She told of her family buying a cow for the village. She said, "It is an investment, rather than a loss." She feels that if everybody gives, someone is bound to give to her.

One respondent, when asked if his family had ever supported individuals in China, remembered the money his mother had been sending: "Oh, yeah. My mother did. She sent money home up until the mid-'60s. I forgot about that. . . . Yes, if one does that, then certainly there is not much money left [for other things]. . . . for a TV, and a bicycle." A student from China said, "Money home? I hope I can in future. . . . I am in discomfort." His parents know that he is not financially able, so if he sent money it would make them uncomfortable.

Bòng is primarily the practice of giving financial and material support to new immigrants settling in the United States. A respondent in her 70s related:

> Some people in need whether it was family or friend, or same village . . . when it became known they were in need, they were given money, or a helping hand. . . . No, when it was given, it was not expected to be paid back, but lots of time my father let people borrow money [for example, to send a family to America], but at the end, people never paid him back. Even when there was a note, some people could not afford to pay back.

The respondent herself said she sent support to family members in China until they all died. The beneficiaries of *bòng* are often, but not necessarily, members of the giver's family or of the giver's community. *Bòng* not only helped immigrants come to America but also developed into the aid given to new immigrants by people who had already settled here.

A student from China who experienced the impact of the Cultural Revolution commented that some of the old customs were frowned upon during the time of Mao, but that after the revolution there was more openness to some customs such as *baai sàhn* and *baai faht* (offerings and prayers to gods and spirits). People needed something to relieve the stress and to give them hope because of the difficult lives they had led. There are no Western-type nonprofit organizations in China. The government is the sole organizational provider of human services. The belief in China is that everyone has difficulties and therefore people must help each one another. The student said:

> If you help someone, that is quite normal. . . . Everybody has equal chance to have difficulties; when not, you should be considerate at that time—it will be fair. . . . In China, the society, I think the basic idea is different. Here people should be individual, but in China all the people have the common benefit. They are equal, there is not much need for organization. But due to the government, they want to help more because they live in close community contact. The sense of helping is more than here. Normally, I don't like to give [money]; food equals money and respect. Make use of little money and connections to spend [people take the time to get and give something special—the time and effort are seen as more important than the money]. . . . In America, money becomes a very common measure. If you have a lot you can buy, but in China, with a lot of money, and want a house— you cannot. Therefore I think that is why in China, people would rather spend time to choose a gift.

The student described a personal experience: "In my childhood there was a time I was sick and needed sugar and a friend went and collected it for me. That meant a lot to me." He understood the inconsistency between the old ways and the behavior during the time he was raised, as well as some of the negative aspects of *bòng*:

> When I was growing up, I must keep the relation—so I must do to respect— I would out of respect and responsibility. . . . I should teach it. There is a drawback that if you care too much—you can lose yourself. How can you find the balance? Great capability but busy helping [so one cannot advance as much for self]. We cannot go to the extreme. Selfishness is original [people are born with it], therefore the father must teach kids to care.

The core of giving remains caring for each other, and there is probably more investment of time than money; Chinese place higher value on the giving of time. When asked about *bòng*, an elderly respondent said, "Somehow, you know, if I were in their position, hopefully they would do the same for me. Because I feel if you don't help, don't expect them to help—but I am not expecting a return. Of course not, I don't want to be in that position."

An 18-year-old female said her family helps out whomever they can. They practice both *yéuhng ga* and *bòng*. They feel that they are doing well, they are obligated to share and "want to be the senders of better things." Her family shares with relatives and friends in China and Hong Kong, and relatives and neighbors in America. Another respondent stated, "My parents gave money to bring family members [and their entire families] over with no expectation of return. . . . They gave what was to be considered loans to start businesses, but people never paid them back." One respondent recalled that even in a competitive business like food service, when his parents' restaurant ran out of an ingredient for cooking, other Chinese restaurants helped out.

Chinese Americans, likewise, often furnish room and board to students who are family members. These family members may be as much as three times removed. Several respondents mentioned sending money to home villages to build schools. *Yéuhng ga* and *bòng* reveal the continued sense of obligation the Chinese feel to share what they have and help other Chinese do better for the sake of the family and community.

∞ CELEBRATIONS

Traditionally, people waited to celebrate a birth because it was a costly affair, and there was no certainty that the newborn would survive. *Mún yuht laih sih* is money given to the newborn by all married individuals in attendance at the Red Egg and Ginger Party (birthday party). *Laih sih*, given in little red envelopes, represents luck and prosperity for the receiver. The family and friends usually bring gifts and/or jewelry to the baby. In the past, the jewelry was usually a piece that had been in the family, especially jade. The jade present signified giving part of oneself to the receiver. However, it is common practice today to give a new piece of gold jewelry, often with Buddha or a Chinese zodiac sign on it. The red egg represents fertility (hopes that another child will come along soon) and the ginger is felt to benefit the new mother's health. At these parties, it is common for Bay Area families to make a public donation to their benevolent association—for example, the Chinese Hospital, or some other favorite like On Lok Senior Center or Self-Help for the Elderly.

A respondent, when asked about the giving of large sums of money, stated:

> At events such as weddings, funerals, birthdays, and business openings, there are usually large donations to particular organizations, such as On Lok or the Chinese Hospital. These donations in celebration of the events are essentially in celebration of life. They go to things that increase longevity, places of new life [birth], and care of the elderly.

The area where one is raised impacts one's giving behavior, and variations of giving customs develop. A fourth-generation respondent reared in a rural area had not really followed Chinese giving customs. His interest in Chinese customs was sparked by one of his daughters, who requested a Red Egg and Ginger Party for her new baby. Since that time, the father has made an effort to learn about Chinese customs.

It is a Chinese custom to celebrate an individual's *daaih sàang yaht* (Big Birthdays). Chinese Americans usually wait until 50 before a formal banquet is given in celebration. Then, after another decade, an individual may have another *daaih sàang yaht*. *Daaih sàang yaht* is never celebrated at the fortieth birthday, because the sound of saying the number four sounds like the word for death. Formal public donations to organizations may also be made at these banquets.

Sàn nihn laih sih is a monetary token given to children by married adults for good luck during the New Year celebration. Once married, individuals no longer receive *sàn nihn laih sih*, and unmarried adults are not responsible for giving *laih sih*. A variation of *sàn nihn laih sih* is that on rare occasions, a newly married couple may receive *sàn nihn laih sih* from their parents, in hope of having a grandchild that year.

Baai nihn (literally "paying homage to the year") is a term used when visiting family and friends during the Chinese New Year period. Gifts of food are brought to the host's house when visiting. The visits reaffirm the social relationship between the families involved. Often the visitors will be invited to stay and share a meal. Food serves as the center of many Chinese rituals of social interaction. Originally, the men of the family were the only ones who went visiting, while women stayed home to serve food to the male visitors. Chinese believed that it is bad luck for women to venture out of the house during the beginning of the new year. They believed that if a woman left, so would their luck. Now, the whole family may *baai nihn*. A 21-year-old said: "Traditional things such as *laih sih* my parents do and bringing food to aunts and uncles. . . . I don't know why they bring food everywhere. I never bothered to ask. . . . Chinese New Year, birthdays, weddings, funerals." When this fourth-generation respondent was asked if she would continue the customs, she replied, "I don't know much, but things like Chinese New Year, Chinese Easter, and things like that." Chinese Easter, from her description, is an adaptation from the traditional April visit paid to the ancestors at the cemetery during the Chinese Memorial Day. All of the respondents participated in Chinese New Year giving in one way or another. Chinese have a strong belief in starting the year off right by being generous.

Jaahk fàan is the custom of giving something back (usually food) to the visitors who have come to *baai nihn*. After the visit is over, the gift is given to the visitor to take home. This gift acknowledges the gift offered by the visitor. A first-generation respondent explained:

> Chinese tradition has you as obligated to give things, and that is just part of the Chinese way, whereas the dominant culture isn't obligated to do anything in the way of giving in their culture. The dominant culture can just give and get nothing back, there are no ties. In Chinese tradition, when you give or get something, you know there is an expectation of return at some point. Think about Chinese New Year, for example, you visit relatives and bring things, and you know that they will probably do this back.

One respondent said that each year, all the participants must raise between $5,000 and $7,000 for their entries in the traditional Chinese New Year Parade. The Buddhist Universal Church was built with donations from the community given during Chinese New Year, when fundraising fairs were held each year until it was completed. Other respondents told of giving during the Chinese New Year to support the Chinese Hospital and various benevolent associations.

The *jàm chàh laih sih* (tea ceremony) is given to newlyweds when they pay their respects to individuals of higher status. Gifts given at this time are generally the most generous. The immediate family, and often the extended family, give jewelry to the bride. Heirloom jewelry was once given, but today the gift is usually purchased. The groom receives a watch and new clothes. Parents may give homes or down payments for homes, and they may even purchase the newlyweds' furniture.

A second-generation respondent said,

> Two months before the wedding the groom is supposed to send cakes over to the bride's side, and a roasted pig. . . . On the day of the wedding, the groom's men pick up the bride and pay the requested amount [money for the bride]. . . . A watch, and a pair of shoes, and a new suit, jewelry [given to the groom]. There are some weddings where they donate tons . . . to places like Chinese Hospital, family associations, On Lok, Self-Help.

This respondent added that people donate, "to look respectable in the community . . . to save face. For some it is for the community, and for others, for the respectability."

Sung hàhng is the custom of giving a party for a departing traveler. In the *sung hàhng* party, the traveler usually receives money and goods along with wishes for a safe journey. The custom is similar to the American practice of a going-away party.

Chàh jí refers to monetary and material gifts given upon arrival at a destination. The traveler may also deliver *chàh jí* (received from people that attended the *sung hàhng* party) to others. One respondent said, "That is just like a gift for luck. . . . Yes, my family does *chàh jí*. When they get back there, they give the money to all the family members." A respondent in his late 40s mixed the term *laih sih* with *chàh jí*: "Wishing them well and prosperity. Saving face too. If you don't give going back to your village, your name is shit. People give because it is expected of them, and also a sense of pride, or sharing of the wealth if you want to be magnanimous. I am sure some give for compassion."

A *sái chàhn* dinner party is given when a traveler returns from a journey. At this time, the returnee shares stories about whom and what he or she has seen and heard, and gives presents from his or her trip. It is not the returnee who arranges the dinner party, just as in the case with *sung hàhng*. This custom serves to keep family and friends abreast of what is going on with those in the home country.

∞ SICKNESS AND DEATH

Taam behng means visiting the sick. It is common to bring food to family and friends who are too ill to take care of themselves. In addition to prepared foods, a whole raw chicken and fruit are commonly given. Money may be given to help carry them over until they are well.

Upon the death of an individual, a funeral is the last time the immediate family may pay homage to the remains of the physical body. As such, great expense is incurred, especially if the deceased is a parent or grandparent. To do otherwise would result in a loss of face to the family. It is customary for extended family members to give *fùi gàm* (ash gold) or *baahk gàm* (white gold) monies to the bereaved to help defray the funeral costs.

No formal record is taken at the funeral, but names are noted, so that responses of "thank you for your sympathy" and thank-you *laih sih(s)* may be sent. A respondent said, "*Fùi gàm* or *baahk gàm* is given, without expectation of payback." Furthermore, some Chinese Americans give large public donations at the funeral banquet. A second-generation, 27-year-old respondent who became the head of his family because of his father's recent death had to manage many details revolving around his father's death. Thus he had a great deal to share about funeral practices: "We wrap up [from 10 to 25 cents, in white envelopes with a piece of candy] and it is given, and then another coin is given in a red envelope. I think it is because they have gone to a funeral and the candy is because of the bitterness, and the candy takes the bitterness away, and the money is always for luck."

He stated that the family received flowers from those that did not give *fùi gàm*. "We made donations to a few charities, to family church, the American Lung Association, the American Heart Association, and Goodwill." (The medical donations stemmed from the fact that his father died from emphysema.) The donation of his father's belongings to Goodwill came just after the 1989 Loma Prieta earthquake. They gave a banquet for those who paid their last respects and wished to attend. "I remember that we had to have Chinese white wine. In the morning before the funeral, the closest relatives came over for a breakfast, consisting of roast pork and *jaai* [a vegetable dish], with rice. I had to put a coin on my Dad's lips. When the coffin was lowered, we had to throw rice into the grave."

People came to sit with his mother a week before and after burial.

> People came to cook for us, and stuff like that. Actually, two ladies helped my mom go shopping for yarn, candy, bowls and chopsticks, blankets [sheets of colored cloth], and even help us go around to mortuaries. [All the things purchased are used in ritual or traditional ceremonies.] Many people did not come over, they just made phone calls.

An elderly respondent provided clarification regarding the use of white and red envelopes. "White color is for death, and when you enter back to the living it is red [when entering a wake or funeral you are given the white envelope, and when you leave, you are given the red one]. Therefore, red and white *laih sih*."

One respondent remembered death rituals (candies and *baahk gàm*) with the burning of incense and money (folded gold and silver paper offered to the deceased). Another respondent remembered that her grandparents were Buddhist and that they burned things (clothes, cars, houses, and so on, made of paper). The colored sheets of cloth or blankets are placed on the deceased arranged from dark to lighter shades, with the final blanket being red, to represent happiness and life. A fourth-generation respondent said it is a way "you give to your ancestors. That may be spiritual insurance for some . . . as form of paying homage."

∞ GIVING TO ORGANIZATIONS

Heung yàuh gàm (incense oil gold) has its origins in temple donations, but has been adapted by Chinese Americans to represent both charity and philanthropy. Donations were used to maintain the temple, pay respect to ancestors, as well as to help those in need, but today these donations are also given to family associations for redistribution. *Chìh sihn gàm* is the Cantonese phrase that is closest to the dominant culture's meaning of philanthropy. It is usually a donation given directly to organizations. However, it may also be given to one's family association for redistribution to both ethnic and dominant-culture formal organizations.

An elderly respondent often traveled to and from China as a child. When asked what individuals have done for religious organizations, she responded, "In the old days [in China], it [donation to the temple] was for burning of incense and to take care of the temple." When asked why, her response was, "Taking care of the ancestors in between time." (Money was given to the monks to burn incense for the ancestor, until the donors could return to burn incense themselves.)

Bòng sáu or *boh hau* refers to volunteering services. It means "lending a hand," or donating time to an institution. An executive director for a service organization stated:

> I have found the older generation gives a lot of both time and money. But the younger generation is more selective, and give more time than money; few give both. Based on their own interest, I do what I can to match their skill with our needs. Another thing is, there is limited time, so they are selective [because the youth have more options today]. But, there are those that only give money. This is different from a group formed 40 years ago. They raise 60 percent of the funds . . . over and above the United Way allocation. In fact, they have established an endowment fund. . . . Then there is another group of youth who say, "If I give, what do I get in return?"

Another administrator stated:

> For myself in the past . . . it is more of the donation of time at the YWCA and Survival English School. I give financially to street people. When I give on the street there is direct connection to the face and person; with United Way it is abstract. The amount varies. It kind of depends on if I am wishing for something, then I give more.

The young people at his organization put on fundraisers, such as fashion shows, to help. At the youth center he administers there are programs in on-the-job training, family and youth counseling (mediation), and drug and gang prevention. Their service area is 70 percent immigrant, and they have more than enough volunteers.

A respondent who worked for many years as a fundraiser for Cameron House, affiliated with the Chinese Presbyterian Church, said:

> Asians are church-giving, both to the Chinese and to the church. For self-development monies, there is more manpower from Chinese volunteers, and it is easier to create an awareness. There is a recent switch in the last ten years from the Hong Kong church and switch in work style. It is easier if it is a coexisting situation like Cameron House and the Chinese Presbyterian Church. Another thing, you can get both money and volunteers that cross generations.

Elderly Chinese American respondents said that their motives for volunteering included continuing to learn, keeping busy, doing things for the less fortunate, a sense of belonging, and the satisfaction they derived from volunteering. Many of the younger volunteers expressed similar motives.

Respondents appeared to feel that giving time is more important than giving money. One respondent said that her volunteer work at the YMCA was part of a class requirement at San Francisco State University. A younger respondent said, "I have a lot of free time right now, and I should use it. I could be sitting at home watching TV, but if you actually help someone, you feel a sense of accomplishment and value for your time. I'm willing to work, because I can gain self-fulfillment through volunteering." A third-generation respondent said, "When a group of people work together on a project they become like a new family." He has been volunteering at the same place for 14 years and feels the people there are part of his family. His father is critical of organizations requesting money and is more likely to give time. As another respondent put it, "I think that volunteering is more satisfying than to give money. I almost feel that I have to give or else I won't get something in return. You give and then you get." He enjoys knowing that his work makes a difference. Another respondent feels one of his personal flaws is giving too much. He sees this in his family as well.

A second-generation respondent commented that the primary reason for volunteering was paying off debts to the people who came before her and the need to be busy and participate: "Yes, volunteer work is important, because they did that for me when I was in the youth programs. And if you have the time, you should use it. You've done your share when you volunteer, rather than leaving it to someone else." Another respondent described Chinese volunteers:

> Of the Chinese volunteers, they seem to be interested in the children. They seem to think that it is important to build a pseudo home for the kids. Of the Chinese who donate money, they seem more concerned that the money

somehow filter back to the community. . . . Either they come from a highly Asian American family or a traditional Asian family that is trying to break away from the family. . . . If you want the beaches clean, then teach the children to keep them clean and eventually they will be.

A third-generation respondent who also said that volunteerism is clearly the preferred method of contribution saw participation partly as control of the involvement. Not only is there social interaction and a sense of belonging but also the satisfaction of seeing the work done. The giver can control the effect of the giving, thus creating a sense of empowerment.

☙ ASSOCIATIONS

In addition to community survival, the primary purpose of a *sihn tòhng* (family association) in the early Chinese immigrant community was management of burials (which were free to its members). After ten years, the bones were retrieved and sent back to home villages in China via Hong Kong. Attached to each packet of remains was $5.00 (U.S.) for the families. There have been changes since the early days, but burial is still a concern of the *sihn tòhng*, though to a lesser extent. Retrieval of the bones is generally not done, unless there is a request for the service, and no money accompanies the remains.

One respondent recalled that during the depression years in the United States, one meal a day was provided for members of his *sihn tòhng*. "There was no shame. It's not like welfare." In the past 15 years, his *sihn tòhng* has had more money and has set aside a large amount that is donated to charitable organizations.

One respondent is part of the Leong *sihn tòhng* and contributes annually but also contributes when there is a special request. She said that the *sihn tòhng* sponsors scholarships and social activities. On the other hand, a fourth-generation respondent stated that his family did not belong to a family association: "That was not common for people who lived in the suburbs."

Each *sihn tòhng* is within the domain of the Chinese Six Companies (CSC), which began in 1854. Subsequently, the regional CSCs came together to establish the Chinese Consolidated Benevolent Association (CCBA) of U.S.A. One respondent, a retired engineer and a current administrative officer of CSC, stated that there were no mutual benefit associations in China. They were developed in America out of necessity: "In the old days you needed to belong for protection. Now, if you don't have money, you go and borrow from the savings and loan. In the old days, you had no credit. In case of emergency, who is going to help you? In the old days, it was mutual benefit; now it is social and charitable *sihn tòhng*." This same respondent told of a giving practice of the CCBA in the early migrant days. Immigrants returning to China were asked for a donation by the president of the CSC, prior to leaving:

The association would get together with the steamship company, then they would send the president [of CSC] to bid farewell. . . . In fact, he was asking for a donation. . . . It was almost mandatory to pay. If you don't pay, the record would go back to China. . . . Otherwise when you get back to China, shame [for not upholding his social status obligation].

The San Francisco CSC has changed its goals over the past 140 years, and now focuses on three areas: education of Chinese children, management of the Chinese Hospital and its charitable affairs, and management of various projects benefiting the community. The CSC in San Francisco has conducted collections for earthquake victims, United Way, earthquake preparation education for Chinatown, YMCA, Self-Help for the Elderly, On Lok, YWCA, and other organizations. Recently, a television advertisement sponsored by several of the family associations asked for donations to help the flood victims in China. The CSC does not sponsor but endorses other charitable projects. One respondent said, "If you don't go through the CSC, you may not attain your goal. We endorse, then people will participate."

CSC connects three kinds of organizations: (1) family associations—people from the same district in China; (2) people associated by their surnames, of which the largest in the San Francisco Bay Area is the Wong Family Association; and (3) people in the same business or profession. About half of the respondents in this study acknowledged a connection with CSC. Most were connected via the family or surname association. One respondent stated: "*Sihn tòhng* was to insure, to protect themselves, a way of getting job, but it was also a place to be a hang-out. . . . Yeah, they pay dues. It was also for the men that came originally; it was their place, and the family associations were almost like a union."

Chinese Americans call their rotating credit association a *wúi*. Rotating credit organizations provide a form of collective banking. Each member makes small monthly payments. Each month, the "pot" or total collection of money is given to one member as a disbursement. Each month, a different person will receive a large payment. A great deal of trust exists among rotating credit association members because if someone received funds and refused to continue making contributions until each member had received funds, there would be no recourse for the other members. As the payments rotated around the membership, each member eventually received a large sum of money with which to buy things, start a business, make a down payment on a house or fulfill other financial obligations. It is a form of savings or investment. Similar to a loan but without the requirement of collateral, these credit associations are essential in building communities. Chinese Americans in San Francisco have been able to survive, even without being able to speak English, by utilizing the support network of family and rotating credit associations.

One respondent summarized giving in the Chinese community: "A major difference is the expectation to care for the extended family rather than the more abstract United Way." He further stated,

There is shift from time to money. The Asians feel the pressure, it is like a contest—there is a high correlation between minority presentation and the goal to increase designated donations. For the Chinese, donating is like face recognition—presentations by Asians give United Way creditability; they know where the money is going. Therefore, pressure plus ethnicity enhance donation. Before presentations, they would take the guilt without giving. With presentations, donation increased by $10,000.

Another respondent said,

I don't think the Chinese community really reaches out for donations that they want from the general public, so I really don't know what they want, as far as the Chinese culture is concerned. There is very little appeal from whatever charities that are Chinese. I really don't know if any organizations really want donations, other than Chinese Hospital, I really don't think that the organizations reach the public. . . . I would have to know what they are about and believe in their cause and know that they are legitimate. There are a lot of organizations that come up to you for donations and these organizations don't mean anything. I don't think I would give to something that I don't know. The Salvation Army, I always give to them, because I went to their camps when I was a child, so I always give to them, because that touches me. . . . I think that everybody should give back to society, whether they take from society or not. The very fact that if they did good, they should contribute to the welfare of the group, so if they can't donate time then I would certainly donate money. Money is easy to give and then the people who have time can give it.

This respondent sees Chinese causes as something to support on special occasions, such as for celebrations or commemorations, whereas he sees causes of the dominant culture as an everyday, general sort of charity to give to at any time.

A respondent who dealt with at-risk youth feels that the more traditional organizations do not adequately address the more modern needs of the community, such as youth drug and gang problems, which are not consistent with traditional Chinese values. Another respondent confirmed this observation but said that an organization like Self Help for the Elderly "is not controversial, [whereas] Chinese for Affirmative Action [an advocacy organization] and education are more nebulous."

Political contributions within *wúi(s)*, *tòhng(s)*, and *sihn tòhng(s)* have a long, established track record. Formerly, it was the Nationalists who were the beneficiaries of Chinese American contributions. One respondent gave some historical perspective for the donations made to the Nationalists:

The first immigrants established *sihn tòhng*, and Chinese Six Companies. With the latter was the first time Chinese were willing to give money toward a group interest [protecting Chinese rights]. Then at the turn of the century came Sun Yat Sen, and he came to the U.S. to get donations to fight the Manchu government. Then came the Kwok Ming Dong [KMT], which is the current version and continues efforts which were started by the father of the Republic, Sun Yat Sen. The Chinese Six Companies and KMT still get the first-generation monies [old and new immigrants—it is an established track]. However, since normalization with the U.S., the money is now used to provide schools and education for the young.

He said that there are political factions within Chinatown that are very skilled at getting donations. "They tend to raise money by picking on their pain. And after, those that have normalized [naturalized] return their focus to the *wúi* [associations], and they reconnect to the homeland." This is consistent with the general phenomenon of third-generation immigrants wanting to go back to their roots. His reference to fundraisers focusing on past pain is illustrated by boat people giving more than established Asians:

> As I said, historically, this is in the context of a fundraiser, the fundraising idea or donating money idea, that from a historical context, there were people that were willing to give money out of their hard earnings or whatever for several causes . . . it dates back to the Taipei uprising and the overthrow by Dr. Sun Yat Sen. He was able to come over to this country, and also to Hawaii to raise quite a substantial sum of money for the overthrow of the Manchu government in China. So, therein was set a historical precedent for fundraising in the overseas communities, the Chinese American communities. This is probably pretty well utilized by what we call the KMT facet of our community. . . . Sun Yat Sen, well, he started the party. So as I said, there is that tradition of being able to raise large sums of money to fight war in China, to fight all kinds of issues in China. And, I think that is still with us today. . . . These people have been giving since that early period, it is a regular practice that they have . . . at least once a year, as a member, they go through the type of ritualistic process of giving to their own association. So that is one big group, the Chinese Six Company, the KMT, they probably together would draw the most money in Chinatown. Still today. The second development, after China normalized with the U.S., is [giving] to schools and education, scholarships, and make sure these people learn something before they come over here. The third track is the work investment, but that is not donation, but business. Chinese use celebrations to raise money, i.e., auctions. . . . To save face the bids get higher and higher. It is to save face, and the relationship that person has with the cause or organization. . . . Thus, the very distinct giving patterns that we see politically are pro-KMT group, pro-Mao group, and pro-normalization group. Those are the groups that galvanize the people.

He said that Chinese Americans support both Nationalist and Communist governments.

The two Chinese political celebrations, October 1 and October 10, no longer play a great part in politics when celebrated in America. A respondent who is very active in the Chinese community said that the emphasis is now more social and is used to maintain ties with China and Taiwan in a symbolic rather than monetary manner. A man in his 60s, who until a decade ago was not interested in Chinese customs, reflected, "Yes, they brought Chang Kai-shek [war bonds] a lot. I had a whole chest of them when [my father] died, but worthless. I donated it to a cultural center. They probably used them for wallpaper." Another respondent, in her 20s, remembered seeing the bonds when her grandmother was sorting out old things to be discarded.

CHAPTER SEVEN *Japanese*

- Confucianism and Buddhism are significant influences in Japanese giving behavior.
- For Japanese, time and money are given with equal readiness due to a strong sense of payback, or of doing one's share toward community survival.
- Japanese donate to both Japanese and dominant-culture organizations.
- Japanese mutual aid associations, originally established for economic survival and political advocacy, have become more social, focusing less on giving assistance and more on preserving the culture.
- *Koden*, consisting of monies given to defray funeral costs, is probably the most common Japanese giving practice. Some of these monies are then donated back to the community.

Kinship, maintenance of culture, politics, and health are focal points of giving for Japanese. The Japanese have been in the United States for over 100 years, but they have not become totally assimilated (Fugita and O'Brien, 1991). They are one of the most homogeneous groups of people in the world and have a strong nationalist identity. The typical Japanese immigrants were independent small farmers seeking to avoid political instability and excessive taxation in Japan. They came to capitalize on new agricultural economic opportunities in the United States. The Japanese have been able to maintain strong ethnic identity while at the same time becoming highly involved with the dominant culture. This same pattern is exhibited by Japanese in their giving behavior (Fugita and O'Brien, 1991; Lyman, 1986).

Unlike the Chinese, the Japanese had family support since they first came to the United States. Many were able to bring their wives and families. Those who came as bachelors often were able to send for "picture brides" (matchmakers used pictures to arrange marriages). Family unity affected charitable behavior. The Japanese focused on family needs and community development. Japanese families already in the United States supplied new immigrants with food, lodging, and employment assistance. At the same time, monies were sent back to relatives in Japan.

Discrimination, including internment during World War II, played a significant role in preserving traditional Japanese culture and social organization (Fugita and O'Brien, 1991; Lyman, 1986; Okazaki, 1985). The Japanese emphasized traditional cultural giving patterns as a way of creating social bonds. The new immigrants remembered giving practices that they had experienced in early childhood and made attempts to replicate them in America. Japanese practices that developed centered on the family, kinship, and community for mutual support and survival. Japanese were forced into a small-scale agriculture because American labor unions discriminated against them. Continued discrimination slowed the pace of assimilation, and giving behavior generally stayed within the family and community.

World War II demolished the niche the Japanese had created in California agriculture and devastated Issei (first-generation) authority. The Nisei (second generation) became upwardly mobile following the war and entered professional and managerial positions. The process continues today (Fugita and O'Brien, 1991).

Much of Japanese giving behavior is rooted in Confucianism and Buddhism. Both provide the framework for deeper and more complex meanings than simply giving something. *Kodomo no tame ni* (for the sake of the children), respect for elders (Confucian philosophy), *giri* (debt of obligation), *oyabun-kobun* (master/disciple or pupil), harmony, and mutual dependence are traditional values wherein the framework for appropriate reciprocal behavior is learned. The early immigrants were deeply involved in Christian and Buddhist church activities. "They had a difficult time, the Depression, language barrier, but they were into giving to the church and to *kenjinkai* [prefecture associations]," said one respondent. Another stated:

> The first generation not only built churches here, but were still sending money back to Japan for the churches there. . . . The church was still the key, and they built the Japanese Cultural and Community Center of Northern California. They had a harder time, because they had fewer ties to Japan. They really had a situation of *gaman* [struggle] and they are conservative.

Linkages outside the family were made through traditional social organization forms. Two of these forms are the *ie* and *iemoto* (Kitano and Kikumura, 1980; Hsu, 1975). Hsu (1975) likens the *ie* to a corporate residential group that takes on the job of managing the affairs of its members. It is one of the strongest elements in the Japanese social system. Farmers in a new land benefited from having the experience of working together with neighbors in an *ie*. The *iemoto* extends linkages further by creating overlapping and interlinked social organizations. Members of both *ie* and *iemoto* are considered quasi-kin (Hsu, 1975).

The following description of Japanese philanthropic concepts and customs is based on interviews with 40 individuals from the Japanese community.

∽ KINSHIP AND COMMUNITY

The Japanese term for charity is *hodokoshi*. With Buddhist roots, there is emphasis on compassion and giving alms. *Kifu* means donation, endowment, and, by extension, philanthropy. The term *boluntary* is derived from and means voluntary. One long-term resident said:

> I really don't think there is too much of this strong traditional charitable giving or donating unless you are very, very devoted believer [Buddhist] in

particular. That is why I think the Japanese companies have only just recently began this kind of philanthropy. . . . Japanese companies, because there is so much pressure from the United States to be a good corporate citizen, they've started giving, but in terms of history, I don't believe there is too much history. . . . I think the motive of like Judeo-Christian type philanthropy is that you collect money and give money for social causes, the poor, the disadvantaged, the larger community. But the case in Japan—and this is true of many East Asian countries—is basically not necessarily to help the disadvantaged or some general social cause but to help particular segments of society, like kin and community. It is very narrow.

This cultural attitude, which emphasizes giving to kin and community, may help explain the ethnocentric giving prevalent in the Japanese American community. This same respondent continued, "Japanese are doing all of these things not because they really feel this volunteerism is important. They are doing this because they have to create face in the community and maintain good relationships." Maintaining harmony in interpersonal relationships and face are mentioned often by respondents as reasons for continuing charitable practices.

A male respondent said that Japanese family ties are stronger than those of the dominant culture, but that Western culture is more generous outside the family. He sees Japanese volunteers as preferring personal interaction and social benefit for their giving and immediate benefit from their work; if they don't see results they at least want a party after the work is done. He added, "Japanese expect something coming back, something where you get benefit immediately."

The emphasis placed on elders and youth continues to have high priority for the Japanese community. A lounge on the bridge of the Japanese Cultural Center in San Francisco was built for Issei who wanted to rest on their trips into Nihonmachi (Japantown). This lounge functions with the aid of volunteers and has become a gathering place for elders.

The major form of Japanese giving revolves around care of elders. Care of the elderly is not considered charitable activity by Japanese but is more of a duty reflecting Confucian, Buddhist, and other traditional values. A Nisei in his 70s related that he and his wife care for his mother-in-law who is over 100 years old. If they did not assume the duties to address this need, who would? Yet a Sansei (third-generation) respondent, born in San Francisco, stated:

> Now, the family is prime. Before, it was the *ie* household unit [which includes neighbors] for the Issei and Nisei. . . . It is what the first generation expected the second generation to do [care for parents]. Therefore, the second [generation] would feel guilt. There was a lot of *gaman* [perseverance] involved, and therefore [they did] not expect the third generation to care for them [the Nisei].

There were other Sansei who related similar experiences and the value they place on family and elders.

This care of the family extends to the community, as shared by a Sansei respondent:

> I think respect to the elders is important. . . . Family is important, basic responsibilities, and family responsibilities. . . . I think it's a tradition of [being] older, like one being able to live a long life and being respected because you survived a long life. At the same time I think there is a lot of compassion involved. I think family tradition is important as far as the community is concerned. I think the extended family is very important. . . . We have members of my family who are not blood line either and people that I work with and other good friends; we share responsibility for each other.

The giving behavior, reciprocity, and mutual dependence learned primarily in early childhood are not restricted within the family, but spread out to the community. When individuals share responsibility for each other, there is less need for dominant-culture social services.

Five respondents continue to send money back to their families in Japan. One respondent mentioned that upon the death of his father his mother gave three homes they owned to relatives in Japan. She felt that her children and grandchildren would not return to Japan to live and that it was proper to give the homes to the relatives there. A similar situation was described by a Sansei after the death of his grandfather. Asked about the importance of giving, one respondent replied:

> The reasons why are value-based for me. It is layered with political belief that everything should be equal and that those that have should help. I think there is a cultural base to it. My grandparents were farmers. There is an increased sense of community. They support each other. This was brought over with them and transferred to me, maybe not financial support but for things like emotional support.

Japanese recognize that giving and sharing is tied to a web of interlocking relationships. As one respondent put it:

> We can't survive without helping each other. The only way people can survive is to help each other. . . . I think that the dominant white culture is strongly based on independence, while, I think this is true with other Asian cultures, but Japanese culture is more based on interdependence and from that basic point the interpersonal relationship is so different, more of the "You scratch my back and I'll scratch your back" sort of thing going on and it is more accepted in the Asian cultures.

Since the war, Japanese Americans are no longer tied to the farms. No longer are Japanese living in high concentrations with other Japanese, nor has there been any substantial emigration of Japanese to America since the 1970s (Fugita and O'Brien, 1991). Yet there remain indications of intergenerational continuity in traditional values of respect, obligation, reciprocity, harmony, mutual dependence, and observance of hierarchy, all of which are acknowledged, to some extent, through giving and sharing. Sansei have more discretionary resources available. Respondents articulated many formal dominant-culture donations. As linkages made by Japanese to the dominant-culture organizations increase, it may be that dominant-culture forms of charitable activity will further increase.

A *happa* (half Japanese) commented on differences between the Japanese and dominant culture's giving patterns:

> I think there are a lot of differences due to internment. There is a cautiousness in Japanese Americans that is not in mainstream communities. The Japanese American community is meshing very rapidly, but they are also concerned with maintaining the Japanese American identity. . . . They have a very insular identity; there is us and them.

Several respondents related that there still remains a degree of mistrust toward the American system of giving. A second-generation respondent who is very active in both the Japanese and mainstream communities said, "One thing with Asians, both with foundations and trusts, monies go to American causes, and little to Asian; it bugs the heck out of me."

Several comments from third-generation respondents gave further insight into the continued ethnocentric interest in giving:

> I think in the '60s I realized that there were needs that the government wasn't addressing and that communities must work for themselves. As ethnic minorities, we must work for ourselves. . . . A place that has gone to the community to find out what their needs are does not just set up and say we are here to help. I think that in big organizations we lose control. I prefer community agencies where control isn't taken from the people. I feel it is important, because if we are talking about the Japanese community in general, it is important to maintain contact and identity within the community. We don't want to lose our ethnic identity. Through giving time and money we can maintain the identity of the community through programs and events. The younger generation is becoming more and more assimilated into white culture and has lost much of the ethnic identity. There has been increased resentment against Japanese nationals. I think people are afraid of confusion between Japanese Americans and Japanese nationals due to the increased racism. Japanese Americans as a whole are worried about dilution. There is not much immigration, and there has been an increase in *happa* children. There will be a scarcity of full-blooded Japanese Americans.

A respondent said about the third-generation Japanese:

> They are just as happy to write one check out to United Way. . . . The mobility, they have all moved away and then there is the out-marriage. Their sense of community is not as strong. The older ones, they are used to giving. I read in the community a sense and ability to contribute. So I do, but other third-generation people don't seem to have the same feeling.

Another respondent commented: "I think that part of the problem is that the ethnic community perceives itself outside of the mainstream community, and therefore feels that it does not benefit, or have direct benefit from mainstream philanthropy. It makes me feel good to give—doing good for others."

∞ CELEBRATIONS

Most Japanese Americans celebrations revolve around the New Year (*oshogatso*). Two prominent New Year gift-giving customs are *nenshimawari* (the New Year walk-around) and *otoshidama* (New Year's monetary gift to children). Part of *nenshimawari* was traditionally practiced by only the males visiting different homes of friends and family while the women stayed home to prepare food and drinks provided for the visitors. This tradition has changed over time to include women and children.

Otoshidama, a present for good luck, is money given to a child in a white envelope with a red band on it. This is usually practiced until the child is between 12 and 18 years old. One Issei in his 80s mentioned the practice of children giving money to elders after receiving money themselves. The idea behind this type of giving is to wish their elders another year of prosperous living. This Buddhist practice was described by one respondent:

> There is this custom of *otoshidama* in which the senior people like grandparents give money to the grandchildren or children. New Year is one of the biggest and holiest of all times and a time that you celebrate fertility and harvest, a most sacred and happy time. Of course harvest is much earlier, but symbolically speaking we celebrate at the beginning of the year. The birth of a new year is a happy occasion and it symbolizes some kind of rich fertile year, so it is a time of generosity.

It is believed that generosity breeds plenty. Many of the respondents were aware of *otoshidama* but did not practice it or had never received it. One elderly respondent felt the reason he never received *otoshidama* is because his family was not well off. Though he was aware of the custom, he never thought of giving it to his children. A Sansei gives his daughter *otoshidama* in an American New Year's card. Some do *otoshidama* and some do not. The continuance or disconstinuance of this custom may be related to religious affiliation on one hand and the celebration of Christmas on the other hand. There was no relationship seen between the age of the giver to generation or length of residence in the United States.

∞ TRAVEL

Senbetsu refers to a gift given when people are relocating their residence or going on a trip. One respondent said, "*Senbetsu* is a little bit sad occasion, so we use the white envelope (for money). *Senbetsu* is a farewell, good-bye money." When asked if he expected anything in return, he replied:

No, no. Maybe if I have received the *senbetsu*, when I go to the United States of America from Japan, I buy something in the United States and bring it back as a return to the man who give me *osenbetsu* [honorific form of *senbetsu*), even if it a very small thing, one handkerchief or one tie. *Senbetsu*, they give us maybe 10,000 yen, I buy for him maybe just about 1,000 yen or 100 yen, but it means symbolic, but it shows my thanks to person who gave me the money when I make travel to the United States. . . . Both way, when I go back to Japan, after a few years, on assignment. . . . The second- and third-generation Japanese, they don't know that. Also, they misunderstand.

A 96-year-old woman still practices *senbetsu*. However, she stated that things became less formal after the World War II. She will continue the Japanese giving customs as long as she can; she is not sure if her children are still practicing. A first-generation male said he is aware of *senbetsu* but that it is not expected of him (he has not married). An 83-year-old second-generation respondent, still practicing *senbetsu*, said that when an individual goes back (to Japan), the traveler is the one who receives the gift. Though a token gift may be returned, it is not of the same value as the money given. When asked if cultural giving practices were expected of her, she stated, "*Koden*, of course, and *senbetsu*, if I want, but not as much anymore." Another second-generation female said there is not as much *senbetsu* now because of the obligation to return something. There was little awareness of *senbetsu* among third- and fourth-generation respondents. When a Sansei was asked about *senbetsu*, she said that she did not practice it. However, when the practice was described to her, she said she had experienced it.

Omiyage means a souvenir, a parting present. It is given by the person or persons that one has visited. The term *omiyage* is also used to describe a gift given by the traveler to the people he or she is visiting. There is a trend to refer to any gift giving solely as *omiyage*.

⮾ SICKNESS AND DEATH

Omimai is a gift of money as a gesture of sympathy, usually when someone is ill. At times, food may also be given. The money is to help defray any medical costs and to assist the family if the person is unable to work. The money is also an expression of well-wishing and hope for a swift recovery. *Omimai* is Buddhist in origin and connotes caring for and helping others. Today, *omimai* could also be given to a group that is recovering from a fire, flood, accident, and so forth. These gifts and donations may also be given as a form of spiritual insurance—I give to you so that the same thing doesn't happen to me.

Koden is the practice of giving money to surviving members at the funeral of a family member. It is a Buddhist practice arising from the desire to be compassionate and ease the suffering of others. *Koden* is one of the most widely practiced of the Japanese customs in the San Francisco Bay Area.

Koden monies are used to defray funeral costs, to establish a memorial in the name of the deceased, to give to organizations in the name of the donor, and to give money to the church. The money is traditionally presented at the funeral in a special white envelope with black and white bands and ideographic writing on it. (One year later, money to memorialize the deceased is given wrapped in an envelope with yellow and white bands.) There is a table when one enters and *koden* is received by relatives, friends, and *kenjinkai* members helping the family. Both the amount of the donation and the name of the giver are recorded at the time it is given. This record serves as a reminder, so that when the need arises the appropriate amount of *koden* may be returned to the givers during their time of need. The amount of money given and the return required is determined by an individual's role and status in the community and the social distance or intimacy of their relationship as well as "face." Not giving *koden* would result in a loss of face, respondents related.

In addition to *koden*, prepared food is often brought to the family's home. A 40-year-old third-generation woman said, "After the ceremony we bring prepared food to the family so they don't have to worry about cooking." Another 40-year-old third-generation respondent stated: "You just do it. It is a cultural way of taking care of people in need. It is a nice way of taking care of people, a lot of support. It's just such a nice thing. I didn't realize how much such a small thing meant until my mother died and we received *koden* and people brought food by so we didn't have to bother with small worries."

One respondent described *koden* as a way to repay the bereaved family for their hospitality during the funeral events as well as to provide some financial support:

> At funerals you have to entertain the guests. . . . so partly *koden* is collected to repay this entertainment and food, but also for the community or family to help the family of the deceased with expenses as well. It is a time where community of family members, relatives and kin, help each other financially. There are two aspects, financial support for the family of the deceased and also paying back some of the things that the family has done for the guest.

This same respondent felt that *koden* "presumes that you will return the favor, so, in a way, its function is to strengthen the community relationship." This sense of returning the favor is consistent with the Japanese value of balance and fairness. An 83-year-old woman called it "some form of helping the family out, like *koden*—redistribution." A third-generation, 47-year-old man said:

> When my mother died, it was the biggest funeral that there had ever been. There were seven Buddhist priests that officiated. There was an incredible amount of *koden* given. . . . Dad donated back to the community: $10,000 to JACL, $10,000 to Hamilton Senior Center, $10,000 to Japanese Cultural and Community Center of Northern California, $10,000 to Kimochi, and $10,000 to the church, etc., [plus] . . . something for the living.

When asked about the importance of giving *koden* and why he practices it, a first-generation respondent raised in a Christian family replied: "If it is *koden*, even if I only have $5.00, I would borrow the rest out of respect; it is an obligation and symbol of being connected in the brotherhood. . . . By own internal motivation . . . social conditioning to express self as part of community that goes to extended family and friendships."

The majority of third-generation Japanese Americans continue to practice *koden*, even those that have married out of the Japanese ethnic group. When questioned as to why, respondents gave various answers. In many cases it has to do with family obligation. As one respondent put it, "You just do it. *Koden* is an important part of respect for the family." The cultural obligation to give *koden* is so strong that an insurance broker felt it necessary to perform *koden* for his clients as part of his regular business contact with them. He said that the IRS had accepted it as a business expense during a recent audit, after he explained the cultural basis for the practice.

A respondent who had lost his father in early childhood had recently lost his mother. He did not know what to do, but the family belonged to a *kenjinkai*. "They took care of it all, the food, even what to do with the *koden*."

The cultural sense of obligation to give *koden* was expressed by all but one of the Japanese respondents. As one respondent stated, "I would expect the kids to do *koden*, but the rest I don't care about." Though traditional practices are not as frequent, nor as elaborate, there is a strong sense that it is important to continue *koden*.

Orei is a monetary or material token of thanks for any favor, service, or help given. This can be any favor or service, but it has special prominence used in regard to thanking a person for attending a funeral. Originally, the Japanese, like the Chinese, gave a banquet for those who attended the funeral. An 83-year-old respondent recalled that, in the old days, the family would give a can of tea to those who came to the funeral (given to the head of the family). After World War II, tea was too expensive, so they changed to a can of coffee (Masumoto, 1987). When her father died, she gave a can of coffee to each of her bosses who attended and, because of the cost, candy to the coworkers. When her mother died, she sent books of stamps in varying amounts to those that gave *koden*. It appears that the current trend is the giving of books of stamps, in thanks for *koden*, and for those who attend the funeral.

⌒ RELIGIOUS CUSTOMS

Religion has had a great impact on Japanese charitable activity. Though Japan has had some contact with Christianity since the sixteenth century, Buddhism, in particular, has for at least 1,500 years provided a model that defines charity for the Japanese. And, as in other Asian cultures, Buddhism plays an integral part in society. Buddhism is not just a religion but a philosophy of life. It encompasses "numerous elements which define the good life and appropriate social, religious and ethical actions" (Lohmann and Bracken, 1991, p. 419).

Buddhist customs permeate funeral observances. The term *ofuse* means offering at a temple: money is placed in an envelope and donated to a temple or church. *Gobutsuzen* is a funeral donation to the temple; it means "placed before" Buddha or someone who has died. *Gobutsuzen* is used when visiting other temples, and is placed in front of the altar of the Buddha. *Goreizen* is a family offering, usually food or incense, for the soul-spirit. *Gobutsuzen* must be given first, then *goreizen* is offered after burial.

These terms were not initially used by respondents. Instead, there was always a general reference to the "church." For example, one respondent told us, "[A Buddhist temple] is referred to as church because, in an effort to become American, the Japanese Americans formed an Americanized Japanese sect of Buddhism. This sect is called the Buddhist Churches of America."

A respondent shared what he gained from his religious participation: "If a member [of a temple or church], you should do your share if you have the means. I feel I am willing to give. You receive when you are a member [a sense of belonging]. It is a sense of responsibility. Almost every month, there is a request for a donation." Another respondent learned from religion, "There are a lot of people that need help out there. People should help other than themselves. You have to look beyond the self." In his 70s, this second-generation man stated:

> I feel an obligation to continue the practice [giving money to the church]. . . . Cultural practices are important, because I'm a product of that culture. Feeling that to belong to a group which is ethnic is not a barrier. . . . you try to do your share and participate in meeting that need. . . . a sense of loyalty to what you think is important.

A Sansei said:

> There are basic principles . . . founded on [Buddhist] religious principles. . . . We strongly believe that your internal strength comes from within, so we want to pass that on to our children, not look away from yourself for support, but look for inner strength. The importance of the family unit, although they are stereotypically Asian principles, and even though I'm relatively removed from my Japanese culture, I still think they are valid principles.

A Yonsei (fourth generation) from Hawaii related how Buddhism transfers to the community:

> Being a Buddhist, there is a oneness of community. You don't operate separate from the community. Your behavior reflects on everyone. . . . It is important being involved in the community. Service and compassion was definitely part of the teaching. We are taught to serve others. . . . It must be based on feeling interrelated, so that resources should be shared. It wouldn't feel right if someone amassed wealth without realizing the needs of others. A sense of community, belonging, having contributed, because without that what is there? You become disconnected.

Another Yonsei respondent put it this way: "I guess having a background related to immigration where there was a struggle, if you benefit from that struggle, you should give back to the community and help others going through it now. . . . My family is very people-oriented and active in voluntary groups. Church was important."

Thus there is a strong sense of payback or doing one's share toward community survival. Though many Japanese have converted to Christianity since coming to America and before, they continue to practice Buddhist giving customs. The temple may not have as many attending weekly, but those who do appear to be heavily involved. A possible reason that traditional giving behavior is being maintained is that most Japanese who attend a church (Buddhist or Christian) belong to a congregation whose members are of the same ethnic background, and the church is the most important voluntary association in the Japanese community (Fugita and O'Brien, 1991). The proximity of others from the same background probably fosters the continuance of religious giving practices. A third-generation respondent said, "Religion gives to the community. They make small grants to social service agencies. There are Kimochi Kai [senior center in Japantown] women's groups within the churches. They take turns volunteering to the Kimochi."

∽ GIVING TO ORGANIZATIONS

The formation of mutual aid associations is common among immigrant populations to help with survival and adaptation to a new environment and culture. Japanese associations provided a feeling of belonging and the framework for values, norms, beliefs, and behavior. Group traditions, mottoes, and slogans reinforced the "we" so that tightly knit groups, group consensus, and a lack of individuality were characteristics.

Beginning in the 1890s, the Japanese formed many prefecture associations (*kenjinkai*). Similar to these was the *nihonjin kai* (Japanese people association). The voluntary nature of the *kenjinkai* facilitated the integration and assimilation of Japanese Americans into the dominant culture because the individuals would not be excluded from the community if they became involved with a dominant culture group or organization (Fugita and O'Brien, 1991). This is in contrast to the Chinese where membership during early immigration was a requirement. The *kenjinkai* helped newly arrived immigrants with food, lodging, and other needs. The association sponsored fundraising activities to help new members get established in America. It helped with marriages and funerals, as well as with paperwork needed to ensure legal residency (Okazaki, 1985).

Around 1900, Japanese American charitable activity began to take on a more formal appearance. The Nippon Jikei Kai (Japanese Charitable Association) was formed to assist the needy. Monies were solicited from Japanese who had become prominent. The group later established the Japanese Cemetery and maintains its premises up to the present (Okazaki, 1985).

Issei immigrants worked hard to keep in touch with each other and provided mutual support through the *kenjinkai*. At the same time they formed the Japanese Association of America to keep communication open with the Consulate of Japan. Whenever there was a major disaster such as an earthquake or major fire, many Issei sent funds, clothes, and survival goods back to their homeland. San Francisco was pleasantly surprised when, after the 1906 earthquake, the Japanese government reciprocated by sending goods and money to the victims of the disaster (Okazaki, 1985). A respondent said, "Japanese nationals gave more aid after the 1906 earthquake to San Francisco . . . than all other countries combined. After the 1989 quake, they gave more than $10 million, the largest; the [San Francisco] *Examiner* stated that they were buying friends." One of the Japanese advisory committee members of the present study stated that the $10 million was not from corporations but from the people of Japan. He suggested that it was probably due to the sensitivity the Japanese feel about earthquakes and because Japan remembers that San Francisco was the first city to come to their aid during a major earthquake they experienced 75 years ago. He pointed out that the monies were sent to the City of San Francisco, not just to Japanese Americans.

An 83-year-old second-generation respondent said that her family belonged to the Kochi *kenjinkai* and that is where most of the single men came from. Many of these single men from the *kenjinkai* were extended assistance by her parents. The assistance ranged from a meal to lodging and assistance in finding work. She said that much of the *tanomoshi ko* (rotating credit association) activity took place in these associations. In earlier times, immigrants were unable to obtain credit. Rotating credit associations became a method of acquiring enough money to start a business, to cover the cost of a sickness, educate the children, and so forth.

Formal associations began in 1918, with the American Loyalty Club, which helped its members claim their rights as American citizens in San Francisco. A united front was formed against a hostile society that resulted in the Japanese American Citizens League (JACL), which was established in 1930. After the war, the ultimate goals of JACL were to gain citizenship for the Issei and establish a nondiscriminatory immigration law, as well as repayment for material losses suffered in the evacuation (Okazaki, 1985). Payments in compensation for internment during the war were begun in 1992.

According to a 72-year-old respondent, at the turn of the century the *kenjinkai* and the *nihonjin kai* were similar mutual aid associations. "All I can remember are the picnics. It was a big thing. People even bought new cars for the event to show off." She had much clearer memories of JACL activities. "In the old days, JACL was a big attraction. They had amateur shows, community affairs, and they would announce the donations, a banner—like the roll of distinction in the lobby of Kimochi Kai [today]." She feels that banners were used to address the face aspect in the Japanese American community, because people wanted to donate, to show that they were doing their share. Other mutual benefit associations were the Nihonjinmachi Improvement Association, the Japanese Association of San Francisco, and business and professional associations (Okazaki, 1985).

Many groups were formed to unite the community by providing activities for women and children and assisting the community endeavors at large. By 1941, women had formed the San Francisco Mothers' Society, Kinmon Gakuen Mothers' Society, a YMCA Mothers' club, a Sokoji Fuinkai, a Women's Home, and a Sister's Home. The groups provided care for the newly arrived, helping them (adults and children) learn about American society and American social skills (Okazaki, 1985). A respondent related that the Satsuki Kai was formed under the sponsorship of the "Y" to assist Japanese businessmen's wives learn about the American way of life.

When an economic niche was established, prewar Japanese Americans began to reduce their ethnocentric giving behavior. With basically Japanese American donations, YMCA, YWCA, and Salvation Army structures were built in Japantown (Okazaki, 1985). All of this was lost during World War II. A first-generation Japanese American said: "In Japan the *kenjinkai* are social and in America it is political, social, and financial. . . . *tanomoshi* were probably in the *kenjinkai* too. It is an obligation to benefit the needy, done because otherwise one would be made to lose face for not complying with the social unit. It is like 'social insurance.'"

The *kenjinkai* has changed its purpose since the coming of the immigrants. It is no longer primarily for group survival. The need to belong to one has weakened. A first-generation male respondent in his sixties said that he donates only when his older brother tells him to. A second-generation respondent who belongs to the Wakawama *kenjinkai* said the activities are social now, but in the past it was mutual aid. "In fact, [in the 1920s] you had to marry someone from the same *kenjinkai*. There are annual dues, and picnics." Another respondent, who is a third-generation male, tells us that his family came to the U.S. in the late 1800s. His family never belonged to a *kenjinkai* or the JACL, but he says, "I belong to a *kenjinkai*. Kanagawa, started by a Keibei Nisei [a second-generation, American-born Japanese, educated in Japan]. The current president is the first Sansei to be president of any *kenjinkai*. And we receive support from Japan."

At one time, there was a great need for the *kenjinkai* as mutual aid associations to assist immigrants in the United States. It appears that their present purpose is primarily social. The resurgence of interest in the *kenjinkai* has more to do with the association's ability to act as a vehicle for the preservation or promotion of the Japanese culture than to provide assistance to the Japanese community.

Japanese American organizations work hard to obtain funds from Japanese national foundations. One respondent states:

> We take for granted that because our ancestors are all Japanese that we somehow share the same value system, but actually we don't. I mean, there are some elements of Japanese values in the Japanese American culture, but if

you put everything together, it is a totally different culture. I think Japanese culture and Japanese American culture is very different. If you think in terms of first-generation Japanese Americans' culture, Issei, there is a intuitive understanding. You know what's going on, even though it is old fashioned, but second- and third-generations' culture they are all mixed together and it is very difficult to understand, so it is kind of difficult for Japanese to work with Japanese Americans, because of the intercultural communication. I myself am still in the process of understanding.

Another respondent, who is an experienced fundraiser, shared:

I think people give to organizations that they feel comfortable with. I receive a lot of individual donations, small donation to medium-size donation from the Japanese elderly, working people, younger people. Families from the Japanese community, and Asian communities, because we have a large interracial marriage population. The Japanese American community is different from the Japanese community in a lot of ways. We get a lot of support from the Japanese American community, as far as the larger grants and donations are concerned. I receive it much more from the American community than I do Japanese corporations. . . . I attribute that to their fear not to be identified as an ethnocentric program when they are interested in a different public image campaign.

On the other hand, when a chief executive officer of a prominent Japanese national organization was interviewed, he stated that his company "does not favor hiring Japanese officers. . . . We are Japanese, but we keep the American identity. If we want to make a donation . . . we don't give some privilege and don't have some privilege to give the donation to Japanese [American] organization here."

Given the decades of separation from Japan, one might expect wide variation in Japanese American giving customs. This was not the case. There were no practices identified by Japanese Americans that Japanese nationals were not aware of, even if they are no longer practiced in Japan. Several of the Japanese nationals said they felt Japanese Americans were "old fashioned" in their giving behavior. One commented:

Japanese American community, one thing is very mysterious . . . value system or social structure, on one hand they are very American, on the other hand they are Japanese. But this Japanese cultural thing that comes out of Japanese Americans is a very old fashioned one of the late nineteenth century. It is much more traditional, so it is a mixture of these two things.

A recent study (London, 1991) notes that Japanese still prefer to give to persons or groups within the donor's immediate circle or closer in social distance. Japanese American philanthropy remains largely a mutual benefit type. There still exists loyalty toward groups with whom there is a relationship, and community self-help remains strong.

- Much Korean sharing and helping takes place within the extended family.
- First-generation Koreans give primarily to Korean ethnic organizations and Korean Protestant churches.
- Giving practices in the Korean community are strongly influenced by social relationships.
- Koreans are not generally expected to participate in giving traditions until they are married.
- Koreans sometimes give indirectly by buying something not really needed from a relative or friend.
- Protestant and, to a lesser extent, Buddhist churches are a focal point in Korean giving practices.

Koreans started immigrating to the United States in 1885 to escape political turmoil in Korea (Melendy, 1977, p. 121). A second wave began in 1902 when Hawaii was looking for sources of cheap labor for its sugar plantations. As a result of the Gentleman's Agreement of 1907, only picture brides from Korea were allowed to enter the United States. From 1924 to 1948 Korean immigration to the United States dwindled to twenty non-laborers per year. During this period, Korean immigrants managed to send money back to their homeland, some of which was intended to support the Korean independence movement.

Since the restoration of Korean independence in 1945, the largest wave of immigrants came after 1965. In 1952 the U.S. government began allowing eligibility for citizenship to those born in the United States. Subsequently, a large number of Korean professionals and students flocked to the United States for economic and educational opportunities. According to the 1990 census, the Korean population has more than doubled in the United States, California, and the San Francisco Bay Area from 1980 to 1990.

Until recently, Koreans in this country have frequently been lumped together with the Japanese. For example, in 1905, the *San Francisco Chronicle* began an attack against Japanese and Koreans in response to growing anti-Asian sentiment. A few months later, the Japanese and Korean Exclusion League, later renamed the Asiatic Exclusion League, was organized, maintaining that both Koreans and Japanese were "undesirable alien elements" (Melendy, 1977, p. 132).

During the periods of early immigration, Koreans formed numerous associations in the United States. Korean immigrants were encouraged to join these organizations and their membership dues were used to support the struggle for independence in Korea as well as to promote the welfare of Koreans in the United States. The organizations worked to further the intellectual and economic development of Korean immigrant communities by setting up schools for children and by publishing textbooks for Korean language schools as early as 1909.

In addition to these organizations, numerous Christian churches were built by the early immigrants, most of whom had converted to Christianity while they were still in Korea. Korean interest in Christianity did not originate from missionary work; they sought it out and adopted it. Since the beginning of this century these churches have been closely involved with education, social services, political and social activities, and the economic needs of Korean Americans. For example, it was through these churches that a large part of the money to support Korea's independence movement was raised. Second only to the Philippines, Korea is the Asian nation with the largest population of Christians: 25 percent of Koreans profess Christianity. About 70 percent of Korean Americans are Protestant.

The following comments on Korean philanthropic customs are excerpted from interviews with 20 individuals in the Korean community.

❧ KINSHIP AND COMMUNITY

The family unit is very important to Koreans. The traditional family unit is based on the clan system, which is most commonly defined as parents, siblings, grandparents, uncles, aunts, and cousins. Grandparents play the central role. The greatest obligation assumed by individuals is toward the parents. The importance of the family unit to Koreans was expressed by one respondent, who stated, "When a family member is in need, it's wrong not to help."

The vast majority of Korean Americans, with the exception of those residing in Hawaii, are either first- or second-generation. First-generation immigrants give to their family members both in the United States and in Korea and to the Korean ethnic organizations and Korean Protestant churches. Their contribution to the Korean community is dictated by a sense of duty, tradition, and social customs of the old country as well as by religious beliefs.

Many respondents used the term "1.5 generation" to refer to those who had recently moved to the United States with their families. This group is the most bilingual and bicultural of the various generations. They have assumed much of the new culture but have retained the traditional Korean culture as well. This generation tends to give more to mainstream organizations than first-generation immigrants do.

Supporting and helping parents is viewed as one's chief duty, especially if one is the eldest son. Koreans retain a strong sense of filial obligation toward their parents. Some believe that taking care of their parents is paying back for what their parents have done for them. One first-generation Korean said:

> In old days, at least three generations lived in a household. Serving your
> parents and grandparents was almost a sacred duty. Still, today, I think sup-

porting your parents with money and other forms of help is something you must do. You should value your parents and do things for them. Your children will do the same for you when you get old.

The 1.5-generation Koreans have to be independent and efficient and at the same time fulfill obligations toward their parents. Some feel the pressure of their parents' expectations. First-generation Koreans want their children to assimilate and to be accepted by the dominant society. At the same time, they expect their children to conform to traditional Korean values.

Sang-hwal-bi is money sent or given to parents for daily living expenses such as rent, food, and utilities. Many Koreans send monthly *sang-hwal-bi* to their parents in the United States and in Korea. The actual amount depends on the economic status of the children. *Yong-don* is pocket money sent by children to their parents. While it is not *sang-hwal-bi*, it is given to supplement whatever income their parents have. *Yong-don* is given either regularly (once a month, for example) or randomly. This practice of giving an allowance to parents is widely practiced in the Korean community.

In Korea, most aging parents live with their children. For many older Koreans, this is the only form of retirement plan. In the United States, many Korean parents live with their children, but some live by themselves in separate apartments. Social security payments as well as *yong-don* and *po-jo-bi* (helping money) are major income sources. One first-generation Korean senior said:

> Now I live here in the United States. I don't speak enough English to take care of things on my own. I need help in that regard. But I think the United States has really good plans and security systems for elderly. Therefore, I really don't need much financial help from my children. I am more independent from my children than others. I live with only my wife. I really don't expect the same kind of parental support expected in Korea here. I just need some help now and then. I think young Korean people here are forgetting the beautiful customs and traditions of respecting and taking care of their parents. Maybe it's the influence of the American culture. Even though I can't help my children financially and there isn't too much I can do for them anymore, I still take care of my children in my own ways. I always worry about them. Children are busy with their lives and their own children. I guess they have no time to spend time with their parents anymore.

One first-generation respondent's attitude toward helping others within the community or even outside the community is typical of many Koreans:

> I collect used furniture, clothing items, dishes, and other used articles from people who are replacing them or moving away and store them in my storage space in the basement of my apartment. When new immigrants or students arrive from Korea, I give these items to them. When people first come here they can't afford to buy everything new at once. Those people can use the items I collected. I live on social security benefit and the pay I get from [the Korea Center], and so I can't give money to everyone; this is my way of helping others.

Another concept, *pu-ma-ssi* (exchanging work), originated in the farm communities of Korea. One person said: "We got help from our friends and neighbors during busy seasons of rice planting or harvest. Then we had to pay back with our labor, doing the same kind of work our friends did for us."

Korean women often help one another whenever they need extra help in cases like *jan-chi* (a party) or *che-sa* (a ritual where food is prepared for ancestors). The tradition for helping one another has changed with time. One respondent stated: "Those traditions [of helping each other] are changing both in Korea and in the United States. In Korea, with the use of the modern farm machines, they don't need as much manpower as they used to. In the United States, people lead busy daily life, they can't help each other as much as they used to."

Koreans use various terms to describe money given to help others. *Po-jo-bi*, *chee-won-bi*, and *gi-bu-kum* all mean money used on various occasions to help. *Mo-kum* means collecting money to help. On special days like Christmas, or for natural disasters, Koreans pool their financial resources and collect money (*mo-kum*) to help those in need.

Outside the clan and *chin-ji* relations, the rationale for giving becomes less clear. One respondent related it to times of hardship, when Korea was poor. During this period, many people gave knowing that others would give to them someday if and when they needed help.

Recency of immigration affects Korean giving patterns. An older first-generation respondent said: "I believe that the longer the person lived in the United States, the less he/she is involved in traditional giving practices; also, the giving practices of those people are simpler, perhaps less, than the people living in Korea."

Generational differences were observed in the giving practices between the first-generation, the 1.5-, and the second-generation Koreans. Second-generation Koreans, born only recently, are generally too young to participate fully in Korean giving practices, because Koreans are not expected to practice the giving traditions until they are married.

Traditionally, Korean society is strictly governed by Confucian philosophy and norms of conduct. Duties to each other in relationships are clearly defined. Being good sons, daughters, brothers, sisters, relatives, and friends is important in Korean culture. Interpersonal relationships and harmony within the community play a major role in the giving practices of Koreans.

When deciding on beneficiaries, most Koreans first consider their families, then neighbors and the Korean community, and then the local churches, school alumni associations, and business and political associations. After these, they will consider giving to other ethnic communities and mainstream organizations. A first-generation respondent summarized this view: "There is a home with family first, then community, society, country, and world exist in that order. Therefore, family is the most basic and important unit. If you don't respect and help each other within the family, you can't achieve anything as a nation."

Besides formal and informal giving practices, Koreans also give indirectly within their communities. This is done to save the pride or face of the person who is being helped. A respondent explained the practice in the following way: "It is quite common. They don't give money directly, but they buy something from the store whose owner needs help. It's indirect giving because people buy things that they do not really need just to help their friends or relatives."

Korean giving practices center around holidays and special personal occasions, and around religious and public events supported through the Korean churches in the community. On these occasions, family and friends gather for a celebration and give money or necessary items. When a person loses a business or job, friends and family members gather funds to help out. One respondent summarized giving practices in the following way:

> Attending weddings, funerals, and *hwan-kap jan-chi* [60th birthday party] and contributing money is important. It is a duty or obligation as a family member or friend. It is also a form of *pu-ma-ssi* [exchange of work, taking turns to do work for one another] even though we don't work physically, we contribute financially as well as emotionally. It is our Korean tradition and culture, a very good tradition, I think. Even if you can't attend the party, wedding or funeral, you have to send money; you have to contribute. *Bu-jo* [contributing money] is almost an obligation. Exchanging *bu-jo* between friends and relatives is very important; it is almost like a law. It's unthinkable not to. Even if there is no shortage of money, you still have to send money to show your concern and respect for each other.

Besides the holidays such as the New Year's Day, Koreans tend to divide their giving occasions into two main categories: happy and sad occasions. Money given on happy occasions is called *chuk-ui-kum*, and money given on sad occasions is called *cho-ui-kum*.

∞ HAPPY OCCASIONS

When a woman gives birth she is taken care of by her mother at her parents' home (*chul-san*). She stays there at least a month, sometimes up to three to four months after the baby's birth. Some relatives or family members give money to help out with hospital expenses. Food items and baby clothing are given as presents by relatives and friends.

Paek-il is the celebration of the baby's first 100 days. Money and presents are given at this occasion by the family, relatives, and friends. In the old days, there was a high rate of infant mortality and it was believed that if a baby survived 100 days, he or she was out of significant danger. Parents therefore celebrated this day with a big party to announce the birth formally. Party guests would bring presents such as baby clothes, toys, and gold rings. Today, people also give money to the parents for the baby. The parents save the money and the gold rings for the baby's future, and send some rice cakes and other party food to neighbors and relatives who live close by. In the old days, parents used to distribute one hundred rice cakes to people passing by their house. This was to ensure the baby's health and longevity by doing good for the community.

Dol is the baby's first birthday. Family, relatives, friends, and neighbors gather for the birthday party. Money, clothes, or gold rings are given to the baby. In times of economic hardship gold rings were considered a means of securing the child's and the family's future financial status. For the celebration, a large table with traditional food is prepared for the family and guests. Later, objects symbolizing various desirable traits, such as wealth, health, longevity, intelligence, and academic success are presented to the baby. It is believed that the particular trait associated with the object that the baby picks up will be transferred to the baby for his/her future success. After the party, the parents again send rice cakes and other party food to neighbors and nearby relatives.

Regular birthdays (*saeng-il* or *saeng-shin*) are usually celebrated at home with nuclear family members, close relatives, and friends. Occasionally, for convenience, a birthday is celebrated outside of the home. Mostly, it is celebrated quietly; small gifts are presented to the celebrant by the family members and others who are invited.

Hwan-gap is a person's 60th birthday. In the old days, reaching one's 60th birthday was a significant event in one's life since many died before reaching that age. For the occasion, family members and relatives threw a big party, organized by the children of the person turning 60. No formal invitations were sent, but everyone was expected to come. Often, even homeless beggars passing by were invited to join the feast. Now, the pattern of celebration has changed. Only family, relatives, and close friends are invited. Money and presents are also given by the children, relatives, friends, and other invited guests. Children usually give a large sum of money or an expensive present, such as travel abroad or a diamond ring. Relatives and friends also contribute food and service for the party. In most cases, the occasion is now celebrated outside the home for the convenience of the family and guests. Sometimes, the party is held at the Korean community church after the regular Sunday service, and all church members are automatically invited.

One 1.5-generation respondent described her experience with *hwan-gap jan-chi* (60th birthday party) in the following way:

> When I was about eight or nine, my grandfather had his *hwan-gap*. My grandparents lived in a small village in a southern farming province at that time. My parents took me and my brothers to our grandparents. We stayed there for two weeks. My mother was busy preparing for the party for days. There were other uncles, aunts and cousins. The party went on for five days. There were at least several hundred guests. We all were wearing pretty *han-bok* [Korean traditional dress] which my mom bought for the occasion. All adults were also wearing matching *han-bok*. During the *hwan-gap-jan-chi*, many

strangers and even homeless people came in and joined the party. The food tables were set up everywhere, from rooms, *ma-ru* [living rooms], to *ma-dang* [big yard]. My mother, aunts, and other relatives were really busy working. People said that my grandfather's *hwan-kap-jan-chi* was the biggest and best in the village. I guess if your children throw a big *hwan-kap-jan-chi*, it shows that they are *hyo-ja/hyo-nye* [a filial, dutiful son and daughter; a good son and daughter].

According to a first-generation respondent, the elaborateness of the *hwan-gap-jan-chi* depends on the children's economic situation. Taking care of one's parents is a moral, not a social, issue:

> Even if the children don't give the parents a big party or no party at all, it's not something the parents should feel ashamed of. It is the children's shame. The children's reputation will be at risk by not giving the best party they can afford. Children celebrate the parent's *hwan-kap* to fulfill the duty as children. Respecting and taking care of old parents has been Korean tradition and propriety, courtesy for thousands of years.

Every tenth birthday is also celebrated in a significant way, but in a smaller way than that for *hwan-gap*.

A first-generation Korean American respondent said he goes to weddings to congratulate the person who is getting married and to celebrate with the person's parents. He views going to weddings and giving money as a form of "exchanging and expressing care and respect." He went on to say: "If the person invites me to a wedding or a party, I will [have to] invite the person to my party and the weddings of my children. That is the way it works. When one gives something to me, I have to return the favor someday."

Ye-dan is a gift given from the bride's family to the groom's family before the wedding. Presents are clothes or dresses for the groom's parents and grandparents, and for siblings of the groom's parents. *Ye-mul* is a personal item given to the bride by the groom's parents. It is sent to the bride's home in a wedding present box called *haam* a week before the wedding day. Various pieces of jewelry (the more, the better), dresses, purses, cosmetics, and other fine items are sent as *ye-mul*.

Pe-bek is the traditional greeting and acceptance of the bride into the groom's family. During the process, the newlyweds bow to the senior members of the groom's family, including grandparents, parents, aunts, and uncles. A table with many colorful foods signifying wealth, health, longevity, togetherness, prosperity, and birth is prepared by the bride's family for the occasion, even though they do not attend the ceremony. *Jul-gap* is a monetary gift presented by the groom's family to the newlyweds during *pe-bek*. It is usually used to pay for the honeymoon or for establishing the new household.

Traditionally, the groom's family is responsible for providing the newlyweds' living quarters. The younger couple may simply move in with the older one, but more commonly a house is purchased or rented for them by the groom's parents. Furnishing the necessary household goods (everything from bedding, kitchen utensils, and dishes to electronics) is the responsibility of the bride's family. Many Koreans save for years to pay for their children's wedding expenses.

Family members, relatives, and family friends give presents or money to prepare a person who is getting a job for the first time after graduating from high school or college (*ip-sa; chui-jik*). The presents usually include suits, dresses, shoes, purses, and other necessary items. Money is also given so the person can purchase whatever is needed.

When one gets the first paycheck, it is customary, in turn, to buy little gifts for one's parents and grandparents. The presents are usually clothing items or money. These gifts signify the beginning of the child's role as caretaker for the older generation. This also means that the older generation, especially the parents, have accomplished their responsibility of raising the child since he or she can now make a living without support from the parents. In many cases, money from the first payday is also given as an offering to the church.

Help with finances from extended family members is frequently given when one starts a new business or store. Sometimes interest-free loans are given to friends or relatives (*chee-won kum*). These practices were frequently reported in the interviews. They are considered a social courtesy.

Before someone in the family, a relative, or a close friend goes on a trip, money or necessary items are given as tokens of one's regard. A bon-voyage party or farewell party (*Hwan-song-hui*) or farewell party (*song-byul-hui*) is held, at which time time the gifts are presented. This form of gathering is frequently held in the Korean community for the benefit of relatives or friends returning to Korea after their visit to the United States. A welcome or welcome-back party (*Hwan-young-hui*) may also have been given to celebrate their arrival.

The returning traveler brings back presents (*son-mul*) or souvenirs (*ki-nyum-pum*) for the family, relatives, friends, and coworkers. This has become the custom after a significant trip. It is practiced widely in Korea, but in the Korean American community it is practiced only to a certain limited degree mainly owing to the availability of most products in the United States.

⁀ SAD OCCASIONS

When someone is sick or hospitalized, friends (including church members), relatives, and family members pay visits, bringing food. Money may be given to help out with expenses. Relatives and friends also help with money, necessary items, and services when someone has experienced an accident or other disaster such as an earthquake, fire, or robbery.

Money is always given for funerals. Friends and relatives stay with the family for a few days, helping prepare food for the guests. Many dishes are prepared. The family is expected to feed the guests well on behalf of the deceased. Korean Americans send money to Korea if a family member, relative, or friend dies there. Money is frequently given to friends whose parents have passed away. The money given at the funeral is called *cho-ui-kum* (sad or condolence money). One first-generation man explained: "Each person contributes a little, then it becomes the pool of money, capital. It will help out the family or person with the expenses. Even if there is no shortage of money, you still have to send money to show your concern and respect for each other."

Che-sa is a yearly ritual where food is prepared for an ancestor on the anniversary of his or her death. The best food and table settings are used. It is believed that the ancestor visits the *che-sa-sang* (*che-sa* table) and that his soul is nourished and entertained by the descendants. In addition, a smaller version of the *che-sa* called a *cha-re* is given twice a year.

The *che-sa* ritual is performed because it is the son's duty to serve and remember his parents, grandparents, and ancestors. One respondent described the origin of the tradition:

> You had to mourn for at least three years. You had to build a dugout or tent next to your parent's grave and live there for three years. You had to eat only twice a day and for each meal you had to set food table at *sang-suk*. [This is the offertory table in front of a tomb; every tomb has this in Korea.] Food offered to ancestors was called *yu-um* or *hon-dok*.

Che-sa is given for up to five generations. There are some variations depending on the family or the region of Korea. Some people count the current generation when they consider five generations. For example, if a person with children gives *che-sa*, he does them for his parents and his grandparents. His grandson, his son, himself, his father, his grandfather would constitute five generations. Koreans also spend much money in general on their ancestors, especially on their parents' tombs. The better the tomb, the more the son (or descendent) is regarded as a good one who fulfills his obligation.

Che-sa is the extension of the *hyo* principle, which emphasizes the importance and value of the filial duty of children. When children or descendants give *che-sa*, it is believed that the ancestors will bless them with prosperity and happiness. *Che-sa* is given at the house of the eldest son. Other relatives and family members contribute money, food, or time to help with cooking and preparations. Koreans who still give *che-sa* have simplified the process, but they still retain most of the ritualistic aspects. Many Christian Koreans do not have the traditional *che-sa*, but they do have a memorial service at home with family and relatives, and the service is frequently followed by lunch or dinner.

☜ RELIGIOUS CUSTOMS

Hun-kum is money given to religious organizations such as churches and temples. Many Koreans regularly contribute a significant amount of money to their churches as well as for special religious occasions. Christmas is the time of the year when many contribute to the social organizations for the poor. Most contributions are made through the Korean churches, which then donate the collected money to the appropriate social organizations, both within and outside the Korean community.

On the Buddha's birthday (*Cho-pa-il*), Buddhists donate money to the temple to buy lanterns so that their wishes will come true and to honor their ancestors. This is one of the days when most Buddhists try to go to a Buddhist temple. Because there are few Korean Buddhist temples in the San Francisco Bay Area, many Korean Americans continue to send their support to the temples in Korea that hold their ancestral memorial tablets. Occasionally, these Korean Americans visit these temples when they go to Korea.

Outside their extended family, Koreans give most generously to Korean Protestant churches. Church members are more likely to participate in social giving practices within the Korean community. Most Korean churches in the United States are run by first-generation immigrants with strong traditional cultural beliefs. Within the Korean community, churches and, to a lesser degree, temples play a central role in organizing social activities. At the churches, information is rapidly distributed and necessary social or community activities are discussed, planned, and organized. One first-generation respondent stated that "Korean Americans give to YMCA and other Christian activities . . . any causes associated with giving in church."

∞ GIVING TO ORGANIZATIONS

More traditional Koreans feel a strong sense of duty to their community. One respondent said: "We all exist as a whole. It is like a human body. Just because you have ugly legs, you can't cut them off; in fact, you can't even ignore them. You have to depend on them to get yourself wherever you want to go." In contrast, a 1.5-generation respondent said that if the recipient is in the family, then it is based on "love and concern for the person." However, when giving outside the family, the biggest concern is "what the person, institution, or organization can do for me as a result of my contribution."

Kye is a traditional rotating credit group which is used extensively by Koreans. Since Koreans are relatively new to the United States, many face credit problems when they try to start a business. *Kye* is a way of acquiring enough money to start a business. A *Kye* group can grow out of a *chin-mok-hoe* (social club), *dong-chang-hoe* (school alumni association), or business association such as a fish-market or laundry association.

Korean groups and associations also provide networking opportunities. School alumni associations also play the role of "hometown" associations because, in general, people who went to the same high school came from the same geographical area. Donations (*chee-won / cheewonkum*) are often given to educational institutions through school alumni associations. College alumni associations play the role of more professional associations. At these gatherings and meetings, *hoi-bi* (a membership fee) is collected to fund the group's activities, which may include beneficial works for the community.

Many Korean businesses buy advertisements in Korean-language newspapers and on television and radio stations. All of the Korean-language media are operated commercially with the exception of the Korean-language Christian radio stations, which are supported by individual donations. These Korean-language media in turn provide community services by supplying both entertainment and vital information to those without adequate English skills. At a time of crisis or need, they also serve as coordinating centers for fundraising.

Business associations double as political and social clubs (*chin-mok-hoi*). Members regularly sponsor parties and gatherings as well as political activities. In many cases, these associations serve as support groups and sources of business information. In 1988, when a Korean owned grocery store in New York was boycotted for over a year by members of other ethnic groups, the Korean Greengrocer Association and its members sent money and stock to keep the store going. After the 1992 Los Angeles riot, Korean business associations collected money and other items to help the victims. One first-generation respondent who has been in the United States more than twenty years stated:

> In the Korean American community, helping and giving are done through the personal association and relationship. For example, when someone needs help in your extended family, it is expected that you will help. If not related, Koreans also willingly give through any form of [social] association. . . . In order to be expected to help [or be helped], one has to have some personal tie through a kinship or association. If you don't have this tie, you don't participate in the giving, helping process. If you are not part of the association, it's not even expected that you will help.

Conclusion

Philanthropy is often associated with wealthy people giving large amounts of money to a charitable organization and indirectly to people they do not personally know—for example, Andrew Carnegie's and Bill Gates's commendable support of libraries. Ethnic philanthropy is almost totally different: it consists primarily of people sharing modest or meager wealth with other people, most of whom the givers know well.

This book reports an ethnographic, cross-cultural study of giving and volunteering in eight communities of color in the San Francisco Bay Area, based on focused interviews with 260 individuals from those communities. The main purpose of the study was to throw light on the little-researched phenomenon of ethnic philanthropy. The focus was on practices of sharing and helping as experienced and expressed by members of the communities studied. Several major findings emerged from the study:

Ethnic philanthropy is inextricably linked with family and kinship. Ethnic charity, like other charity, truly begins at home. While transactions involving money, goods, and services within the nuclear family cannot be considered "philanthropy" or "charity," they powerfully prepare family members for charitable activities that go beyond the nuclear family. In the eight communities studied, there is typically a seamless transition between intra- and extrafamilial sharing and helping. Parents' care for their children, children's care for their parents, and sharing and helping among siblings move almost imperceptibly outward to grandparents and grandchildren, aunts and uncles, nieces and nephews, cousins, friends, neighbors, fellow church members, coworkers, classmates, other members of the ethnic community, relatives and friends living in the homeland, and finally people and organizations in the larger society both in the United States and abroad. Many stories told by participants revealed a steady addition of beneficiaries in ever-widening circles of sharing and helping.

The dominant culture's definition of (nuclear) family as parents and children, and the distinction between family and extended family (including also some relatives and fictive kin), are largely ignored by the ethnic communities studied. As one participant put it, family means "people you truly love who love you back." Blood relationships begin but do not end the concept of family in the communities studied. Several respondents went out of their way to criticize the dominant culture's notion of family as narrow and lacking appropriate scope of love and responsibility.

Family broadly defined is not only the prime teacher and model of ethnic philanthropy but also its prime recipient. The great bulk of philanthropy (giving money, goods, and services outside the nuclear family with no expectation of economic return) in the eight communities studied comes from and goes to the family broadly defined and the ethnic community, including churches and other organizations primarily serving the ethnic community. While this study made no effort to quantify ethnic giving and volunteering, a reasonable estimate based on the interviews is that 80–90 percent of time spent helping and money and goods shared were directed toward the "family" and the ethnic community.

Respondents volunteered many reasons for this: One's primary obligation is to one's own: "family" members and fellow members of the ethnic community. To paraphrase many responses: "These are the people you know best and love most. These are the people who have given or will give you most in return. These are the people whose needs are most evident and immediate; they need help right here, right now. These are the people who count on you for help, and on whom you may count some day." There was also, in all eight communities, a strong sense of the special needs of the community, resulting from poverty, discrimination, language differences, or all of the above. Obligation to family came first, obligation to the community a close second. To many respondents, it simply did not make sense to support mainstream charitable agencies while there were such pressing needs in one's "family" and community. Charity was not a matter of the best use of discretionary income; it was a matter of the survival of loved ones.

Families and kinship groups practice reciprocity as well as charity. People care for their elderly parents at least partly so that they will be cared for when they are old. Families give elaborate and expensive wedding gifts to cousins and neighbors partly so that their own children will receive similar help as they start families. The family is the first teacher of reciprocity as well as charity: as you give, so will you get.

Fictive kinship was important in all the communities studied. In the African American community, for example, much emphasis is placed on helping one's "brothers" and "sisters," who might be relatives, former classmates, friends, members of the same church, or simply other members of the black community. In Latin American cultures, "uncle" might mean your father's brother or simply his good friend. These fictive kin are also "family" who help and are helped in times of need.

In most of the communities studied, there were overlapping kinship groups such as family-surname associations and homeland-district associations. Many such kinship groups and ethnic mutual benefit associations were created in America for support and solidarity in response to discrimination and other hardships. In such groups, as in the nuclear and extended family, charity and reciprocity are almost inextricably mixed.

Research on charitable behavior, as well as common notions of philanthropy in the United States, rightly excludes gifts of money, goods, and time within the nuclear family. However, ethnic philanthropy cannot be understood without careful reference to family and kinship interactions. The social context of philanthropy for most Americans is quite different. As a result of urbanization, industrialization, and other socioeconomic changes, the roles of family and kinship group in caring for the aged, providing relief for the poor, and other such activities have increasingly been assumed by government, nonprofit, and some for-profit institutions including soup kitchens, homes for the elderly, schools, and insurance companies (Mintz and Kellogg, 1988; Espiritu and Hunt, 1964; Dalton, 1971). But nearly two-thirds of the world's population still lives in villages in close association with large numbers of their kin (Shoumatoff, 1985, p. 204). The countries of origins for the ethnic groups studied here have reached various stages of modernization. In all of them, however, kin networks are much more important than they are in the dominant culture of the United States. Even in Japan, which has become heavily industrialized based on the American model, kinship is very important, far more so than here. Not long ago, in many of the countries of origin represented in this study, the kinship system completely dominated all forms of social action. This is relevant to understanding not only the local but also the international dimensions of American ethnic philanthropy. Many respondents described how they support relatives and friends who remain in the homeland.

Religion plays a very important role in ethnic philanthropy. In all eight communities studied, religion plays an important role in shaping the philanthropic behavior of community members. In four of the groups (Mexican, Guatemalan, Salvadoran, and Filipino), Catholicism is the dominant religious influence. In two groups (Korean, African American), Protestantism is dominant. In the Chinese and Japanese communities, Confucianism and Buddhism play an important but different, less direct role, and many community members also belong to Protestant churches.

Catholicism provides a sacramental context, model, teacher, and recipient of ethnic philanthropy. Sacramental events tied to major life changes—baptisms, confirmations, marriages, funerals—are the occasion for many forms of giving and volunteering, as are religious/cultural practices such as *compadrazgo* (co-paternity, godparenthood) and *quinceañera* (a girl's fifteenth birthday and coming-out celebration). But the church's role in ethnic philanthropy goes far beyond such events and practices. The weekly collection at mass, parish food drives, Catholic schools and religious education programs, religious festivals, church societies to help the poor, church efforts to assist immigrants and refugees, and many other activities are occasions for ethnic giving and volunteering. Through its charitable activities, the church practices, teaches about, and receives philanthropy. Ethnic philanthropy in the Catholic tradition, like family and kin interactions, also mixes charity and reciprocity: gifts to the *santos* (saints) bring benefits in return.

Catholicism has had a profound effect on the cultures of Mexico, Guatemala, El Salvador, and the Philippines in recent centuries. Though recently losing ground somewhat to secularism and evangelical Protestantism, Catholicism continues to exert considerable influence in shaping the values of people living within these countries, values which are then brought to the United States when people immigrate here. In addition to their devotional aspects, religious ceremonies and festivals in the home countries promote communal solidarity. This emphasis on community, and attendant customs such as *compadrazgo*, reflect and reinforce similar values of the communal and kin-based societies of Latin America and the Philippines.

Catholicism in the groups studied ranges from traditional folk religion to highly intellectualized religious philosophy. The church plays very different roles in the lives of different respondents. Most who attend mass with some regularity donate money to the collection and often volunteer their time. For many respondents, Catholicism helps support traditional family and community values. Some respondents' practice of Catholicism was stronger than in the country of origin, probably because the religious values and practices lent support in a foreign environment. For many respondents, religious giving was primarily devotional. This was especially true among the Guatemalans interviewed and some of the more recent immigrants from Mexico and the Philippines.

Protestantism is the religious choice of 70 percent of Koreans, with Buddhism attracting most of the rest. The church is a very important part of Korean philanthropy and is active in the educational, social, economic, and political lives of Koreans. Korean churches helped raise money to support the independence movement in the homeland.

Protestantism is also the overwhelming choice of African Americans, although in recent decades Islam has attracted a sizable number of blacks. The church is by far the most important philanthropic organization in the African American community. Charitable church programs include food and clothing drives, services to the sick and elderly, college scholarship funds, day care and after-school centers, tutoring, counseling, recreation, and many others. In addition to formal church charities, much of the personal and family-based philanthropy within the black community is inspired and organized by the church. As one respondent said, "You know, it'd be 'Sister Jones is sick and shut in, so therefore we'd like to have you take her a meal.'"

The black church also plays an important role in directing charitable resources to other organizations, both within and outside the African American community. Such is the influence of the black church that Carson (1989) believes the future of African American charitable organizations will depend on the support and endorsement of black religious leaders.

Confucianism and Buddhism teach and support philanthropic values but do not play the same activist philanthropic role that Catholicism and Protestantism do in the communities studied. Both Buddhism and Confucianism provide centuries-old ethical precepts relating to charity. In particular, these wisdom traditions convey the central importance of community, oneness, connection with others. As one respondent said, "You don't operate separate from the community. . . . Service and compassion was definitely part of the teaching. We are taught to serve others." In the course of collecting data from Asian respondents, it became clear that the majority of those interviewed did not distinguish between what is Confucianism and what is Buddhism.

Often the customs remained as a family tradition rather than a religious practice.

In all the groups studied, it was clear that the philanthropic aspects of religion could not be seen as separate and distinct from family, kinship, and ethnic group. Local religious congregations were largely composed of members of the same ethnic groups, and the congregations included many families related to each other by kinship or fictive kinship ties. In other words, it is difficult and probably impossible to isolate the specific effect of religion on ethnic philanthropy, since for religiously active people of color, religious influence continually and extensively interacts with the effects of the ethnic group, family, and kinship. Religion both shapes and expresses culture (Geertz, 1973). There is no way to separate fully religion and culture. As a 21-year-old second-generation Chinese American said, "Part of the Buddhist teaching is to give, and to sacrifice. Religion mixed with our culture is what makes us give the way we do."

Little ethnic philanthropy is directed toward mainstream charitable organizations other than churches. Most ethnic philanthropy is informal and probably goes unrecorded in tax returns and Gallup surveys because it is given directly by one person to another. Respondents mentioned giving to or volunteering for a number of non-church charitable organizations, both ethnic agencies (National Association for the Advancement of Colored People, Mexican American Legal Defense and Educational Fund, Japanese American Citizens League, Chinese for Affirmative Action) and mainstream nonprofit organizations (YMCA and YWCA, Boy and Girl Scouts, Red Cross, March of Dimes, Easter Seals, Salvation Army, Goodwill Industries, United Way), as well as organizations in the countries of origin. However, giving and volunteering to secular charitable organizations constitute a relatively small portion of ethnic philanthropy, most of which goes to the extended family, including fictive kin, and the church. Several respondents expressed distrust of mainstream charitable organizations, seeing them as large, impersonal institutions operated by strangers and benefiting strangers. A young second-generation Guatemalan woman said bluntly, "Latins do not follow the American model of charity; we do not give to strangers."

National surveys of giving and volunteering as well as the heroic tales of philanthropic lore, such as John D. Rockefeller's gifts that led to the elimination of hookworm, create the impression that philanthropy is largely if not exclusively a matter of giving money to and volunteering for charitable organizations. The present study found that philanthropy in the eight minority communities studied had very little to do with giving to organizations other than churches and temples. Nearly all giving and volunteering, or sharing and helping, within these communities of color was person to person, family to family, neighbor to neighbor, church member to church member. Much of this ethnic philanthropy consisted of bringing food, visiting, taking in someone who didn't have a place to stay—all activities that are difficult to place a monetary value on, difficult to measure. It is easy to record the value of a donation sent to Amnesty International or clothes given to Goodwill Industries, but it is difficult to record the value of bringing shoes to a neighbor's nephew in Guatemala. Defining charity or philanthropy as giving to and volunteering for incorporated nonprofit charitable organizations simply excludes most of the reality of ethnic philanthropy. Survey research based on such a definition becomes a Procrustean bed, to accommodate which major parts of philanthropic behavior are cut away. The present study suggests that this approach does great disservice to the understanding of at least minority philanthropy and probably other philanthropy as well. While survey research cannot take the time to catch all the nuances that are possible in an ethnographic study, at least the survey questions can be modified to allow for a more accurate view of informal as well as formal philanthropy. If, for example, philanthropy is defined as "giving money, goods, and services outside the nuclear family with no expectation of economic return," without *necessary* reference to charitable organizations, it is possible to get a clearer, fuller, and more comparable picture of philanthropic behavior practiced by people from all social, economic, cultural, ethnic, and religious groups. Comparability is a key issue. If, hypothetically, the dominant philanthropic pattern of white Americans is to give to charitable organizations and *not* to relatives, friends, and members of their ethnic/national origin group, while people of color give primarily within their extended family (including fictive kin) and ethnic group, research focused largely or exclusively on giving to organizations will always "prove" that whites give much more than people of color.

At the very least, interviews with the 260 participants in this study make it clear that a definition of philanthropy like the one used in this study is essential to describing and understanding sharing and helping within these eight communities of color. It is also clear that even formal philanthropy (giving to organizations) must be understood within the larger context of informal philanthropy within these communities.

There is a similarity of giving-related customs (and even terms) across the groups studied. The eight groups studied have very different histories, both in their lands of origin and in the United States. The differences go back centuries and are expressed in social, political, and economic structures; art, music, and literature; philosophy, religion, and culture. Some of the countries of origin have warred with each other, and in the United States some of the groups have had tense relationships with one another. In spite of all these differences, there are strong similarities in the groups' customs, practices, and even terminology related to sharing and helping. Part of the similarity may be explained by common religious traditions (Catholicism, Buddhism) or common history of colonization (Spanish). But the extent of similarity may indicate more generalizable characteristics of sharing and helping.

In most of the groups studied, much giving and volunteering takes place in connection with major life events such as birth, coming of age, marriage, moves, and death. The obvious explanation is that people need extra money, goods, help and emotional support at such times. A communal response helps ease the burden. For example, the birth of a baby occasioned giving in different forms: the Filipino *pakimkim* (money and gifts to the godchild at baptism), the Chinese *Mún yuht laih sih* (money given to the newborn by all married individuals in attendance at the Red Egg and Ginger birthday party), the Japanese *oiwai* (money and gifts of congratulation), the Mexican *bolo* (money thrown to children at the baptism), *batea* (tray full of gifts given to the parents and child), *aguacero* (shower for the newborn; gifts and money for the mother), and so forth.

Respect for parents and the elderly in general was a common philanthropic theme in the groups studied. Such values and practices clearly go back to times and countries where the extended family is the sole means of support for the elderly, but the values have remained strong even in the United States of the 1990s, where different values and support systems are in place.

Customs and terms such as *compadrazgo, padrino/a,* and *quinceañera* appear in the four groups with a Catholic Hispanic background and clearly reflect the language and culture of that background. They are, however, similar to godparenthood and coming-of-age practices in the other four communities studied, and other religious and cultural groups.

A detailed comparative list of customs and terms for five of the eight groups (Chinese, Japanese, Filipino, Mexican, Guatemalan) may be found in Smith, Shue, and Villareal (1992, pp. 227–49).

Significant amounts of money and goods are sent to family, kin, and communities outside the United States. With the exception of the African American community, all of the groups studied directed a significant part of their philanthropy to their countries of origin. This pattern of giving is strongly reminiscent of the practices of European immigrant groups (Irish, Italian, Polish, Jewish, and so forth) during the nineteenth century. If the first rule of philanthropy is "charity begins at home," the second is "people help their own," both here and in the homelands. Sending money abroad is clearly related to recency of immigration: Americans of English, Irish, German, French, and African descent send little money to their countries of origin, whereas Americans of Mexican, Filipino, Guatemalan, Korean, and other ancestry do, because of the recency of direct family and kinship ties.

In the groups studied, there was a continual flow of visitors and migrants back and forth between the United States and the countries of origin. These people were carriers and often recipients of ethnic philanthropy. Money and goods sent abroad mostly went to relatives and friends, but some went to more general causes. For example, people who had done well economically in the United States might build a new school or clinic in the town they came from. Sometimes there are sending-off parties and welcome-back parties. These events both help pay the expenses of the trip and provide the travelers with gifts to people in the homeland. Visiting the homeland can be expensive. One Filipino respondent said that the required gift-giving there usually cost more than the plane tickets.

Any attempt to quantify American ethnic philanthropy must take into account this large-scale transfer of money and goods out of the United States. Some respondents estimated that these transfers account for a significant percentage of revenue flowing into some of the countries of origin. If the practices reported by the 240 respondents from seven groups here (not counting the African American group) are any indication of general practices within these communities, the total annual value of these philanthropic transfers would be in the hundreds of millions of dollars, and possibly higher.

Members of ethnic communities often report caretaking activities which in the mainstream society are more likely to be performed by government and nonprofit organizations. This study did not systematically compare ethnic philanthropy practices with those of the dominant culture, but some apparent differences were revealed in participants' statements with regard to care for the elderly, children and youth from troubled homes, and the needy. In some cases these differences were rooted in strong cultural values, such as respect for the elderly. Generally the ethnic caretaking practices were brought over from the homeland. In many cases there was a noticeable element of reciprocity: people care for elderly parents partly in the hope that their children will care for them in later years.

Many respondents expressed surprise and even shock at the way mainstream Americans dealt with the elderly and other vulnerable populations. To some respondents, it was unthinkable that one's parents or grandparents would have to finish their years in a nursing home. Some respondents saw American customs as indicating greed, selfishness, and lack of love. However, there were some "minority" opinions on this matter. The longer one had been in the United States, the more likely one was to follow the general American custom of elderly parents and grandparents living separately. A few of the elderly themselves said they preferred it this way. Length of time in the United States was related to giving habits in general. One 47-year-old Japanese male said that the first generation of Japanese Americans gave to the *kenjinkais* (mutual aid groups) and the Buddhist church, the second generation gave to Japanese nonprofits and several churches, and the third generation "are just as happy to write one check out to United Way."

Higher income respondents consistently spoke of their obligation to help others in their community achieve success in the same way they themselves were helped by members of their family and community. While people of color are disproportionately represented in lower income groups, some groups and some members of all groups have achieved significant economic success. Do these people help the less fortunate in their own ethnic groups? The self-reports in this study suggest that this is generally the case. Many participants expressed strong feelings of obligation toward those in "the community" who had not fared so well. The assistance comes in many ways. Frequently people spoke of professionals who could have made more money by leaving the ethnic community but who took lower pay to serve in the community. Some of the successful made financial donations, as to college scholarship funds. Volunteering was a common form of "payback": tutoring, coaching, providing other services to young people. Jobs are an important form of payback. People in jobs that hire others try to hire some members of the ethnic community. Shop owners sometimes hire extra workers even when they don't need to.

Knowledge of people's ethnicity does not help to predict the proportion of their total yearly household expenditures or total number of hours a year they give outside their nuclear family; but knowledge of people's ethnicity does help to predict the forms and beneficiaries of giving and volunteering outside the nuclear family. One of the major conclusions of the study is that the apparent disparity between white and minority giving may be largely spurious, a result of the way questions are worded in national surveys. The national surveys report that whites give twice as much as blacks and Hispanics: whites give about two percent of their income to charity, while blacks and Hispanics give one percent or less. The present study showed that members of eight communities of color, including blacks and Hispanics, are extensively involved in sharing and helping. In these communities, these activities are usually personal, direct, informal and of their very nature not likely to be recorded and reported in tax returns and Gallup polls. The key question may turn out to be a definitional one: what do "charity," "philanthropy," "giving," and "volunteering" include? If the definition is restricted largely or exclusively to activities directed toward organizations, people of color will fall short. But if all giving of money, goods, and service outside the nuclear family is counted, people of color may turn out to be as generous as whites, if not more so. It must be stressed again that the present study did not test but rather generated this hypothesis.

It seems appropriate to end this report with a brief discussion of the concept of social exchange. It is clear to most who study charitable activity that there is some form of exchange in any act of sharing or giving (see, for example, Mixer, 1993). People get something out of giving their money and time. Giving is not simply asymmetric; it is at least partly a transaction, an exchange. As Blau (1964, p. 17) remarked, "An apparent 'altruism' pervades social life; people are anxious to benefit one another and to reciprocate for the benefits they receive. But beneath this seeming selflessness an underlying 'egoism' can be discovered; the tendency to help others is frequently motivated by the expectation that doing so will bring social rewards." Capitalist economies are based largely on the idea and practice of economic exchange, but the interviews reported here clearly verify that other types of exchange are common. For example, contributions of money and time often result in social approval. Within the Asian communities, in particular, there is an explicit discussion of "face" or the dignity, prestige, and respect a person maintains in the community. Giving can bring prestige to the giver; conversely, giving must be done in a way that preserves the dignity and self-respect of the recipient. This process of maintaining "face" in the community is observed in all social groups, though perhaps with less self-awareness and discussion than found in the Asian groups studied here.

A related issue is the value of social cohesion, which can bring many benefits to the individual: identity, security, a feeling of belonging, protection from threats from outside, and the like. People want acceptance and recognition, want to feel part of a group. Helping and sharing create social cohesion and generate for individual givers the resulting benefits. Many of the giving customs identified in this study are used to establish and maintain social ties.

Finally, there is often an implicit social contract in giving and volunteering. Gifts of money and time are often made with the understanding that an obligation is being created that will be repaid at some time in the future or that an obligation is being discharged that was established at some time in the past. The notion of "payback" was present more or less subtly in all the groups studied.

Appendix A ∽

Methodology and Research Staff

The principal investigator holds a doctorate in sociology and has extensive experience in managing social science research projects. The Asian project manager is a third-generation Chinese American with a doctorate in multicultural education; she is bilingual in English and Cantonese. The Hispanic project manager is a Mexican American, active in the Bay Area Hispanic community; he has a degree in applied history. The African American project manager joined the original research team for the second phase of the study in April of 1993; she is an African American with a master's degree in African Diaspora history. There were two research assistants during the second phase of the study, a Chinese woman with a degree in anthropology and a bilingual Guatemalan woman attending college in the Bay Area. During the first phase, the project had the assistance of two volunteers, a second-generation Filipino woman with a doctorate in multicultural education and a third-generation Japanese American woman with a master's in educational psychology. There were five student research assistants during the second phase of the study: an African American woman, a bilingual Korean American woman, a Thai American woman, a bilingual Salvadoran man, and a bilingual Salvadoran woman.

Prior to the development of the interview protocols, a literature search was conducted. An annotated bibliography of approximately 150 references was developed and used throughout the study.

The fieldwork during the first phase was carried out from January to September of 1991 and involved 40 focused interviews within the Chinese, Japanese, Filipino, Mexican, and Guatemalan communities, for a total of 200 interviews. The interview protocols are included at the end of this Appendix. During the second phase, fieldwork took place between June and September of 1993 and included 20 focused interviews within the African American, Korean, and Salvadoran communities, for a total of 60 interviews. Resources were not sufficient to conduct 40 interviews within each community during the second phase of the study. The focused interview was utilized because: (1) it does not suggest particular answers; (2) it permits the researcher to find out whether or not the respondent has any attitudes toward the object in question; (3) it aids the discovery of a variety of attitudes that might not have been anticipated; and (4) it enhances rapport by allowing the respondent to talk about the topic in a way that is natural and interesting to him or her (Scott, 1968). Each interviewer employed culturally appropriate questions (language used reflected the interviewers' acquaintance with cultural norms) for the corresponding ethnic group, taking into account its special cultural characteristics, traditions, customs, and norms.

A list of individuals known by Institute for Nonprofit Organization Management staff constituted the initial list of contact persons. These individuals provided additional referrals for our snowball sample. (A snowball sample is created by asking initial respondents for the names of potential respondents, who are, in turn, asked about additional respondents. The sample "snowballs" as respondents suggest others to be interviewed.) The interviews typically took an hour and a half; most were completed within one to two hours. Most of the interviews were conducted in English; bilingual translators were present when needed. The majority of Chinese respondents came from Cantonese speaking-backgrounds. The interviews were typically one-on-one; a few included more than one interviewee. Some respondents were interviewed on more than one occasion. The interviews with 260 individuals provided the major corpus of data upon which the results of this study are based. During the second phase of the project, interviewers spoke again with several of the original respondents from the Chinese, Japanese, Filipino, Mexican, and Guatemalan communities.

Following an explanation of the purpose of the study, the interview process began. Six areas of inquiry were developed and put into an order that led informants to talk about giving:

1. Family histories and current giving practices
2. Religion/spiritual influences
3. Where and why monetary contributions are made
4. Where and why volunteer efforts are contributed
5. General philosophy about giving; what others and the community are doing
6. Personal demographics

Each of the questions was extended and became more specific over the course of the focused interview process. The researchers were interested not only in the cultural giving customs but also in the possible cultural meaning behind the customs, the respondents' attitudes toward the observed practices, and the participation or lack of participation in giving practices. About a third of the way through the interviews in the first phase of the study, the demographic questions were moved to the beginning of the interview; the researchers felt this improved rapport with the respondents.

Behavioral cues during the interviews provided feedback to the researchers as to whether the respondents understood the question and were comfortable with the interview process, or whether the researchers needed to provide clarification and more guiding questions to maintain rapport. The researchers were also on guard for situations where respondents were overly courteous and may have been providing biased responses in order to maintain a positive image. Further, the researchers made conscious efforts to dress and act in keeping with the expectations of the setting at all times.

Voluminous notes were taken during interviews, and verbatim quotes are utilized in the presentation of the study. Minimal encouragers such as, "Thank you for being patient while I write exactly what you have said," and "Your comments are really adding to this study," were used to inform the respondent as to his/her role in the study. Other statements made to the respondents such as, "I want to know as much as I can about your culture's giving customs, what you do in the way of giving, and what you think others do" were interspersed during the interview to reinforce the kinds of information being sought.

Notes were reviewed immediately after the interviews and conclusions/impressions were made about interrelationships, socialization procedures, norms, and anything else believed to be of significance. The original handwritten notes and verbatim quotes were entered into a computer database. The interviews were then labeled.

Demographic data as well as conclusions and impressions were entered into a separate file to facilitate the development of categories. Points noted were used for the follow-up exploration in subsequent interviews.

All Chinese, Japanese, and Korean interviews were conducted by the Asian researchers and all Mexican, Guatemalan, and Salvadoran interviewers were conducted by the Hispanic researchers. Approximately 80 percent of the interviews were conducted by one of the researchers who belonged to the same community as the respondent. The Filipino interviews were split evenly between the Asian and Hispanic researchers because the Philippines are geographically an Asian country, but the culture of the country is, to a significant extent, Catholic and Hispanic. General agreement concerning the Filipino practices of sharing and giving was found among the researchers.

An advisory committee with three members representing each of the eight ethnic groups was formed to review the written products. All of them as well as several of the respondents who requested the opportunity to help with the study provided valuable feedback.

The Interview Protocol follows.

INTERVIEW PROTOCOL

Name:
ID:
When:
Time:
Where:

Do you feel it is important to give time/money to help the less fortunate, or to aid the community?

CATEGORY OF INQUIRY #1—HISTORY OF, BELIEFS IN, AND FAMILY PRACTICES OF PHILANTHROPY

What did your family practice in the way of giving time and money?

Do you continue any of these or other traditional practices?

Have these practices changed in form?

What types of philanthropy are expected of you, as the result of your culture or family today?

What are the primary values, priorities, and concerns, as you see it, in your culture regarding "giving" behavior?

What do you think is important in life?

What do you see in your culture that is different from the dominant culture in the way of giving?

What do you consider a family?

Do you feel you have the same perception of family as others in your cultural group?

What do you think of cultural giving practices?

Will you continue to practice these types of giving and to transmit (teach to your children) them to others?

CATEGORY OF INQUIRY #2—RELIGION

Do you think of yourself as a religious/spiritual person?

What religion/spiritual affiliation are you, if any?

How large a role does this play in your life?

Do you attend church/temple regularly?
Always ___
Moderate (1–2 times/month) ___
Sometimes (a few times a year and holidays) ___
Never ___

How involved in church activities/programs are you?
Active ___
Moderate ___
Sometimes ___

Do you believe that philanthropy should be a prime goal of organized religion?

Are you aware of any contributions that churches/temples may have made to your community?

Are you aware of any contributions that an individual/group/or community has made to a religious organization?

Is it expected of you to be involved, and by whom?

CATEGORY OF INQUIRY #3—MONETARY CONTRIBUTIONS

To which organizations do you contribute monies?
    Asian/Hispanic:
    Not Asian/Hispanic:

Can you rank-order your priority of the organizations?

Why that priority?

Why don't you give (monetarily)?

CATEGORY OF INQUIRY #4—VOLUNTARY (TIME) CONTRIBUTIONS

Do you now do, or have you ever done, volunteer work?
Yes ___ No ___

Where did/do you volunteer?
    Asian/Hispanic:
    Not Asian/Hispanic:

Can you rank-order your priority of the organizations?

Why that priority?

Do any of your family/friends do volunteer work?
Yes ___ No ___

Why don't you volunteer?

CATEGORY OF INQUIRY #5—GIVING TIME AND MONEY, AND THE COMMUNITY

What is your general philosophy on giving time or money?

When you contribute money or give time, is it done consistently or at random?

Are you more likely to give to an ethnic organization?

What do you see others and the community doing?

Who do you believe should be taking care of the needy, or new immigrants, etc. (government or community)?

If a family or extended family member is in need, are you or your family expected to help them?

Do you have much contact with your homeland? Do you give to causes/organizations in your homeland?

Do you donate anything other than time and money?

What kinds of organizations would you consider giving either time or money to?

Please describe what you think might be worthwhile causes to give to.

Is there anything else that is relevant that we have not touched on?

CATEGORY OF INQUIRY #6—DEMOGRAPHIC DATA

Gender:
Age:
Marital Status:
Number of Children:
Birthplace:
Ethnic Background:

Are you a citizen of the U.S.?
Or what status:

How long have you been in the U.S.?

What generation are you?

LANGUAGE USAGE and BACKGROUND

English ___ Mandarin ___ Cantonese ___ Japanese ___ Any Filipino Language ___
Other(s) ___ (Bi-, Tri-, Multilingual)

Educational level:

Occupation (p/f):

Who lives with you?

Do you support any other than the nuclear family? Yes ___ No___
Why?

Where do these people live?

SELF-IDENTITY

Do you consider yourself:
a) American first, African American, Asian, or Hispanic second
b) Equally African American, Asian, or Hispanic and American
c) African American, Asian, or Hispanic first, American second

Why do you feel this way?

Describe the neighborhood you live in (SES and ethnic mix):

Address:
Or Street coordinates:

Appendix B ∽

Census Statistics

Table B-1: Resident Population of the United States, by Race and Hispanic Origin: 1980 and 1990

Race and Hispanic Origin	Number (1,000)		Percent		Change 1980–1990	
	1980	1990	1980	1990	Number (1,000)	Percent
All Persons	226,546	248,710	100.0%	100.0%	22,164	9.8%
RACE						
White	188,372	199,686	83.1	80.3	11,314	6.0
Black	26,495	29,986	11.7	12.1	3,491	13.2
American Indian, Eskimo, or Aleut	1,420	1,959	0.6	0.8	539	37.9
Asian or Pacific Islander	3,500	7,274	1.5	2.9	3,773	107.8
Chinese	806	1,645	0.4	0.7	839	104.1
Filipino	775	1,407	0.3	0.6	632	81.6
Japanese	701	848	0.3	0.3	147	20.9
Korean	355	799	0.2	0.3	444	125.3
Other Asian or Pacific Islander	865	2,575	-	0.3	-	-
Other race	6,758	9,805	3.0	3.9	3,047	45.1
HISPANIC ORIGIN						
Hispanic Origin	14,609	22,354	6.4	9.0	7,745	53.0
Mexican	8,740	13,496	3.9	5.4	4,755	54.4
Salvadoran	-	565	-	-	-	-
Guatemalan	-	270	-	-	-	-
Other Hispanic	5,868	8,023	2.6	3.5	-	-
Not of Hispanic Origin	211,937	226,356	93.6	91.0	14,419	6.8

Source: Bureau of the Census, *Statistical Abstract of the United States*, 1992, p. 17.
Note: Persons of Hispanic origin may be of any race.

Table B-2: Resident Population of California, by Race and Hispanic Origin: 1980 and 1990

Race and Hispanic Origin	Number		Percent		Change 1980–1990	
	1980	1990	1980	1990	Number (1,000)	Percent
All Persons	23,667,902	29,760,021	100.0%	100.0%	6,092,119	25.7%
RACE						
White	18,221,353	20,555,653	77.0	69.1	2,334,300	12.8
Black	1,818,660	2,198,766	7.7	7.4	380,106	20.9
American Indian, Eskimo, or Aleut	231,702	248,929	1.0	0.8	17,227	7.4
Asian or Pacific Islander	1,312,973	2,847,835	5.5	9.6	1,534,862	116.9
Chinese	325,882	713,423	1.4	2.4	387,541	118.9
Filipino	358,378	733,941	1.5	2.5	375,563	104.8
Japanese	268,814	320,730	1.1	1.1	51,916	19.3
Korean	102,582	259,908	0.4	0.9	157,326	153.4
Other Asian or Pacific Islander	257,317	819,833	-	2.8	-	-
Other race	2,083,214	3,908,838	8.8	13.1	1,825,624	87.6
HISPANIC ORIGIN						
Hispanic Origin	4,541,300	7,557,550	19.2	25.4	3,016,250	66.4
Mexican	3,613,167	6,070,637	15.3	20.4	2,457,470	68.0
Salvadoran	-	338,769	-	1.1	-	-
Guatemalan	-	159,177	-	0.5	-	-
Other Hispanic	928,133	998,967	-	-	-	-
Not of Hispanic Origin	19,126,602	22,202,471	80.8	74.6	3,075,869	16.1

Source: 1990 Census of Population and Housing Summary Tape, File 3A

Note: Persons of Hispanic origin may be of any race.

Table B-3: Resident Population of the San Francisco Bay Area, by Race and Hispanic Origin: 1980 and 1990

Race and Hispanic Origin	Number		Percent		Change 1980–1990	
	1980	1990	1980	1990	Number	Percent
All Persons	5,367,925	6,253,311	100.0%	100.0%	885,386	16.5%
RACE						
White	4,106,512	4,341,175	76.5	69.4	234,663	5.7
Black	467,823	535,477	8.7	8.6	67,654	14.5
American Indian, Eskimo, or Aleut	39,063	40,804	0.7	0.7	1,741	4.5
Asian or Pacific Islander	468,100	928,026	8.7	14.8	459,926	98.3
Chinese	169,691	332,033	3.2	5.3	162,342	95.7
Filipino	139,676	260,394	2.6	4.2	120,718	86.4
Japanese	68,585	81,504	1.3	1.3	12,919	18.8
Korean	18,870	41,813	0.4	0.7	22,943	121.6
Other Asian or Pacific Islander	71,278	212,282	1.3	3.4	-	-
Other race	286,427	407,829	5.3	6.5	102,532	33.6
HISPANIC ORIGIN						
Hispanic Origin	660,173	945,070	12.3	15.1	284,897	43.2
Mexican	418,297	647,495	7.8	10.4	229,198	54.8
Salvadoran	-	52,438	-	0.8	-	-
Guatemalan	-	13,153	-	0.2	-	-
Other Hispanic	241,876	231,984	-	-	-	-
Not of Hispanic Origin	4,707,752	5,308,241	87.7	84.9	600,489	12.8

Source: 1990 Census of Population and Housing Summary Tape, File 3A
Note: Persons of Hispanic origin may be of any race.

References ✑

Anima, N. 1978. *Childbirth and burial: Practices among Philippine tribes.* Quezon City, Philippines: Omar Publications.

Aschenbrenner, Joyce. 1975. *Lifelines: Black families in Chicago.* New York: Holt, Rinehart and Winston.

Baker, Hugh D. R. 1979. *Chinese family and kinship.* New York: Columbia University Press.

Banks, James A., and Jean D. Grambs (eds.). 1972. *Black self-concept: Implications for education and social science.* New York: McGraw Hill.

Blau, Peter M. 1964. *Exchange and power in social life.* New York: John Wiley & Sons.

Boorstin, Daniel J. 1969. *The decline of radicalism: Reflections on America today.* New York: Random House.

Boulding, Kenneth E. 1981. *A preface to grants economics: The economy of love and fear.* New York: Praeger.

Bowen, James G. 1990. Attitudes toward fundraising and volunteerism within the Filipino community of Moreau High School as a microcosm of Southern Alameda County. Master's thesis, University of San Francisco.

Carson, Emmett D. 1987a. *Black philanthropic activity past and present: A 200 year tradition continues.* Washington, DC: Joint Center for Political Studies.

———. 1987b. *The contemporary charitable giving and volunteerism of black women.* Washington, DC: Joint Center for Political Studies.

———. 1987c. *Pulling yourself up by your bootstraps: The evolution of black philanthropic activity.* Washington, DC: Joint Center for Political Studies.

———. 1987d. "Survey dispels myth that blacks receive but do not give to charity." *Focus* (March), pp. 5–6.

———. 1989. "Church support of individuals and organizations: Patterns of black and white giving." 1989 Spring Research Forum Working Papers. Washington, DC: Independent Sector.

———. 1990. *Black volunteers as givers and fundraisers.* New York: Center for the Study of Philanthropy, City University of New York.

Chan, Sucheng. 1991. *Asian Americans: An interpretative history.* Boston: Twayne Publishers.

Chang, Betty L. 1983. "Care and support of elderly family members: Views of ethnic Chinese young people." In William C. McCready (ed.), *Culture, ethnicity, and identity: Current issues in research.* New York: Academic Press.

Commission on Private Philanthropy and Public Needs [Filer Commission]. 1975. *Giving in America: Towards a stronger voluntary sector.* Washington, DC: U.S. Department of the Treasury.

Cortés, Michael. 1991. "Philanthropy and Latino nonprofits: A research agenda." In Herman E. Gallegos and Michael O'Neill (eds.), *Hispanics and the nonprofit sector.* New York: Foundation Center.

Crouchett, Lorraine J. 1982. *Filipinos in California: From the days of the galleons to the present.* El Cerrito, CA: Downey Place Publishing House.

Dalton, George. 1971. *Economic anthropology and development.* New York: Basic Books.

Daniels, Roger. 1990. *Coming to America: A history of immigration and ethnicity in American life.* New York: HarperCollins.

Eckhouse, John. 1991a. "How the flow of labor changes the world." *San Francisco Chronicle,* July 1.

———. 1991b. "Migrant workers' economic impact." *San Francisco Chronicle,* July 1.

Espiritu, Socorro C., and Chester L. Hunt (eds.). 1964. *Social foundations of community development: Readings on the Philippines.* Manila, Philippines: R.M. Garcia Publishing House.

Foster, George M. 1967. *Tzintzuntzan: Mexican peasants in a changing world.* Boston: Little, Brown.

Fuentes, Carlos. 1992. *The buried mirror: Reflections on Spain and the New World.* Boston: Houghton Mifflin.

Fugita, S. S., and D. J. O'Brien. 1991. *Japanese American ethnicity: The persistence of community.* Seattle: University of Washington Press.

Geertz, Clifford. 1973. *The interpretation of cultures.* New York: Basic Books.

Gibbs, Jr., James. 1973. "Two forms of dispute settlement among the Kpelle of West Africa." In Donald Black and Maureen Mileski (eds.), *The social organization of law.* New York: Seminar Press.

Gulliver, P.H. 1977. "On mediators." In I. Mamnet (ed.), *Social anthropology and law.* New York: Academic Press.

Harris, Robert L. 1979. "Early black benevolent societies, 1780–1830." *The Massachusetts Review,* vol. 20, 608–609.

Hawke, David F. 1988. *Everyday life in early America.* New York: Harper & Row.

Hodgkinson, Virginia A., and Murray S. Weitzman. 1986. *The charitable behavior of Americans: A national survey.* Washington, DC: Independent Sector.

———. 1988. *Giving and volunteering in the United States: Findings from a national survey.* Washington, DC: Independent Sector.

———. 1990. *Giving and volunteering in the United States: Findings from a national survey.* Washington, DC: Independent Sector.

———. 1992. *Giving and volunteering in the United States: Findings from a national survey.* Washington, DC: Independent Sector.

———. 1994. *Giving and volunteering in the United States: Findings from a national survey.* Washington, DC: Independent Sector.

———. 1996. *Giving and volunteering in the United States: Findings from a national survey.* Washington, DC: Independent Sector.

Hollinsteiner, Mary. 1970. "Reciprocity in the Lowlands Philippines." In Frank Lynch and Alfonso de Guzman II (eds.), *Four readings on Philippine values.* 3rd ed. Quezon City: Ateneo de Manila University Press.

Hsu, Francis L.K. 1975. *Iemoto: The heart of Japan.* New York: Halsted Press.

———. 1981. *Americans and Chinese: Passage to differences.* 3rd ed. Honolulu: University Press of Hawaii.

Kasberg, Robert H., and Cheryl Hall-Russell. 1996. *African-American traditions of giving and serving: A study of ethnic philanthropy in the Midwest.* Indianapolis: Center on Philanthropy, Indiana University.

Kitano, Harvey L., and Akemi Kikumura. 1980. "The Japanese American family." In Russell Endo, Stanley Sue, and Nathaniel N. Wagner (eds.), *Asian-Americans: Social and psychological perspectives.* Vol. II. Ben Lomond, CA: Science and Behavior Books.

Ko, Elaine, and Danny Howe. 1990. *The Asian American charitable giving study: A survey of charitable giving in King County's Asian American community*. Seattle: United Way of King County.

Lardizabal, Amparo S., and Felicitas Tensuan-Leogardo (eds.). 1976. *Readings on Philippine culture and social life*. Manila, Philippines: Rex Book Store.

Lee, Robert. 1990. *Guide to Chinese American philanthropy and charitable giving patterns*. San Rafael, CA: Pathway Press.

Lincoln, C. Eric. 1974. *The black experience in religion*. Garden City, NY: Anchor Press.

Lincoln, C. Eric, and Lawrence H. Mamiya. 1990. *The black church in the African-American experience*. Durham, NC: Duke University Press.

Lohmann, Roger, and Mary Sue Bracken. 1991. "The Buddhist charitable commons in Japan and Asia." In ARNOVA 1991 Conference Proceedings. Pullman, WA: ARNOVA.

London, Nancy R. 1991. *Japanese corporate philanthropy*. New York: Oxford University Press.

Low, Victor. 1982. *The unimpressible race: A century of educational struggle by the Chinese in San Francisco*. San Francisco: East/West Publishing Company.

Lyman, Stanford M. 1986. *Chinatown and Little Tokyo: Power, conflict, and community among Chinese and Japanese immigrants to America*. Millwood, NY: Associated Faculty Press.

Lynch, Frank. 1970. "Social acceptance reconsidered." In Frank Lynch and Alfonso de Guzman II (eds.), *Four readings on Philippine values*. 3rd ed. Quezon City: Ateneo de Manila University Press.

McAdoo, Harriette P. (ed.). 1988. *Black families*. 2nd ed. Newbury Park, CA: Sage Publications.

Market Opinion Research. 1989. *The Bay Area volunteers and gives: 1989*. San Francisco: Bay Area Strive for Five.

———. 1991. *Volunteering and contributing in the Bay Area: 1991 follow-up study*. San Francisco: Bay Area Strive for Five.

Martin, Elmer P., and Joanne M. Martin. 1978. *The black extended family*. Chicago: University of Chicago Press.

Masumoto, David M. 1987. *Country voices*. Del Rey, CA: Inaka Countryside Publication.

Mauss, Marcel. 1954 [1925]. *The gift: Forms and functions of exchange in archaic society*. Glencoe, IL: Free Press.

Melendy, H. Brett. 1977. *Asians in America: Filipinos, Koreans, and East Indians*. Boston: Twayne Publishers.

Meñez, Herminia Q. 1980. *Folklore communication among Filipinos in California*. New York: Arno Press.

Mintz, Steven, and Susan Kellogg. 1988. *Domestic revolutions: A social history of American family life*. New York: The Free Press.

Mixer, Joseph R. 1993. *Principles of professional fundraising: Useful foundations for successful practice*. San Francisco: Jossey-Bass.

Mukenge, Ida R. 1983. *The black church in urban America: A case study in political economy*. Lanham, MD: University Press of America.

Necesito, Rodolfo I. 1977. *The Filipino guide to San Francisco: An introduction to the Filipino-American community of San Francisco*. San Francisco: Technomedia.

Nelsen, Hart M., Raytha L. Yokley, and Anne K. Nelsen (eds.). 1971. *The black church in America*. New York: Basic Books.

Nelson, Cynthia. 1971. *The waiting village: Social change in rural Mexico*. Boston: Little, Brown.Okazaki, S. K. 1985. *Nihonmachi: A story of San Francisco's Japantown*. San Francisco: Josten's Printing Publishing Department.

Pitti, Jose, Antonia Castaneda, and Carlos Cortes. 1988. "A history of Mexican Americans in California." In *Five views: An ethnic sites survey for California*. Sacramento: State of California—The Resources Agency, Department of Parks and Recreation, Office of Historic Preservation.

Portes, Alejandro, and Robert L. Bach. 1985. *Latin journey: A longitudinal study of Cuban and Mexican immigrants in the United States*. Berkeley: University of California Press.

Schlesinger, Arthur M. 1944–45. "Biography of a nation of joiners," *American Historical Review*, vol. 50, 1–25.

Scott, William. 1968. "Attitude measurement." In Gardner Lindzey and Elliot Aronson (eds.), *Research methods*. Vol. 2 of *The handbook of social psychology*. Menlo Park, CA: Addison-Wesley Publishing Co.

Shorris, Earl. 1992. *Latinos: A biography of the people*. New York: W. W. Norton.

Shoumatoff, Alex. 1985. *The mountain of names: A history of the human family*. New York: Vintage Books.

Smith, Bradford, Sylvia Shue, and Joseph Villarreal. 1992. *Asian and Hispanic philanthropy: Sharing and giving money, goods, and services in the Chinese, Japanese, Filipino, Mexican, and Guatemalan communities in the San Francisco Bay Area*. San Francisco: Institute for Nonprofit Organization Management, University of San Francisco.

Sowell, Thomas. 1981. *Ethnic America: A history*. New York: Basic Books.

Steinberg, David Joel. 1990. *The Philippines: A singular and a plural place*. 2nd ed. Boulder, CO: Westview Press.

Takaki, Ronald. 1993. *A different mirror: A history of multicultural America*. Boston: Little, Brown.

Tonai, Rosalyn M. 1987. Asian American charitable giving: An analysis of the relationship between demographic, attitudinal, and situational factors and the cash contributions of Asian Americans to nonprofit organizations in the San Francisco–Oakland area. Master's thesis, University of San Francisco.

Van Loo, M. Frances. 1990. "Gift exchange: A brief survey with applications for nonprofit practitioners." 1990 Spring Research Forum Working Papers. Washington, DC: Independent Sector.

Vlach, Norita. 1992. *The quetzal in flight: Guatemalan refugee families in the United States*. Westport, CT: Praeger.

Willie, Charles V. (ed.). 1970. *The family life of black people*. Columbus, OH: Merrill.

Yu, C. Y. 1993. *Chinatown San Jose, U.S.A*. San Jose, CA: Historical Museum Association.

Zografos, Peter J. 1991. A study of the relationship between the socioeconomic effects of recent U.S. immigration legislation and the presence of respect for the fundamental human rights of the Salvadoran and Guatemalan members of the Central American refugee community in San Francisco. Unpublished manuscript, San Francisco.

Index ∞